Discovery Travel Adventures™

DINOSAUR DIGS

Blake Edgar
Editor

John Gattuso
Series Editor

Discovery Communications, Inc.

INSIGHT GUIDES

Discovery Communications, Inc.
John S. Hendricks, *Founder, Chairman, and Chief Executive Officer*
Judith A. McHale, *President and Chief Operating Officer*
Michela English, *President, Discovery Enterprises Worldwide*
Raymond Cooper, *Senior Vice President, Discovery Enterprises Worldwide*

Discovery Publishing
Natalie Chapman, *Publishing Director*
Rita Thievon Mullin, *Editorial Director*
Mary Kalamaras, *Senior Editor*
Maria Mihalik Higgins, *Editor*
Kimberly Small, *Senior Marketing Manager*
Chris Alvarez, *Business Development*

Discovery Channel Retail
Tracy Fortini, *Product Development*
Steve Manning, *Naturalist*

Insight Guides
Jeremy Westwood, *Managing Director*
Brian Bell, *Editorial Director*
John Gattuso, *Series Editor*
Siu-Li Low, *General Manager, Books*

Distribution
United States
Langenscheidt Publishers, Inc.
46-35 54th Road, Maspeth, NY 11378
Fax: 718-784-0640

Worldwide
APA Publications GmbH & Co.
Verlag KG Singapore Branch, Singapore
38 Joo Koon Road, Singapore 628990
Tel: 65-865-1600. Fax: 65-861-6438

Discovery Communications produces high-quality nonfiction television programming, interactive media, books, films, and consumer products. Discovery Networks, a division of Discovery Communications, Inc., operates and manages the Discovery Channel, TLC, Animal Planet, and Travel Channel. Visit Discovery Channel Online at http://www.discovery.com.

Although every effort is made to provide accurate information in this publication, we would appreciate readers calling our attention to any errors or outdated information by writing us at: Insight Guides, PO Box 7910, London SE1 1WE, England; fax: 44-171-403-0290; email: insight@apaguide.demon.co.uk

Printed by Insight Print Services (Pte) Ltd., 38 Joo Koon Road, Singapore 628990.

Dinosaur digs / Blake Edgar, editor ; John Gattuso, series editor.
   p. cm. -- (Discovery travel adventures)
   Includes bibliographical references and index.
   ISBN 1-56331-835-0 (alk. paper)
   1. Dinosaurs--United States Guidebooks. 2. Natural history museums--United States Guidebooks. 3. United States Guidebooks.
I. Edgar, Blake.   II. Series.
QE862.D5D49348 1999
567.9'0973--dc21   99-31541
                                              CIP

Cover: Paleontologist Luis Chiappe unearths a *Protoceratops* skull (see page 41).

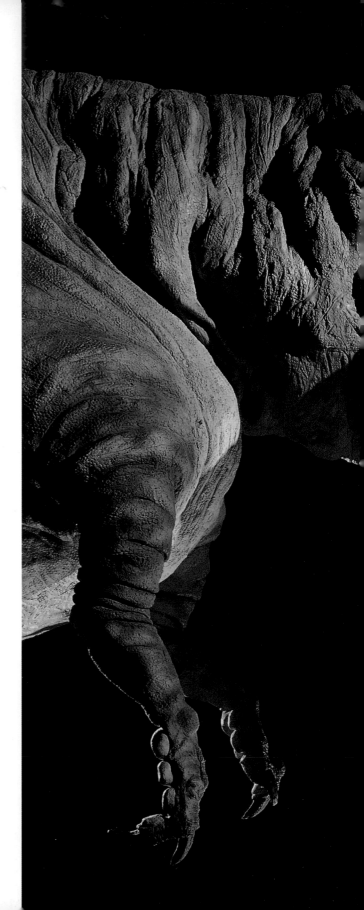

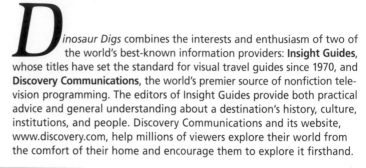

*D*inosaur Digs combines the interests and enthusiasm of two of the world's best-known information providers: **Insight Guides**, whose titles have set the standard for visual travel guides since 1970, and **Discovery Communications**, the world's premier source of nonfiction television programming. The editors of Insight Guides provide both practical advice and general understanding about a destination's history, culture, institutions, and people. Discovery Communications and its website, www.discovery.com, help millions of viewers explore their world from the comfort of their home and encourage them to explore it firsthand.

About This Book

This book reflects the contributions of dedicated editors and writers familiar with North America's most fascinating dinosaur fossil sites and museums. Series editor **John Gattuso**, of Stone Creek Publications in New Jersey, worked with Insight Guides and Discovery Communications to conceive and direct the series.

Gattuso looked to **Blake Edgar**, a science journalist and editor based in Northern California, to manage the project. Edgar knew all about the skeletons in the human closet before he took on the job. He had collaborated with famed fossil hunter Donald Johanson, the discoverer of Lucy, on *From Lucy to Language* and *Ancestors*. This book immersed him in the lore and literature of dinosaurs and prompted a road trip to Dinosaur National Monument and several other sites in the "Dinosaur Diamond" of Utah and western Colorado. "Dinosaurs captivate us like few animals living or dead," says Edgar, "and North America is blessed with many places to encounter them."

He assembled a crackerjack team of 20 science-minded journalists from across the continent to cover the basics on dinosaurs, from what they are to how – or whether – they went extinct, and to profile the best museums, bone quarries, and excavation programs devoted to these charismatic creatures.

One of Edgar's first choices, **Don Lessem**, also known as "Dino Don," runs Dinosaur Productions in Massachusetts and has 15 books to his credit, including *The Complete T. Rex*. For this guide, he profiled several East Coast sites and reported on the state of dinosaur science and what we know of the beasts' behavior and biology.

Robert J. Coontz, Jr., a former editor at *Earth and The Sciences*, chronicled the Great Bone Wars of the late 19th and early 20th centuries as well as the ethics of collecting fossils today. "Early paleontologists were like Gilded Age magnates struggling to corner the fossil market, but they were also staking out territory in people's imaginations," Coontz says. "The bone hunters were discovering a new world, one whose remains had to be hauled, slab by slab and ton by ton, out of bare rock."

Josh Fischman, former editor-in-chief of *Earth* magazine, trekked to Alberta's Dinosaur Provincial Park and spent a day on his stomach in a trench near the Royal Tyrrell Museum surrounded by centrosaur bones and digging carefully through the dirt in search of more. "Eight hours under the broiling sun and all I had to show for it at the end were dirty knees, a tiny piece of amber, and a new appreciation for the painstaking nature of paleontology." Other sites in Canada were covered by photojournalist **Linda J. Moore** and travel writer **Wayne Curtis**.

Mary K. Miller, a writer for the Exploratorium in San Francisco, visited California museums and investigated the bones, eggs, trackways, and other fossil evidence that paleontologists use to reconstruct dinosaur anatomy and behavior. "Even though I work in a museum," says Miller, "I'm always thrilled to poke through the collections of other museums. For this book, I got to heft a mastodon jaw collected by Thomas Jefferson, sit inside a sauropod footprint, and rub my finger on a *T. rex* tooth still razor-sharp after 75 million years."

Oregon writer and editor **Margaret Herring** trekked to the John Day Basin, and Flagstaff-based freelancer **Peter Friederici** tracked early dinosaurs at Arizona's Petrified Forest National Park. **Catherine Dold** and University of Colorado journalism professor **Tom Yulsman** wrote about fossil sites in Colorado.

Alexandra Witze, science reporter for the *Dallas Morning News*, covered New Mexico and Texas, where she swam above sauropod footprints in the Paluxy River. *Billings Gazette* reporter **Michael Milstein** and freelancer **Yvonne Baskin**, author of *The Work of Nature*, wrote about dinosaur sites in Wyoming and Montana, respectively. *San Francisco Examiner* reporter **Ulysses Torassa** explored the Cleveland Museum of Natural History.

On the East Coast, **Sarah Simpson** of *Scientific American* ventured down Maryland's Dinosaur Alley, **Richard Monastersky** of *Science News* wrote about the Smithsonian, *Science* correspondent **Ann Gibbons** covered the Carnegie Museum, and freelancer **JoAnn C. Gutin** took on Manhattan, or at least its American Museum of Natural History.

Geologist and paleontologist **Lowell Dingus**, co-author of *The Mistaken Extinction* and a participant in major dinosaur discoveries in Mongolia and Patagonia, explored what happened to the dinosaurs 65 million years ago. And should you desire to dig up your own dinosaurs, New York City-based freelancer **Beth Livermore** investigated some of the best participatory programs in the United States and abroad.

Thanks to Steve Manning of The Nature Company and the many curators, park rangers and naturalists who reviewed the text. Thanks also to members of Stone Creek Publications' editorial team: Judith Dunham, Edward A. Jardim, Michael Castagna, and Nicole Buchenholz.

Martin Lockley (above), an expert on dinosaur tracks, displays the cast of a *Tyrannosaurus rex* footprint from New Mexico.

Fossil hunter (opposite) Hans Larsson rappels down a cliff to remove centrosaur bones in Canada's Dinosaur Provincial Park.

Primitive predator *Coelophysis* (below) may have eaten its own young on occasion. This skeleton resides at the Museum of Northern Arizona.

Preparators, or fossil technicians (following pages), in London arrange bones of an ornithomimid dinosaur before the massive skull of *Triceratops*.

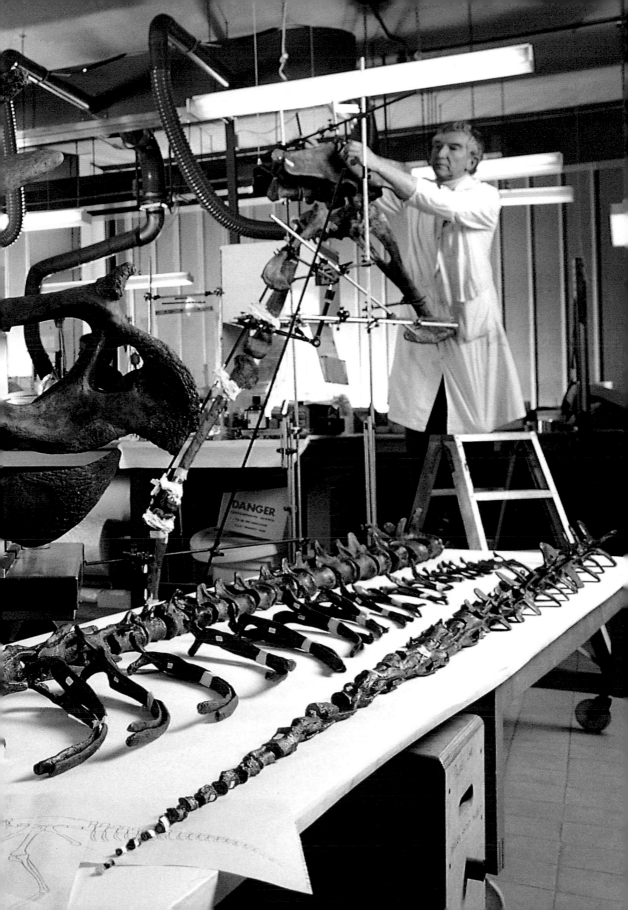

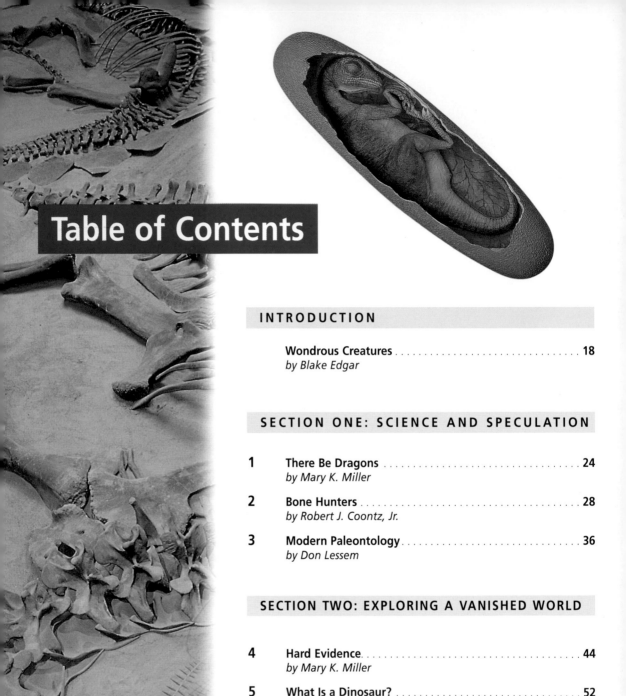

Table of Contents

Continued on next page

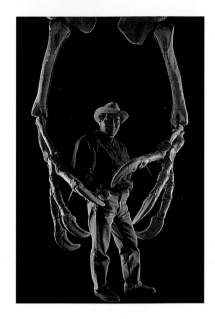

MAPS

SECTION FOUR: EXPLORING MUSEUMS

MAPS

PRICE GUIDE –
Admission to fossil sites and museums
$ = up to $10 $$ = $11–$25
$$$ = $26–$40 $$$$ = $41 and up

n 1802, a farmer with the improbable name of Pliny Moody stumbled upon dinosaur footprints while plowing his father's field in Massachusetts. They were the first ever documented in North America. ◆ Today, dinosaurs are popping up all over the place. From museums to movie theaters, it seems we can't get enough of these fascinating creatures. Pretty impressive, considering that they died out 65 million years ago. Humans may be top dog now, but dinosaurs filled that role for more than 160 million years. You could squeeze more than eight million human generations into the amount of time that dinosaurs trod the Earth. ◆ "With a temporal span of 163 million years," says paleontologist Peter Dodson, "dinosaurs cannot be judged as failures by puny, naked bipeds who have been here for two million years." ◆ Extinct? Maybe not. Some of Dodson's colleagues insist that the Age of Dinosaurs endures. They argue that birds are the direct descendants of certain dinosaurs, and that more than twice

Extinct or not, dinosaurs thrive in our imaginations. There's never been a better time to explore the world of these fantastic beings.

as many kinds of birds exist today as do mammals. Paleontologist Jacques Gauthier has remarked that members of the Audubon Society and members of the Dinosaur Society "actually belong to the same club." ◆ Whether or not you consent to living in the Age of Dinosaurs, there can be no doubt that this is a golden age of dinosaur discovery. About six new species are added to the dinosaur roll call every year. In 1998, for example, newspapers carried the story of a strange new carnivorous dinosaur from Niger, *Suchomimus*, a fish eater with crocodile-like head and jaws. In the same

Sparks fly as a *Tyrannosaurus rex* named Black Beauty gets ready for its museum debut.

Preceding pages: *T-rex* courtship portrayed by Richard Penney; technicians prepare skeleton mounts in Drumheller, Alberta; paleontologist Paul Sereno ponders a human skull from inside the jaws of *Carcharodontosaurus*.

A **sauropod footprint** (left) easily contains young Tommy Pendly. This print is part of a Texas trackway.

Mere ropes (right) would not restrain a real *Allosaurus* but suffice for this fiberglass sculpture on a road trip through the Southwest.

Horned dinosaurs (below) like this *Centrosaurus flexus* formed huge herds 75 million years ago.

week came the announcement from Patagonia of a vast dinosaur hatchery harboring the first sauropod embryos ever found and the first fossil skin from a dinosaur embryo.

Nearly 60 years elapsed between the discovery of the third *Tyrannosaurus rex*, in 1907, and the fourth. In just the last 10 years, however, the number of *T. rex* discoveries has doubled. There are now almost two dozen specimens of the "Tyrant Lizard King," including the most complete skeletons ever unearthed.

There's still plenty to discover about dinosaurs.

The experts think that we have sampled only a small fraction – they disagree on the exact percentage – of total dinosaur diversity. Nearly half of all dinosaurs named are known from just a single specimen of each, and only a fifth have fairly complete skulls or skeletons to study. We know much more about the kinds of dinosaurs living at the very end of their reign on Earth than we do from the beginning, or from several periods of time in the middle.

Readers of this guide will explore some of the world's richest dinosaur country. The United States contains remains of more kinds of dinosaurs than any other nation – well ahead of Mongolia and China – and Canada is among the top five dinosaur-producing

nations. Whether you're on a solo sojourn to fossil-laden badlands or part of an official excavation team, North America is a prime place to search for these ancient beasts. If you prefer to see the successes of yesterday's and today's fossil finders, this guide directs you toward the top showcases for dinosaur bones. Should you become inspired to dig deeper, several programs teach proper excavation techniques at field sites from Montana to Mongolia.

Amateurs like Pliny Moody back in 1802 have contributed greatly to our knowledge of dinosaurs. Even children make important discoveries. Recently, digging in the sand along New Mexico's Rio Puerco with his toy backhoe, three-year-old David Shiffler excavated a tiny fragment from a dinosaur egg laid 150 million years ago. In Montana in 1993, 15-year-old Sherri Flamand found the most complete maiasaur specimen known, while in the same year, 14-year-old Stephanie Willen unearthed the first dinosaur egg from the Mygatt-Moore Quarry in western Colorado. It could be your turn next. Good hunting.

Science and Speculation

Dinosaur discoveries have inspired imaginative tales and incited heated quests for their remains. Today's scientific techniques help clarify our image of these beasts, but there's still room for speculation and creativity.

Long before 19th-century scientists first began to search for dinosaur fossils, people were finding large bones with odd, yet somehow familiar, shapes and coming up with their own imaginative explanations of what they were. The Sioux believed that dinosaur fossils were huge serpents that burrowed into the ground to die from wounds. In Indochina, legend interprets dinosaur bones as belonging to a sacred buffalo that carries the sun across the sky every day and returns to the jungle each night to die. In 1935, a French geologist traveling in what is now Vietnam could not collect any of these "stone bones" without making a sacrifice of livestock to the buffalo.   ◆   In ancient China, dinosaur fossils were regarded as the remains of dragons, venerated beasts with magical healing powers. The Chinese word for these creatures is *konglong*, which still means both "dinosaur" and "terrible dragon." According to a legend from the third century, the

Legends of gold-hoarding griffins and other mythical beasts may stem from early discoveries of dinosaur bones.

dragon failed in its attempts to enter Heaven and fell back to Earth, where it sank into the ground. "Dragon bones" have been ground up for traditional medicine since at least the 12th century; to this day they can be purchased in Chinese pharmacies to bring good luck and strength.   ◆   The ancient Greeks were also fascinated with dinosaur fossils, but the bones elicited more fear than reverence. The mountains of central Asia were thought to be populated with fierce beasts called griffins, part bird and part mammal. An epic Greek poem from the seventh century B.C. describes griffins as silent hounds with sharp beaks and a lion's strength. Griffins guarded gold mines along the trade route between China and what is now Kazakhstan. To avoid

Fire-breathing dragons of legend were partly inspired by dinosaur fossils found in ancient times.

Preceding pages: A bone-filled basement at Humboldt University in Berlin holds fossil *Brachiosaurus* limbs excavated in Tanzania.

the terrible creatures, miners waited until dark to search for gold.

Behind the Myth of Griffins

The Greeks regularly traveled through central Asia, and the griffin became a recurring icon in their art and folklore. Paintings, jewelry, and bronze reliefs depict the mythical beast in stunning detail. For a millennium, particulars of the griffin's anatomy and size remained consistent. Unlike any living bird or beast, griffins were described as being from six to seven feet long, with four legs, two webbed wings, and a hooked beak. Could the legend be grounded in reality?

A Chinese pharmacist (right) dispenses powdered dinosaur bone, which is believed by some to enhance strength and good luck.

Griffins (opposite, bottom), big-beaked mythical beasts with horns and pointed ears, appear frequently in Greek art and folklore, possibly inspired by fossils of *Protoceratops* (above) found in Asia.

A sea monster (opposite, top) stampedes through London to reclaim its offspring in the science-fiction movie *Gorgo*, one of many modern myths inspired by dinosaurs.

During a collecting expedition to the fossil-rich Gobi Desert in the 1920s, Roy Chapman Andrews and his team from the American Museum of Natural History discovered a vast nesting ground and skeletons of *Protoceratops*, a dinosaur about seven feet long with four limbs, claws, and a vicious-looking beak. Later expeditions to the mountains of central Asia found the fossilized remains of psittacosaurs, primitive horned dinosaurs with parrot-like beaks. The white fossils are abundant and conspicuous against wind-swept red sands. Folklorist Adrienne Mayor suggests that ancient nomads and traders could easily have come across the intact remains of these lion-sized dinosaurs, drawing their own fearful conclusions about why they lived among the rich gold deposits.

Theropod Tracks and Biblical Birds

Dinosaur tracks have also long intrigued observers. African Bushmen, themselves

skilled trackers, recognized that dinosaur footprints were made by a large, two-legged predator not unlike current notions of theropod dinosaurs. Native peoples in Brazil and North America sometimes depicted dinosaur tracks in their rock art; at one site in southern Utah, a pictograph shows a three-toed footprint like those at a nearby theropod track site. Australian aborigines have incorporated dinosaur track sites into their song lines, stories of sacred sites, and events with deep religious and cultural significance. The recent theft of stegosaur footprints from such a site in the Australian Outback is considered a huge cultural and scientific loss.

When the first documented dinosaur tracks in North America were discovered by the Massachusetts farmer Pliny Moody in 1802, the three-toed tracks were interpreted by religious authorities as belonging to "Noah's raven," a bird of truly biblical proportions. More tracks uncovered in New England spawned the science of ichnology, the study of fossil tracks; ichnology's father, Edward Hitchcock, described countless dinosaur tracks in the Connecticut River Valley from 1836 to 1865. Hitchcock also believed that the tracks were made by giant flightless birds and never accepted the notion that many were left by dinosaurs. His ideas have been somewhat redeemed, as many paleontologists now consider birds to be directly descended from some dinosaurs.

They Might Be Giants

The first scientific citation of a dinosaur bone dates to 1677. In his work, *The Natural History of Oxfordshire*, Robert Plott drew and described a petrified bone fragment with two rounded ends. At first, he thought it resembled the thighbone of an ox or elephant, but with a 23-inch diameter, the fossil was far too large to be either. Failing in his attempts to identify the bone by comparing it to living creatures, Plott concluded that it had belonged to one of the biblical "giants of the earth." The actual specimen was lost, but scientists now believe that it came from *Megalosaurus*, a carnivorous dinosaur known to have been from Oxfordshire.

In 1763, Robert Brooke published a more precise – though no more accurate – interpretation of Plott's specimen. In his *Natural History of Waters, Earths, Stones, Fossils, and Minerals*, Brooke named the fossil *Scrotum humanum* for its pendulous resemblance to male genitalia. This ribald moniker was the first name applied to the specimen and, under the strict rules of scientific nomenclature, should have remained the scientific name for what we know as *Megalosaurus*. Cooler heads prevailed, however. Since Plott's bone was lost, there was no way to prove its identity, and *Scrotum* did not survive as the first generic dinosaur name.

To sensation-seeking readers, the story that appeared in the *New York Herald* on January 12, 1890, was almost as good as a high-society murder. The article trumpeted, "Scientists wage bitter warfare. Prof. Cope of the University of Pennsylvania brings serious charges against ... Prof. Marsh, of the Geological Survey ... Learned men come to the Pennsylvanian's support with allegations of ignorance, plagiarism, and incompetence." ◆ To the "learned men," this was old news. The two scientists at the center of the conflict, Edward Drinker Cope and Othniel Charles Marsh, had been savaging each other's reputations without letup for more than two decades. Each had set his sights on becoming the preeminent vertebrate paleontologist in America. Their personal duel, which stretched from the smoke-filled back-rooms of the nation's capital to the fossil-rich badlands of the West, left its mark on two generations of scientists and gave a name to the first great era of American dinosaur exploration: the Great

Bitterness between scientists in the 19th century sparked a fossil feud and an unprecedented rush for bigger and better bones.

Bone Wars. ◆ At the start of the 1870s, the men were well matched. Cope was an independent scientist with ties to the Academy of Sciences in Philadelphia; Marsh was a professor at Yale University and director of the university's Peabody Museum. Both were boundlessly energetic and ambitious, and, just as important, both had money. ◆ Cope had been a scientific boy wonder. Born in 1840, the son of a wealthy Quaker shipowner, he quickly became known as an expert's expert on anything that walked, crawled, swam, or slithered. At the age of 18 he published the first of more than 12,000 scientific papers, articles, essays, and books, many of which dealt

Walter Granger examines the hind limb of a *Diplodocus* at Wyoming's Bone Cabin Quarry. This site and nearby Como Bluff produced a bounty of dinosaur bones.

Othniel Marsh (left) poses with Chief Red Cloud, who let Marsh's fossil prospectors cross Sioux land. In exchange, Marsh spoke on the Sioux's behalf with President Ulysses Grant.

Duckbilled *Anatotitan* (below) was collected in South Dakota for Edward Cope in 1882. This illustration by Erwin Christman shows the skull from above.

Edward Cope (opposite, top), a brash and brainy pioneer paleontologist, had to sell his vast fossil collection to pay off debts.

Marsh's motley crew (opposite bottom) of fossil hunters scoured badlands throughout the West for dinosaur skeletons to stock the Peabody Museum at Yale University.

Clash of Titans

Cope and Marsh met when they were students in Berlin, Germany. They struck up a correspondence and, after the American Civil War, spent a week collecting fossils together near Cope's home in Haddonfield, New Jersey (where Leidy had discovered the first American dinosaur, *Hadrosaurus*, in 1868). But their two drives – Marsh's need to be first, and Cope's need to be right – made a quarrel inevitable. The spark hit the tinder when Cope showed Marsh his restoration of a plesiosaur, a long-necked marine reptile called *Elasmosaurus*. Marsh pointed out, correctly, that Cope had attached the beast's skull to the end of its tail. Mortified, Cope scrambled to buy up every copy of the journal in which his paper had appeared. He never forgave Marsh for what he considered an impertinence.

After that it was gloves off, as the two scientists vied to smear each other's reputations and build their own. The formula: find new fossils, rush their names and descriptions into print, and seize on your opponent's mistakes. The campaign focused on the American West, which Indian Wars and railroads had opened up to large-scale scientific exploration for the first time. Cope spent most of the 1870s prospecting for fossils as an

with evolutionary theory. Cope, taking issue with Charles Darwin, believed that animals could *choose* how they would evolve, an idea he considered compatible with a divine master plan for life.

His theories won him many disciples but few friends. Cope was a loner, sharp-tongued and short-tempered, with a jutting jaw that a biographer called "an affront to the peace." Even his scientific mentor, the renowned anatomist Joseph Leidy, said, "He does things in an unnecessarily offensive manner."

Marsh, by contrast, was a slow starter. Nine years older than Cope, he was plucked

from idleness by his uncle, the self-made millionaire financier George Peabody, who sent young "O. C." to Yale at the advanced age of 26, and later bought him a professorship as a condition for endowing the university's museum of natural history. Marsh, however, was no dilettante but a methodical scientific worker, a collector and categorizer rather than a theorist. Formal and status-hungry, with a genius for networking and self-promotion, he pursued his scientific career with the cool determination of a business magnate taking over an industry.

unpaid volunteer with government survey teams. Marsh, meanwhile, organized field trips for Yale seniors, who took time off from fossils to hunt bison with army scouts (among them "Buffalo Bill" Cody) and to flirt with the 22 daughters of Mormon leader Brigham Young. In 1874, in exchange for safe passage across Sioux territory, the Sioux leader Red Cloud made Marsh promise to meet with President Ulysses S. Grant and pass on complaints about corrupt government agents. Marsh did indeed meet with the president and leaked details of his encounter to the press. Heads rolled, and the resultant burst of

publicity may have propelled Marsh into the National Academy of Sciences (with one dissenting vote – undoubtedly Cope's).

The Bone War simmered throughout the early 1870s as Cope and Marsh built up their research machines. In the West they recruited agents – freelance fossil hunters who were tough, resourceful, and ready to dig for the highest bidder. In the East they cultivated the editors of scientific journals, offering big scoops in exchange for permission to send in papers, often by telegraph, on the brink of a deadline. *The American Journal of Science* got so tired of resetting its type to accom-

modate Marsh's multiple last-minute submissions that it started running his papers in a special appendix. Cope wound up buying his favorite outlet, *American Naturalist*. In addition, Marsh had one

luxury Cope could not match: a museum staff to prepare and study his fossils, work for which Marsh blithely neglected to share credit.

In 1877, three big fossil strikes brought the war to a rolling boil. In Colorado, near the town of Morrison, an English-born schoolteacher named Arthur Lakes reported finding some enormous dinosaur bones, crates of which he sent to both Marsh and Cope. While Cope was still studying the bones, Marsh had dispatched his agent Samuel Wendell Williston to buy Lake's loyalty for $100. Cope had to surrender his specimens to Marsh. The dinosaur, which

Marsh called *Titanosaurus* (since renamed *Atlantosaurus*), was the biggest ever found.

Hot on the heels of that discovery, another Colorado schoolteacher, O. W. Lucas of Cañon City, wrote to Cope with a similar report. Cope promptly hired Lucas and wired money for a field crew. The resultant dinosaur was even bigger than the one in Morrison. Cope called it *Camarasaurus*.

Then came a letter that tipped the war in Marsh's favor: "Dear Sir: I write to announce to you the discovery not far from this place, of a large number of fossils.... We are working men and are not able to present them as

a gift, and if we can sell the secret of the fossil bed, and procure work in excavating others we would like to do so.... We would be pleased to hear from you, as you are well known as an enthusiastic geologist, and a man of means, both of which we are desirous of finding – more especially the latter."

Bounty of Bones

They had found their man. The informants, William E. Carlin and William H. Reed, were the station agent and section foreman, respectively, for the Union Pacific Railroad at Como Station, about 10 miles east of Medicine Bow, Wyoming. Marsh fired off a

Barnum Brown (left), the legendary paleontologist from the American Museum of Natural History, preserves a theropod dinosaur trackway.

Iguanodon (below) and other life-size models were shown at London's Crystal Palace in 1853. Anatomist Richard Owen (right) supervised their creation.

Richard Owen and the Crystal Palace

Twenty-two of Britain's top scientists came together on New Year's Eve in 1853 to dine in the belly of an *Iguanodon*. Their host was Richard Owen, the renowned comparative anatomist. He helped design the 28-foot-long model, along with other life-size dinosaur reconstructions, as lawn ornaments for the famous Crystal Palace, centerpiece of the first world's fair, in London's Hyde Park.

Eleven years earlier, Owen had coined the word Dinosauria ("fearfully great lizards"), in part as a jab at pre-Darwinian ideas of evolution. If the supreme reptiles had died out eons ago, Owen argued, their fate must have been due to divine fiat rather than to some godless natural drive toward perfection.

Owen's theories would soon seem as quaint as his squat, four-legged *Iguanodon*. But at this banquet, he and his models were creatures of the moment – party animals reveling in fleeting glory.

telegram to Williston, who found the men, swore them to secrecy, and put them to work.

Carlin and Reed had found the Jurassic mother lode. Soon Marsh's work crews were shipping back bones by the ton, everything from nearly complete skeletons of giant sauropods and carnivores to the fingernail-sized jaws of the earliest mammals then known. Cope's spies found the spot and opened their own quarry on the fringes of the excavation. Contrary to legend, the rivalry between the crews probably stopped short of out-and-out violence, but the teams were obsessively secretive and jealous of their own turf. They kept a close eye on each other and, on abandoning a quarry, smashed any leftover fossils in it to keep them from falling into enemy hands.

The work was hard, especially during winter, and paychecks could be slow in coming. Backbiting among teammates was rife, and several workers, including Carlin, switched sides. Nevertheless, hundreds of tons of bones made their way back to Philadelphia and New Haven. Cope and Marsh could have spent the rest of their careers studying the fossils they amassed from Como Bluff alone.

Unfortunately, Cope did not get the chance to rest on his laurels. During the 1880s, he watched with frustration as Marsh gained power and prestige. In 1882, Marsh became the first vertebrate paleontologist of the recently organized U.S. Geological Survey. A year later he was elected president of the National Academy of Sciences. Meanwhile, Cope's own star was falling fast. He had to curtail his field expeditions after squandering his family fortune on bad investments in Mexican silver mines, and now, with his nemesis entrenched in a powerful position, he could not count on government support for his projects. To add insult to injury, in 1889 the Secretary of the Interior, spurred on by Marsh, tried to confiscate Cope's personal fossil collection on the grounds that Cope had collected the fossils while on government-sponsored expeditions.

War Without Winners

To Cope, this was the last straw. The fossils were his nest egg; if he lost them, he lost everything. In desperation, he phoned the *New York Herald* and vented the accu-

Cope's field notes (opposite, top) record details of the geologic setting for some of his fossil discoveries.

Automobiles (opposite, bottom) made remote areas more accessible for collecting trips. Barnum Brown, seen at center in the 1930s, led the great era of fossil exploration that followed the Cope–Marsh feud.

Apatosaurus **limbs** (right) supported the first sauropod skeleton exhibited anywhere. This mount went on display in New York City in 1905.

mulated grievances of 20 years. He charged Marsh with stealing credit, plagiarizing results, and packing the National Academy of Sciences with cronies. In effect, he said, Marsh wasn't a scientist at all but a "scientific-political adventurer." Marsh lashed back, accusing Cope of out-and-out fossil theft and resurrecting the story about the wrong-headed *Elasmosaurus*. Supporters rallied around the combatants, and for two weeks the public was treated to the sight of two august paleontologists dragging the skeletons out of each other's closets.

When the smoke cleared, there were no winners. Cope kept his fossil collection, only to sell most of it to the American Museum of Natural History a few years later to pay his mounting debts. He died in 1897. Marsh was reelected president of the National Academy of Sciences, but his job at the Geological Survey was abolished by congressional budget-slashers hostile toward the survey's conservationist

agenda. He died in 1899.

Between them, they had discovered more than 130 species of dinosaurs, as well as flying reptiles, marine reptiles, birds, and ancient mammals. They had pioneered field techniques still in use today. And they had trained a whole generation of

paleontologists – a peaceful generation, for the most part. In the bone rushes that followed, in Montana, Alberta, Mongolia, and elsewhere, the successors of Cope and Marsh made it clear that, as far as they were concerned, nothing like the Great Bone War would ever happen again.

Modern Paleontology

After three and a half years of excavation, paleontologist Dan Chure of Dinosaur National Monument uncovered an 18-foot, juvenile *Allosaurus* skeleton, a rare find in a quarry renowned as the Jurassic jackpot for giant sauropods. But the beast lacked a head, and no one knew whether more digging into a steep slope would expose it. Enter radiation analyst and amateur fossil hunter Ramal Jones, who had built a promising new tool for finding buried bones that contain radioactive uranium. In 1996, Jones brought his dinosaur detector to the site of Chure's excavation. Six feet from where the skeleton had been removed, Jones got a strong radiation reading. A few hammer blows exposed a lovely *Allosaurus* skull – and from a new species to boot. ◆ Nowadays, much of dinosaur science combines old-fashioned prospecting with newfangled gadgetry.

While rooted in rich tradition, paleontologists pursue novel ways to learn more about their quarry.

But old ways die hard. Fossils are still found as they were a century ago, mostly by serendipitous scavenging. Amateurs and volunteers continue to play major roles in discovering, digging, and cleaning dinosaur bones. During excavation, the bones get wrapped in protective shells, or jackets, of plaster, just as pioneer paleontologist Edward Cope did it in the 1870s. ◆ Despite all the media and public attention, the paltry budget devoted to dinosaur science today barely nudges into seven figures. This remains the profession of a small, dedicated bunch, with just a few dozen researchers digging for dinosaurs worldwide. Many go about their work quietly, while others become colorful, celebrated characters: pony-tailed maverick Bob Bakker, ornery college dropout Jack Horner, and dashing globe-trotter Paul Sereno. Conspicuous or not, the leading dinosaur scientists are

High-stepping *T. rex* towers over Bob Bakker, the dinosaur paleontologist who designed this active pose for the Denver Museum of Natural History.

Virtual Dinosaurs

Generations of special-effects artists have fed our enduring desire to give sound and motion to dinosaurs. Rapidly growing computer graphic capabilities continue to produce more realistic dinosaurs on movie screens. Now scientists are getting into the act, using computers to study how dinosaurs moved and sounded.

Paleontologists conceived a computer model to simulate honking sounds from the hollow, trombone-shaped crest atop the skull of *Parasaurolophus*. Chambers in the crest open to the throat, and the crest could have resonated with low, haunting tones or, if this dinosaur had vocal cords, birdlike chirps.

Microsoft technology guru Nathan Myhrvold modeled the tail of a giant sauropod on his computer and made a surprising discovery. It turns out that these supposedly defenseless beasts could crack their tail like a whip at supersonic speeds – generating ear-splitting booms that might have scared off enemies.

Cyberpaleontologist Kent Stevens has looked at the opposite end of sauropods, using computers to infer the potential range of motion in their long necks. Some kinds could hold their necks scarcely higher than horizontal, while others swung their necks nearly upright.

Less exotic but more informative 3-D computer models of dinosaur bones allow experts to peer inside the skeleton or to reconstruct flattened fossils with the click of a mouse. Re-creating dinosaurs in such piecemeal fashion will never fully capture what these creatures could do in life, but the approximations are too compelling to give up.

Model *Maiasaura* (above), built by the Japanese company Kokoro, will eventually move and make noise with the help of human technology.

Paleontologists (opposite, top) haul a plaster-coated piece of a *Kritosaurus*, excavated in New Mexico's Bisti Badlands.

A plastic toy (opposite, bottom) submerged in water helps paleontologist James Farlow estimate that the long-necked *Mamenchisaurus* weighed 23 tons.

revolutionaries, overturning outdated methods and coming up with fresh ideas. Bakker, for example, has steadfastly supported the idea that dinosaurs were as active and agile as today's birds and mammals. Horner's discoveries have opened our eyes to communal nesting and probable parental care among the duckbilled *Maiasaura*. In addition to adopting a new approach to constructing dinosaur family trees, Sereno has uncovered a string of new and unusual species on two continents, including some of the oldest known dinosaurs.

Beyond mounting skeletons and making headlines, modern paleontology involves the integration of the latest discoveries into an ever more detailed portrait of dinosaur life. It also addresses larger environmental questions about the nature of ancient ecosystems and how they changed during the 150 million years that dinosaurs dominated life on land. While it's true that in the past two centuries scientists have identified scarcely 350 kinds, or genera, of dinosaurs – many from a single tooth or bone – we know of twice as many dinosaurs now as we did 20 years ago. On average, at least one new kind of dinosaur gets discovered every six weeks.

Fossils keep emerging from predictable places such as Mongolia, China, Canada, Argentina, and the United States, but also from such surprising spots as Australia, Italy, and Romania. Among the new discoveries in Argentina are the biggest land animal that ever lived, 100-ton *Argentinosaurus*, and the earliest known dinosaur, tiny *Eoraptor*. Pliny the Elder could have been thinking about dinosaurs, too, when he noted that there was always something new out of Africa. The vast Sahara has recently revealed an amazing array of predatory dinosaurs. First came *Carcharodontosaurus*, with a longer skull than the largest *Tyrannosaurus rex*, and slender *Afrovenator* – both relatives of North America's *Allosaurus*. Even stranger is *Suchomimus*, a 35-foot, crocodile-snouted fish-eater.

Renaissance in Dinosaur Science

Along with new bones to study come new ways to study them. Today's paleontologists use radar, radioactivity detectors, and infrared sensors to locate fossils in the ground. Back at the lab, CAT scans are revealing the inner architecture of dinosaur anatomy. Miniature pneumatic drills are supplanting awls and brushes, allowing for more precise separation of precious fossil from encrusting rock. Experts and amateurs alike bring better training and broader knowledge to the

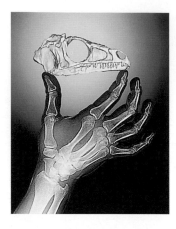

task of interpreting fossils. For dinosaur science, this time will be remembered as a renaissance.

Here's a case in point: Two decades ago, the only known dinosaur nests were to be found in the Gobi Desert of Mongolia. Paleontologists have since uncovered nests of plant eaters and meat eaters in Europe, the Americas, Africa, and elsewhere in Asia. Add to this the magnificent Montana *Maiasaura* hatchery and other finds of babies and adolescents, and dinosaurs begin to take shape as members of families and communities. Their rate and manner of growth can be analyzed and compared with living animals.

A subtle yet significant revolution has also altered our understanding of broad-scale dinosaur relationships and where they fit into the tapestry of evolution. Any kid can tell you that dinosaurs were big, land-dwelling animals that lived only during the Mesozoic. But for a new generation of scientists, classifying dinosaurs requires more meaningful definitions. By comparing a host of distinctive, shared anatomical and behavioral features, they have reshaped the dinosaur family tree. Traits such as an S-shaped neck and locked ankle joints form the basis of this new theoretical framework, known as cladistics.

A frustration for today's experts, but good news for ambitious children, is the fact that thousands more dinosaurs remain buried, along with abundant mysteries about their lives. Some scientists say we've only found about a quarter of all the kinds of dinosaurs that existed during their incredible reign. A long road of discovery lies ahead, but modern paleontologists have covered considerable ground.

An x-ray (top, left) reveals the bone structure of *Eoraptor*, the earliest known dinosaur, dating from about 228 million years ago.

British scientist Terry Manning (left) soaks dinosaur eggs in a weak acid solution that slowly dissolves the rock inside each shell, leaving behind the embryos' bones.

White bones (right) emerge from red sand as paleontologist Luis Chiappe excavates a *Protoceratops* skull from Mongolia's Gobi Desert.

◆

Exploring A Vanished World

◆

From elusive origin to enigmatic extinction,
dinosaurs confront us with many mysteries.
Probing fossils and assembling intricate family
trees help answer at least some of our questions
about their lives and world.

Hard Evidence

CHAPTER 4

Besides being objects of great beauty, fossils offer the only concrete data paleontologists have to reconstruct the lives of extinct creatures. Dinosaur fossils – bones, teeth, eggs, and claws – are usually body parts hard enough to withstand the ravages of time and remain intact or nearly so. Very rarely, casts of internal organs or the brain may be preserved. There are also trace fossils: footprints, mineralized feces, stomach stones called gastroliths, and impressions left by skin or feathers. ◆ The odds are stacked against an animal becoming a fossil. Paleontologists estimate that less than one percent of all animals that once lived on Earth have been preserved in the fossil record. To achieve immortality this way, an animal has to die where rivers, streams, or lakes can supply enough sediment for a quick burial. Mudslides, sandstorms, or volcanic ash eruptions can also do the trick. Once buried, though, even robust bones have no guarantee of success. Soil, peat bogs, and other acidic environments can dissolve bone completely.

Dinosaur science is built on a foundation of fossils – bones, footprints, eggs, and whatever else was left behind.

A carcass that sits too long on the surface will be torn apart by scavengers, which scatter the skeleton or even digest it. A shallow burial may bring bones back to the surface prematurely; too deep a burial, and the bones may never work their way back, despite help from wind and water. ◆ Those tough enough to survive tend to be the more durable body parts from bigger individuals. Discoveries of relatively dainty sauropod skulls, for example, have been few and far between, while their bulky leg bones and vertebrae turn up frequently. When museums first mounted the enormous skeletons of sauropods, the dinosaurs often remained headless or

Dinosaur bone cells, shown behind Armand de Ricqlès, resemble those found in fast-growing, warm-blooded mammals.

Preceding pages: "Bird robber" *Ornitholestes* leaps after a pterodactyl.

Tough substances like teeth (left) stand a better chance of becoming fossils. This ankylosaur tooth was found in Antarctica.

Sharklike teeth (below) of *Megalosaurus* would be replaced whenever they were broken or fell out.

Amber traps insects (opposite, top) and other small animals intact, but no dinosaurs have been preserved in this petrified tree resin.

Fragile fossils (opposite, bottom) like this *T. rex* pelvis being unearthed in South Dakota need a protective plaster "jacket" to be moved safely.

had the wrong skull attached. For more than half a century, the *Apatosaurus* in the American Museum of Natural History wore a *Camarasaurus* head atop its long neck.

Although bones need the deposition of sediment as the first step toward sticking around, at some point erosion must occur for buried bones to be exposed and excavated. Despite the long odds, major dinosaur discoveries occur with pleasing regularity. Remains of species new and familiar are found all over the planet, even in Alaska and Antarctica. North America's richest bone deposits occur in geologically active areas with thick sediments, such as the badlands of the western interior states and Alberta, Canada. During the Cretaceous Period, these desolate lands were foothills along a vast inland sea. Streams flowing down the newly formed Rocky Mountains carried debris that routinely blanketed the surface in thick layers of mud. Deep underground, soft sediments surrounding any bones hardened into rock. Wind and water gradually laid bare vast boneyards. (Paleontologists estimate that nearly three-fourths of Montana's surface consists of Cretaceous sediments.)

Choice fossil beds can be found where old rock layers are exposed: in river canyons, wind-whipped deserts, quarries, road cuts, railway lines, and building foundations. Even the construction of paleontology museums has uncovered new fossils for their collections.

How Bones Become Fossils

Only 60 percent solid, living bone is filled with pores

containing cells, blood vessels, and marrow. Water percolates through these spaces in buried bones, leaving behind minerals such as calcium, silicate, or iron. This process, called permineralization, sometimes happens in a matter of months.

Permineralization makes an old bone look and feel like rock, leading to the common perception that fossils are simply bone turned to stone. But researchers such as Hilde Schwartz dispute that bit of dinosaur dogma. Instead of becoming petrified like wood, with all the bone crystals replaced by minerals, they think that much of the original bone sticks around. "The crucial thing to understand about fossils," says Schwartz, "is that they don't have to 'form' at all. They merely have to somehow survive."

Many rare elements, like phosphate, occur in both living and fossilized bones, suggesting that fossilization doesn't dramatically alter the chemical makeup of the bone. Schwartz and colleagues at Los Alamos National Laboratory examined thin cross-sections of fossils under high magnification and found that 110-million-year-old bones from two different dinosaurs had intact crystalline structure like that of recent bones. Such

evidence leads her to believe that most fossil bone still consists of essentially original stuff. Fossils can become petrified, but most undergo only subtle chemical changes.

What stories do old bones tell? Of course, an entire skeleton is a gold mine of information. Without skin, muscles, or internal organs, it's impossible to know just how the animal looked and behaved, but the skeleton can help determine a dinosaur's size and build, whether it was a carnivore or herbivore, where it lived, who its relatives were, and sometimes its age and sex.

On rare occasions, bones catch long-dead animals in the act of being themselves. In 1971, paleontologists on an expedition to Mongolia found a juvenile *Velociraptor* locked in mortal combat with a *Protoceratops*. *Velociraptor* had jabbed its lethal claw into the belly of its intended

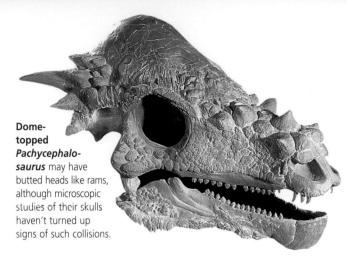

Dome-topped *Pachycephalosaurus* may have butted heads like rams, although microscopic studies of their skulls haven't turned up signs of such collisions.

victim, but *Protoceratops* bit back. Its jaws remained clamped around the predator's right leg. Then a sudden sandstorm entombed predator and prey, forever embraced in each other's death grip.

Paleontologists sometimes dig deeper into bones to reveal new stories. For instance, experts have long assumed that the improbably

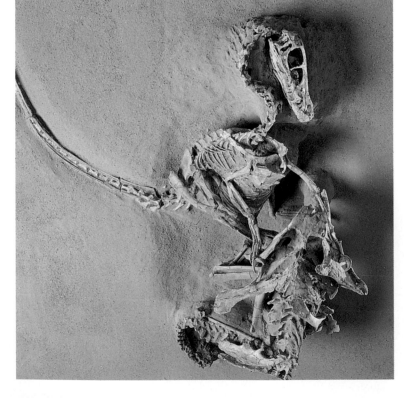

thick noggins of such dome-headed dinosaurs as *Pachycephalosaurus* and *Stegoceras* served to knock each other around during competition for mates, as is the case with bighorn sheep. Mark Goodwin, from the University of California Museum of Paleontology, and Jack Horner, of the Museum of the Rockies, tested the battering-ram theory by looking at thin sections of the skull for signs that the bone had healed from some previous injury. They encountered no evidence of bone stress caused by trauma. Younger dinosaurs had fast-growing, vascularized bone, and older individuals showed slower growth, but none appeared to have sustained a head-on collision.

The dome-shaped skull would have concentrated forces toward, not away from, the braincase, offering no protection from injury. There's still no explanation for the animals' large heads, but they

Entombed together in the Gobi Desert, a *Velociraptor* couldn't release its leg from the beak of a *Protoceratops*, its intended prey.

may have been designed to attract mates or intimidate rivals. Other paleontologists say that Goodwin's and Horner's work doesn't rule out head butting, since three-dimensional computer models show that glancing blows would not damage the skull enough to leave visible traces.

Footprints Fill Gaps

Despite new and clever ways to extract information from them, there are only so many dinosaur bones. Even the biggest name in the business, *Tyrannosaurus rex*, has scarcely a couple dozen skeletons. That's where dinosaur tracks come in handy. Individual footprints, and sequences of footprints called trackways, provide the raw materials for a growing branch of paleontology called ichnology. Trackways give a true snapshot of an animal's behavior and a reliable way to estimate population densities. Following tracks helps paleontologists fill in some of the blanks: how heavy dinosaurs were, how they moved, how fast they ran, how far they roamed, whether they traveled in groups, or stalked their prey. Footprints reveal whether a creature walked on two legs or four, ran on toetips or plodded with flat feet, and

Once Over, Easy

Birds do it, and so did their ancestors, the dinosaurs: They laid hard-shelled eggs. Dinosaur eggs come in a range of shapes and sizes. Some are spherical, others oval, but all are smaller than a soccer ball.

The first publicized discovery of dinosaur eggshell occurred in southern France in 1859. During his Gobi Desert expeditions in the 1920s, the legendary fossil prospector Roy Chapman Andrews uncovered nests full of dinosaur eggs arranged in concentric circles. Since then, dinosaur eggs have been found at some 200 sites worldwide. Besides France and Mongolia, major fossil egg sites occur in China, India, Argentina, the United States, and Canada.

Several kinds of dinosaurs nested in colonies and may have cared for their eggs. At a single site in central China, densely packed nests contain more than 5,000 probable hadrosaur eggs. Hundreds of eggs have been found at Egg Mountain in western Montana, where an adult *Troödon* took the time to build a rimmed nest for its clutch. Paleontologists in Patagonia encountered an extensive hatchery for titanosaurs; the eggs, some with embryos inside, covered the surface for a square mile in layers 16 feet thick. In Mongolia, a mother *Oviraptor* died while incubating and guarding a clutch. Her squatting skeleton was found on top of the unhatched eggs.

It's rare to find intact dinosaur eggs, rarer still to find any with an embryo entombed inside – the only sure way to identify the parent. But eggs and embryos can reveal a wealth of information about dinosaur growth and development.

kept its legs beneath the body like a bird or sprawled to the side like a crocodile.

Trackways with increasing or decreasing stride lengths indicate a slowing or speeding pace; alternating long and short steps suggest limping. Groups of parallel, evenly spaced tracks may have been left by a migrating herd. A dinosaur's speed can be

calculated from its foot size, stride length, and hip height. A Texas trackway captures steps of the fastest dinosaur known, a Jurassic carnivore that could sprint at 26 miles per hour, faster than the swiftest humans.

Footprints constitute the most common trace fossil; in some places they're many times more prevalent than

Erosion exposes a rhyncosaur limb bone (left) in Argentina's Valley of the Moon.

Karen Chin (below) takes a close-up look at fossilized dung at the Museum of the Rockies in Montana.

Dinosaur trackways (opposite) such as these in Alberta, Canada, are much more common than their bones and let scientists ponder how far and how fast the beasts traveled.

bones. Of the thousands of track sites on most continents, each may contain hundreds or thousands of footprints. One megasite, the "Dinosaur Freeway" along the Front Range of the Rockies from Boulder to New Mexico, encompasses an estimated 80 billion footprints in a mile-deep layer that covers nearly 31,000 square miles.

Many trackway sites turn up few, if any, bones. After all, an animal takes many steps in its lifetime but leaves only one skeleton. No dinosaur has ever been found literally dead in its tracks, the only sure way to identify the trackmaker. But dinosaur trackers can make informed guesses, based on clear differences in the size, shape, and depth of footprints from sauropods, theropods, and other major groups. When the track doesn't match any known fossil foot, a new species can be named on the basis of tracks alone.

"For years, there's been a bias in favor of the bone data," says Martin Lockley, a leading dinosaur track expert. "Bone paleontologists have said, 'Here is the skeleton, Martin, where are the tracks of this animal?' So, I'm turning it around and saying, 'I've got the tracks, you guys have to find the animal to fit those tracks.'"

In order to piece together the lives of these captivating creatures, dinosaur paleontologists will no doubt take every piece of evidence they can get their hands on, whether bones, tracks, skin, eggs, or – maybe someday, à la *Jurassic Park* – DNA.

Dinosaur Dung

Dinosaurs left behind more than their bones, eggs, and footprints. Sometimes we find their dung. Fossil feces, or coprolites, of dinosaurs often look like plain rocks, but they can reveal clues to ancient diets and environments.

Chunky gray coprolites from *Maiasaura* nesting grounds near Egg Mountain, Montana, suggest that these duckbills swallowed twigs or bark while plucking conifer leaves. Dung beetle burrows in some specimens confirm the first known interaction between two of the largest and smallest members of a Cretaceous community.

A huge sample of tyrannosaur dung found in Saskatchewan in 1995 was crammed with crushed bone from a young herbivore, most likely *Triceratops* or *Edmontosaurus*. The blade-like teeth and massive jaws of *Tyrannosaurus*, this specimen shows, could shatter bones in a few bites. – Blake Edgar

CHAPTER 5

At first, in 1842, there were just three. In that year the British anatomist Richard Owen confronted the bones of animals known as *Megalosaurus, Iguanodon*, and *Hylaeosaurus*. The trio of huge beasts – *Megalosaurus* was estimated to be about 40 feet long and eight feet high – had been found years earlier and classified as reptiles, but to Owen, who founded the British Museum of Natural History, these particular beasts looked peculiar. ◆ It was, for the most part, their hips. For one thing, their hip sockets weren't completely filled in; there was a hole in the center. Other reptiles, both past and present, had a complete cup of bone. And the whole angle of the pelvis, and the way the thighbone and hipbone met, were different. It looked as if the legs of these animals came up directly underneath them, while other reptiles – like crocodiles and lizards – sprawled, with their legs out to the sides. Since they looked as if they were a distinct group, Owen

Determining where dinosaurs fit into the great parade of life requires attention to details of anatomy.

gave them a distinctive name: the Dinosauria, Greek for "fearfully great lizards." ◆ Now scientists recognize about 350 dinosaur groups, or genera, ranging over 165 million years from the Triassic through the Cretaceous Periods and encompassing a wide variety of adaptations. Some dinosaurs were true giants: *Diplodocus* exceeded 80 feet in length, while *Brachiosaurus* stood 40 feet high and may have weighed 90 tons. Of the two-legged meat eaters, or theropods, the ever-popular *Tyrannosaurus rex* weighed in at about six tons. Yet not all dinosaurs were huge. Some were sleek and agile, and some were no bigger than a turkey. Most scientists believe, in fact, that dinosaurs survive today as turkeys, and as all the other

Hip joints distinguish the two major groups of dinosaurs. This ceratopsian, reconstructed by Rolf Johnson, curator of paleontology at the Milwaukee Public Museum, falls into the bird-hipped group, or Ornithischia.

Primitive *Mussaurus* (left), shown with its furry namesake, lived 210 million years ago in South America. The young may have spent time in a nest under parental care, but they grew to be over 10 feet long. The skull (below) of a baby *Mussaurus* contains some of the smallest dinosaur bones ever found.

members of the bird family.

The origins of dinosaurs are less clear than their eventual fate, if that's possible. About 250 million years ago, there was a diverse group of reptiles known as archosaurs. Some, such as the winged pterosaurs, flew. Creatures something like crocodiles swam through rivers. Other four-legged animals took to the land. What they all had in common was a peculiar skull. It had an opening in front of each eye, another opening in the lower jaw, and serrated teeth. The overall effect was less bone and more room for muscle, which made for some powerful chewing machines – a recipe for success in a harsh world where your next meal is the key to evolutionary survival.

Dawn of the Dinosaurs

One of these creatures was named *Lagosuchus* ("rabbit-crocodile"). What this hare-sized animal lacked in stature, it makes up in scientific significance. For in the skeleton of *Lagosuchus*, paleontologists can see hints of the shape of dinosaurs to come, such as an S-shaped neck and a tail that pivoted up and down. Its hind legs, in particular, were stretched out long and slender in comparison to the front limbs, an anatomical feature that when fully developed is well suited to running on two legs. Those legs were beginning to tuck more directly underneath the hips, forming the contrast to crocodile hips that caught Richard Owen's eye millions of years later. *Lagosuchus* also displays a simple hinged ankle joint and reduced outer toes. But *Lagosuchus'* legs and hips were still too primitive to be considered truly dinosaurian.

Paleontologists, in fact, don't know when the first true dinosaur appeared. They think they have something very close to it in a 230 million-year-old animal called *Eoraptor*. Found in northwestern Argentina, *Eoraptor* ("dawn stealer") weighed in at about 25 pounds and had a slender, upright-walking frame and the three-toed feet that show up in later dinosaurs like the tyrannosaurs or, if you like, chickens. But it was still a fairly primitive beast.

The next major event in the dinosaur lineage was that it split in two. In the decades after Owen coined the name, a wide variety of dinosaurs were unearthed, particularly in the American West, and by the late 1880s scientists began to recognize that the beasts fell into one of two groups.

Reptile Hips vs. Bird Hips

One group's bones bore a superficial resemblance to the hips of lizards. A flat, rodlike bone called the pubis comes off the hipbone (where the top of the thighbone fits into the hip) at a

Feathered dinosaurs (right) called *Caudipteryx* contest in a Chinese forest. They may have fanned their tail feathers for display, but their wings were too short for flying.

Archaeopteryx (below) is known from only seven skeletons. About the size of a blue jay, this oldest bird may be descended from a theropod dinosaur.

broad angle, essentially facing forward toward the front of the body. Since this arrangement follows the pattern in lizards, these dinosaurs

were dubbed the "reptile-hipped" group, or Saurischia. In fact, there was nothing new about the hipbones in Saurischia, but this group

The Flap Over Birds

Standing in the American Museum of Natural History in New York, John Ostrom looked dazed. "I never thought I'd live to see something like this," said the white-haired Yale paleontologist, wiping the sweat of excitement from his brow. What startled him was a small stack of color snapshots of a dinosaur fringed with what looked a lot like feathers.

The year was 1996, about 26 years after a younger Ostrom, while studying the world's oldest known bird, *Archaeopteryx*, had realized that its hands, wrists, arms, shoulders, hips, and ankles bore a striking resemblance to dinosaur bones. Ostrom proposed a then-radical theory: birds had evolved from dinosaurs and were flapping, squawking representatives of animals thought to have died out 65 million years ago. Now a Chinese dinosaur dubbed *Sinosauropteryx*, the creature in the snapshots, bolstered the link by displaying the very birdlike trait of feathers.

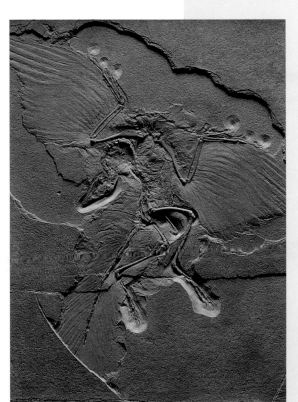

But were they really feathers? Or perhaps some kind of reptilian scales? Maybe the fringe was a frill running along the back. Ostrom and other paleontologists went to China to examine the fossil itself but could not reach a firm conclusion.

For most paleontologists, it almost didn't matter. Researchers have counted about 150 characteristics, such as hollow bones, shared only by dinosaurs and birds. To them, this shared heritage indicates that just prior to 150 million years ago, when *Archaeopteryx* appeared, the dinosaur and bird lineages split from a slender, two-footed common ancestor. One line developed through *Archaeopteryx* into modern birds, while the other produced birdlike dinosaurs such as *Deinonychus*, *Troödon*, and *Velociraptor*

A hard core of skeptics doubted any close tie between birds and dinosaurs, arguing that the two lines split apart much earlier, near the dawn of the Dinosaur Age.

Other new Chinese fossils strengthen the family ties. Bearing strong similarities to the other birdlike dinosaurs, *Caudipteryx* and *Protarchaeopteryx* have small bodies surrounded by barbed, closely packed feathery filaments. The new finds haven't quite knocked the skeptics off their perch, but it's harder for them to hold their balance.

did develop distinctive grasping hands, big thumb claws, and other features that set it apart. Saurischians stood in sharp contrast to a second group, whose hip-bones had changed significantly. In this group, the pubis jutted backward at a narrow angle, almost parallel to the spine and pointing back toward the tail. This pattern resembled the arrangement seen in modern birds, and this second group were named the "bird-hipped" dinosaurs, or Ornithischia.

This name was perhaps not the most felicitous choice. For while "bird-hipped" conjures up images of light, agile beasts, the group actually includes some fairly heavy hitters. *Stegosaurus*, for instance, tipped the scales at two tons and had a double row of arrowhead-shaped bony plates down its back and a tail covered with two-foot spikes. Its hindquarters were so massive that, for a time, paleontologists speculated that a cavity in the hip vertebrae housed a second brain just to control the rear

end. Another ornithischian, *Ankylosaurus*, at four tons, had bands of armor plating from the top of its head to the tip of the tail, which ended in a stout club of bone. And massive *Iguanodon*, one of Owen's original terrible trio, was part of this group.

The "reptile-hipped" group, on the other hand, includes some of the lightest, fleetest dinosaurs known. Take *Compsognathus*. This tiny, bipedal beast was about two feet long and built for speed. It had light, hollow bones, a long neck balanced

Reptile-hipped
Tyrannosaurus (opposite) torments the bird-hipped *Ankylosaurus*. This battle pits members of the two major dinosaur categories.

Taking wing (right) to catch dragonflies, these thrush-sized pterosaurs were flying reptiles but not dinosaurs.

The killer claw (bottom, right) of *Utahraptor* sliced open prey; the fleet-footed predators may have hunted in packs.

by an even longer tail, skinny legs with long shins and bird-like feet, and short arms with grasping fingers. The complete package made for a quick and efficient hunter: one fossil found in Germany had the bones of a tiny lizard in its abdomen.

Reptile-hipped hunters came in larger, fiercer versions, too, like the velociraptors, standing about six feet tall on two legs, each of which ended in a lethal, sickle-shaped claw on the second toe. An even larger relative, *Deinonychus*, had a claw about five inches long, and the killer claw on the recently discovered *Utahraptor* was about twice the size. Researchers think these animals stood on one leg as they slashed their prey open with deadly kicks. *Tyrannosaurus* is yet another member of the reptile-hipped group, an extreme version of a class of carnivorous

killers called theropods.

These large-brained beasts are, in fact, the dinosaurs that share the most features with birds. It isn't that they don't have reptilian hips, but rather that scientists have assembled a long list of features of hand, jaw, and brain anatomy that look more specifically birdlike.

Despite the apparent confusion, some dinosaurs do seem to be in properly named categories. The giant, four-footed sauropods, such as *Apatosaurus*, *Brachiosaurus*, and *Supersaurus*, occupy a branch of the Saurischia which seems to have split off from those that

evolved in the direction of birds. Some of the last members of the bird-hipped group, roaming over North America in herds, were large grazing animals called hadrosaurs whose mouths ended in duckbills. Hadrosaurs and the rest of their ornithischian brethren were knocked into the netherworld of extinction 65 million years ago, and today we alternately admire and do our best to bump off the last of the saurischians – the birds.

One of the first scientists to name a dinosaur, Gideon Mantell, saw *Iguanodon* and its relatives as scaly, bulky, and decidedly primitive animals that plodded around on all fours like reptilian elephants. That was the view of dinosaurs in 1825. In the 1850s, paleontologist Joseph Leidy had the chance to examine the first decent dinosaur skeleton, found in a clay pit in Haddonfield, New Jersey. Leidy put his *Hadrosaurus* in an upright, kangaroo-like posture, but little else had changed. Museum dinosaurs would largely remain lumbering, dim-witted leviathans for the next century. ◆ Now we know better. Dinosaurs were not plodding dolts or evolutionary failures but lively, social, even intelligent creatures perfectly adapted to their environments. Though plenty of gaps and guesses remain when it comes to reconstructing dinosaur behavior, recent research has pro-vided the clearest picture yet of some of their capabilities and activities.

Not simply lumbering leviathans or warm-blooded killers, dinosaurs confound attempts to define their behavior.

And it's clear that to go "the way of the dinosaurs" did not mean embarking on a one-way express to extinction. Dinosaurs can only be considered unqual-ified successes, nearly unrivaled in the history of vertebrate life for their diversity and endurance over time. By comparison, the mammals of the period were small, probably nocturnal creatures that led a marginal existence beneath the dinosaurs' dominating stride. ◆ Did dinosaurs have to be smart to be so successful? If we take intelligence as our measure of advance-ment, some dinosaurs had it, but most did not. Apart from its spiky tail and double row of pointed plates projecting from its back, *Stegosaurus* has a more dubious claim to fame: an adult brain the size of a walnut. It couldn't

Keen smell and eyesight, possibly aided by depth perception, made *Tyrannosaurus* a formidable foe. Experts debate whether it hunted or scavenged for meat.

Bringing Up Baby

Even before he knew her identity, John R. "Jack" Horner suspected that there was something special about the mother of the baby duck-billed dinosaurs he dug out of the Montana badlands in 1978. Horner's discovery of the first known nest of dinosaur babies soon led to an even more startling announcement. The mother of this brood was no lay-'em-and-leave-'em lizard; she had taken care of her young 80 million years ago much the way a modern warbler or robin would. He named her *Maiasaura*, the "good mother lizard."

Mothering maiasaurs (below) keep watch over a colony of nestlings. Adults provided food to the baby duckbills, who doubled in size before leaving the nest.

Fifteen three-foot-long babies had died together in a mud nest. Yet they weren't newly hatched when they died. The tendons that held their tails off the ground, flexible in hatchlings, had already stiffened. Some babies had almost worn out their first teeth. The circumstantial evidence grew as Horner and his crews uncovered at least three *Maiasaura* nesting grounds, along with dozens of nests, eggs, and hatchlings.

The babies more than doubled in size while still in the nest. But how did they get food? If three-foot babies were already capable of grazing at the feet of three-ton adults, why would they have returned to the nest to die together? The only answer that made sense to Horner was that these youngsters had never left. One or both parents had brought them food. A key piece of evidence came in 1988, after Horner put thin cross-sections of leg bones from *Maiasaura* hatchlings under the microscope and concluded that their hip and knee joints had been too spongy for them to walk.

Not everyone is convinced, especially skeptics of the dinosaur-bird link. One study, which Horner and many others dismiss, concluded that the baby pelvis and legs could support a mobile *Maiasaura*. "Most critics haven't begun to look at the specimens and the evidence in detail," says Kevin Padian, a paleontologist at the University of California, Berkeley. Those who have are fairly convinced that there was some kind of parenting going on, he says. But how much, how long, what kind?

Dinosaur parenting will always require a level of inference, says Phil Currie of the Royal Tyrrell Museum in Alberta, Canada, "but it fits consistently with what we're seeing at other sites, and it's certainly changing our view of dinosaurs." – *Yvonne Baskin*

Grinding teeth (opposite, top) of a hadrosaur were anchored in a flexible skull that could chew tough plants in three directions.

Velociraptors (opposite, bottom) were agile predators who may have hunted in groups to kill animals several times their size.

perform calculus. Most dinosaurs do score above certain reptiles on a brain-to-body size ratio that serves as an index to measure smarts (naturally we humans come out very well on this particular index), but few excel.

An exception is *Troödon*, a diminutive North American carnivore that was among the last of the dinosaurs. Before getting to this beast's brain-power, there's a good tale to tell. *Troödon* happens to be one of the first dinosaurs

named, but for a long time it was known only from some teeth. Then in 1983, paleontologist Phil Currie was observing construction of the Royal Tyrrell Museum of Palaeontology in Alberta, Canada. He and fellow dinosaur hunter Jack Horner took a walk in the adjacent badlands, where Horner soon found a dinosaur jaw sticking out from a hillside. Rain put off an impromptu excavation for a week, and when Currie returned, the fossil seemed to have washed away. Two years later, Horner paid another visit, took a walk in the same place, and found the same jawbone of *Troödon*. So in 1986, when Currie was excavating in China, he immediately recognized a bony braincase as one belonging to a similar creature.

The avocado-sized cranium enclosed a brain three times larger than that of any other dinosaur. Some 75 million years ago, no animal could outwit *Troödon* and its ilk. Perhaps as smart as an ostrich, troödontids may have teamed up to hunt prey. Fast, agile, and clever, with dextrous gripping hands and keen vision, this carnivore was up to the challenge, scientists speculate, of hunting small mammals at dawn or dusk.

It turns out that *Troödon* bears one of the closest kinships to birds of any dinosaur, and evidence from Montana indicates that this flightless forebear also laid eggs in nests. A well-preserved clutch found at Egg Mountain contained two dozen eggs, around which a *Troödon* parent had built a five-inch-high circular rim to secure its incubating offspring. According to paleontologist David Varricchio,

who studied the bone microstructure of a *Troödon* embryo, this theropod may have grown after hatching at a faster rate than crocodiles but slower than birds, taking five years to reach an adult weight of about 100 pounds and the size of a full-grown person. Like the duckbilled hadrosaurs *Maiasaura* and *Hypacrosaurus*, *Troödon* nested in colonies and returned to the same nesting site year in and year out.

Different Ways to Keep Warm

Now to the great controversy of the past two decades in dinosaur science: Were they warm-blooded? Thanks to recent cellular analysis and oxygen isotope studies, the contentious and largely factfree debate has come up with an answer: yes, and no. Current evidence indicates that dinosaurs varied widely from one kind of metabolism to another, even shifting

within the lifetime of an individual.

Hadrosaurs, for example, show patterns of rapid bone growth as babies, like warmblooded birds or mammals, but slower bone growth as adults. A huge Triassic herbivore from South Africa called *Massospondylus* has a bone-growth rate akin to cold-blooded crocodilians and other reptiles, while its contemporary, a smaller meat eater named *Syntarsus*, has a pattern similar to modernday, warm-blooded carnivores.

Dinosaur chicks may have hatched hot to grow fast

enough to travel with a herd or to better avoid being eaten. Adults relied instead, perhaps, on their enormous bulk to heat their bodies in a less energy-expending way. Staying warm-blooded would have been detrimental to something the size of a sauropod, but it may have been essential to small, lithe predatory dinosaurs (though at least some warmed themselves with feathers).

Apatosaur and Allosaur Appetites

Without more details of their metabolism, it's hard to know the extent of dinosaur gluttony. Bob Bakker, for one, has argued that

sauropod herds could have cleared the upper canopy of forests, letting in enough light for weedy, flowering plants to flourish in the early Cretaceous; ultimately, flowering plants came to dominate the dinosaurs' environments, and ornithopods and ceratopsians replaced sauropods as the main herbivores. Some sauropods and prosauropods, and perhaps other dinosaurs, swallowed stones to compensate for weak chewing teeth. After the dinosaurs stripped greenery from ferns, cycads, and conifers, these rocks, or gastroliths, ground up the vegetation inside their muscular gizzards and made the food digestible. At the excavation of *Seismosaurus* in New Mexico, more than 240 gastroliths as large as four inches across were found clustered

near the chest and pelvis.

Later herbivorous dinosaurs had all the equipment needed to process food right in their mouths. Ornithopods chewed with a side-to-side grinding motion by rotating either the upper or lower jaw. Duckbilled hadrosaurs possessed a more sophisticated design. A duck-bill's mouth contained several hundred tightly packed teeth with a thick coat of enamel on the leaf-shaped crowns. And flexible skulls let them mash tough, fibrous plants up and down, back and forth, and side to side.

Some meat eaters may have bolted down food with little thought to chewing. A typical carnivorous dinosaur had two powerful legs for speed, long arms for grasping prey (with their amazingly puny arms, the tyrannosaurs were oddballs), and gaping jaws full of teeth that were repeatedly replaced as each broke. A study of bite force concluded that *Tyrannosaurus* could easily have seized and subdued struggling prey. With curved teeth serrated like steak knives – one paleontologist calls *T. rex*'s dental arsenal "lethal bananas" – the king carnivore used a puncture-and-pull biting strategy that probably removed sizable chunks of flesh. Its jaws could chomp down on prey with at least 3,000 pounds of force, pulverizing any bone in their path. Fossilized *Tyrannosaurus* feces found in Saskatchewan indicate that plenty of bone passed through the gullet and guts unchewed and undigested.

Some carnivores may have hunted in packs as a way to tackle bigger prey. Allosaurs were just a tenth the size of some of the adult sauropods they apparently attacked, so having comrades would have helped. Others, maybe even mighty *T. rex*, scared other predators away from their kill sites and scavenged the carcasses.

Scientists have begun to fill in our knowledge of dinosaur biology and behavior in extraordinary ways, but the story is far from complete. We have no idea, for instance, how long dinosaurs could live, but there's plenty of evidence in their bones of painful injuries and crippling diseases. Though dinosaurs were often ornamented with crests, horns, plates, and spikes, one can only guess at their true colors. Could their skin flash warning, welcoming, or concealing colors and patterns? Did hues and horns project an image designed to intimidate or allure?

Many questions will linger while new ones arise, because dinosaurs were varied and complex creatures. Nothing so strange or so enormous ever walked the Earth before or is likely to again. Learn what you can about them, but above all admire them as a testament to the glory and mystery of evolution.

The Skin They Were In

Nobody knows what dinosaur skin really looked like. But this much we do know: They had a variety of pebbly, scaly skin patterns. And they appear to have shared a rosette pattern of raised bumps.

The proof lies in skin impressions left by dead dinosaurs in the surrounding sediment. One of the best examples comes from a mummy of *Edmontosaurus* at the American Museum of Natural History. *Carnotaurus*, a peculiar horned predator common in South America, had even bumpier skin. Ankylosaurs wielded scutes, or plates, of armor. Some sauropods may have sported spines. And at least two kinds of small, meat-eating dinosaurs who roamed in China stayed warm and cozy in a coat of feathers.

Although one paleontologist called it "a subject a mile wide and an inch deep," knowledge of dinosaur skin will be deepened by new discoveries. In late 1998, Argentine and American researchers announced spectacularly well-preserved, 70- to 90-million-year-old embryos of titanosaurs, the first sauropod embryos ever found. Skin impressions from the unborn babies capture amazing details of texture. But we may never know whether dinosaurs were as vivid as birds or as drab as many artists cautiously choose to portray them.

Earth-shaking *Seismosaurus* (opposite, top), the longest dinosaur ever found, towers over a lunging *Allosaurus*. *Seismosaurus* swallowed stones to help grind up plants inside its gizzard.

Tyrannosaur teeth (opposite, bottom) could tear away huge chunks of flesh thanks to serrated edges. This tooth belonged to Sue the *T. rex*.

Skin imprint (below) from a hadrosaur reveals a pebbly texture of scales. Skin color remains a mystery.

The extinction of large dinosaurs 65 million years ago poses one of the most intriguing and enduring mysteries in the history of life. The dinosaurs' dynasty had dominated herbivore and carnivore niches for about 160 million years, but at the end of the Cretaceous Period, the dinosaurs vanished – all except for birds. ◆ It's no surprise, really. Based on the fossil record, more than 99 percent of all species that have ever lived on Earth are now extinct. Dinosaurs were by no means the only group affected by the Cretaceous-Tertiary mass extinction. As many as half the species then alive may have ceased to exist. Many land plants perished, especially in North America and across temperate northern latitudes. Some groups of lizards, mammals, and freshwater fish suffered severe declines. Marine plankton, which form the base of the food chain, certain clams, ammonites, and giant sea lizards called mosasaurs also became extinct. ◆ What caused this wave of

A worldwide catastrophe may have caused the extinction of dinosaurs 65 million years ago.

extinctions? While many ideas have been proposed, recent research has focused on a pair of competing culprits, tied to two of the most monumental events in Earth's history. ◆ One extinction scenario involves the second largest continental lava eruption ever to have occurred on Earth. Almost a half-million cubic miles of lava emanated from enormous plumes of magma deep inside the planet and spewed from cracks in the crust. Evidence of this event exists in massive, steplike deposits of lava such as those in west-central India, where 8,000-foot-thick flows flooded an area larger than California over a period of half a million years between 68.5 and 64.9 million years ago – the same time that large dinosaurs disappeared. Deep beneath the South Atlantic,

Meteor Crater in Arizona formed when an iron meteorite struck the Earth. A crater more than 100 times larger, Chicxulub in Mexico, marks an earlier impact that may have extinguished the dinosaurs.

a submerged mountain range constitutes additional evidence of continuous, widespread volcanic eruptions during this period. Eruptions occurred across Africa, off Australia, and in the central Pacific.

Huge clouds of dust and trillions of tons of carbon dioxide and sulfur were thrown into the atmosphere and could have spawned corrosive acid rain and thinned the ozone layer. The upper layers of the ocean became an acidic bath, killing oxygen-producing microorganisms. Gradually, the subtropical climate to which the dinosaurs had adapted began to change. Along North America's Western Interior Seaway, the shoreline that had helped to buffer temperatures receded. Days grew hotter and nights colder. Seasonal extremes in temperature became more pronounced. Extended darkness from air pollution also may have cooled tempera-

tures, followed by greenhouse warming. Over hundreds of thousands of years, such effects could certainly have extinguished the dinosaurs.

Asteroid Theory Makes an Impact

The second extinction scenario implicates one of the largest asteroid or comet collisions ever to strike the Earth. The giant object streaked across the Caribbean sky at speeds approaching

Volcanic eruptions (left and right) that pumped toxic gases into the sky, unleashed massive lava flows, and caused acid rain could have contributed to the mass extinction of dinosaurs.

Terrified *Tyrannosaurus* (below) watches as a flaming asteroid streaks across the sky. Much evidence suggests that such an impact triggered the extinction of dinosaurs at the end of the Cretaceous.

150,000 miles per hour, tearing through the atmosphere in seconds. Herds of duck-billed and horned dinosaurs stampeded in panic.

The six-mile-wide meteor crashed near the shoreline of the Gulf of Mexico, unleashing an explosion 10,000 times as powerful as the world's nuclear arsenal. This incredible impact triggered an earthquake a million times stronger than any ever recorded. Three-hundred-foot-high tsunamis pummeled the coastline.

As if that weren't enough, a huge cloud of dust and debris was blasted into orbit – 1,200 times the amount of ash ejected from Mount St. Helens. At first, the particles heated up the atmosphere and ignited fires on the ground. Then, accumulating dust and smoke obscured the sun for months, perhaps years. Without sunlight, temperatures plummeted.

Freezing temperatures or persistent acid rain probably drove many plants to extinction. The lack of vegetation in turn hastened the demise of large herbivorous dinosaurs. Carnivores like *Tyrannosaurus* traveled farther in an unsuccessful search for prey and finally perished. Dinosaurs, which had endured for eons, vanished in a geological instant.

Evidence of such a devastating impact consists of high concentrations of an element called iridium found at several locations on different continents. The iridium occurs in thin bands of clay sandwiched between rock layers dating to the end of the Cretaceous and those from the subsequent geologic period. Because iridium and other heavy elements such as iron and nickel sank toward the center of the planet early in Earth's history, iridium is rare in rocks at the surface. But since comets and asteroids contain relatively more iridium, scientists conclude that the iridium-enriched clay captured fallout from a cataclysmic impact.

Further evidence of an extraterrestrial impact in these clays includes microscopic crystals of fractured quartz, small glassy spheres that may be molten droplets of rock blasted from the impact crater, and soot from vast fires

The Rise of Mammals

Mammals were no strangers to dinosaurs. The earliest known dinosaurs, such as *Herrerasaurus*, lived about 228 million years ago. The first mammals weren't far behind, appearing in the fossil record about 200 million years ago.

Unlike many around us today, the first mammals were no larger than rats. Not until after the Cretaceous-Tertiary (K-T) mass extinction did any mammal grow bigger than a beaver. By dominating many ecological niches, dinosaurs may have delayed the evolution of larger fur-covered creatures. Only about 10 million years after the demise of large dinosaurs did large mammals become commonplace.

Fossil evidence places the origin of most modern mammal groups no earlier than the late Cretaceous, which began about 97 million years ago. But marsupials (pouched mammals) existed earlier, and sloths, hoofed mammals, and some meat eaters may have, too.

The fossil record reveals how different groups of mammals fared in the K-T extinction. Marsupials were hammered: about 90 percent became extinct. So did half of the small, rodentlike mammals called multituberculates. But placentals, the group that would later include humans and most living mammals, appear to have emerged almost unscathed.

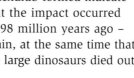

A dilophosaur (above) dines on an early mammal. The furry little creatures grew no larger than house cats during the Age of Dinosaurs.

Paleontologist Dale Evans (right) ponders a model of Dinosauroid, a hypothetical creation that represents his idea of an animal that would have evolved from smart, two-legged dinosaurs like *Troödon*.

ignited by burning debris.

Finally, a massive impact crater was found buried beneath the coast of the Yucatan Peninsula in Mexico. The crater, called Chicxulub, measures somewhere between 110 and 175 miles across,

and just after the impact it was between 18 and 35 miles deep. Rocks that melted when Chicxulub formed indicate that the impact occurred 64.98 million years ago – again, at the same time that the large dinosaurs died out.

Unanswered Questions

For nearly two decades, a scientific debate has raged between advocates

A layer of clay (below, indicated by rock hammer) in Alberta's Red Deer Valley marks the Cretaceous-Tertiary, or K-T, boundary. The layer coincides with the dinosaurs' last days.

of the two catastrophic scenarios. The fascinating and often fractious debate involves paleontologists and geologists, physicists and astronomers, and many other scientists. Among the public, the impact hypothesis has gained wide recognition, and a majority of scientists now accept that an asteroid impact played a role in the extinction of large dinosaurs. But a significant minority still doubts that the impact caused the extinction, and proponents of the volcanic alternative remain convinced that catastrophic eruptions were responsible. Some scientists even suspect that both events – one terrestrial, the other extraterrestrial –

combined in a coincidental one-two punch to wipe out the dinosaurs.

An earlier and much larger episode of extinction may help scientists figure out exactly what happened to the dinosaurs. The largest mass extinction in Earth's history occurred about 250 million years ago, at the end of the Permian Period; more than 90 percent of all species were wiped out. Curiously, this extinction coincided with the biggest volcanic eruptions ever. These massive eruptions spewed about 720,000 cubic miles of lava – half again as much as the Cretaceous eruptions – enough to cover the planet's entire surface with a layer 10 feet thick.

Dating of the volcanic rocks indicates that the eruptions happened 250 million years ago. This is a compelling coincidence, and there has so far been scant evidence of an asteroid or comet impact at this time.

While the extinction debate has been exciting, it may not be resolved anytime soon. Two major problems still confound attempts to pin the Cretaceous-Tertiary mass extinction on either eruptions or a cosmic impact. First, since each would have resulted in similar killing mechanisms – acid rain, short-term cooling, long-term warming, and so on – how can we discriminate between the two from the evidence?

More important, our inability to date ancient events precisely prevents us from knowing how quickly the extinction took place – a key clue as to which event was to blame. The major pulse of volcanic eruptions is thought to have occurred over a 500,000-year period at the end of the Cretaceous. But the effects of the impact would have lasted for centuries at most. If we could tell time at the level of decades or centuries, then we might learn whether the extinction happened as hastily as the impact hypothesis predicts. Until we obtain a more precise method of dating, the extinction debate will continue.

Ready for a quiz? Try this one: You're driving down a gravel road in central Montana, and you stop for a stretch. Looking around, you see, weathering out of a nearby hillside, the skeleton of a dinosaur – the tyrannosaur-like *Albertosaurus*. Trembling with excitement, you dig out the bones, whisk them off to paleontologists at a nearby field site, and then, glowing with pride, fly back home and tell the newspapers about your once-in-a-lifetime discovery. You are: (A) a hero, (B) a criminal, (C) a klutz. ◆ This "hypothetical" example actually happened to a family of amateur fossil hunters in 1994. The answer, once the returns were all in, was somewhere between criminal and klutz. Though they didn't know it at the time, the fossil lay on private ranchland. That meant that the would-be benefactors had trespassed and stolen private property. In removing the fossils from the rocks, they had destroyed the context of the remains – an

Pith helmets are passé: Today's dinosaur diggers carry sophisticated gear and need to know the law.

irreplaceable loss of scientific information. And because they weren't trained in excavating fossils, they damaged the bones beyond repair. Quite a record for an afternoon's work. ◆ Yet they so easily could have been heroes. All it would have taken was a little thought and a smattering of legal knowledge. The laws and regulations affecting fossil collecting can be hard to read and harder still to interpret, but the basic rules are simple. Everything boils down to knowing where you are. ◆ If you parachute at random into the fossil-rich badlands of the American West and want to collect dinosaur bones, the rule wherever you land is likely to be simple: You can't. Most western land is federal property managed by agencies such

Eva Koppelhus, a paleobotanist, displays a fossil fern found on the banks of the Red Deer River in Alberta. Ferns formed an essential part of some dinosaurs' diets.

as the Forest Service, the National Park Service, and the Bureau of Land Management. All of them, along with most Indian tribes, require that you get a permit before collecting vertebrate fossils. To do that, you must be a scientist attached to either a university or a museum that is certified as a "fossil repository." In many places, you don't need a permit to gather non-vertebrate fossils such as shellfish, trilobites, or petrified wood, as long as you don't plan to sell them (commercial fossil hunters are barred from federal public land). And, of course, you don't need a permit if you are part of a team working for a scientist who has one.

The other major category of public land is that owned by the states. There the laws vary from restrictive to liberal. Wyoming, for example, has thrown out the welcome mat to private and commercial collectors interested in the spectacular fossil fish found in beds near the Green River. Colorado, on the other hand, requires a permit to pick up any fossil. A lot of road cuts

Eroding bones (left) are like gold nuggets to collectors, but whether it's legal to gather a fossil depends on where it lies.

This gorgosaur tooth (right), still encased in rock, was collected during an official museum expedition to New Mexico. Gorgosaurs were a primitive relative of *Tyrannosaurus*.

fall under state jurisdiction, so it's wise to phone state authorities to find out what rules apply.

In Canada, where vertebrate fossils are considered part of the country's cultural heritage, you need an export permit to take large or valuable ones out of the country. Other nationwide laws forbid collecting in federal or provincial parks. Apart from that, fossils are administered by Canada's 10 provinces and territories, and their approaches vary widely. British Columbia, for instance, takes a fairly laissez-faire attitude toward fossil collecting, while dinosaur-rich Alberta and Saskatchewan severely restrict it. In Alberta, all vertebrate fossils, whether found on crown (public) or private land, belong to the province. Apart from "float" (eroded-out fossils lying loose on the ground), they may be collected only with

Sue's discoverers (left) learned the hard way about knowing who owns fossil-laden land. The federal government confiscated the *T. rex* skeleton, which later went up for auction.

A sign posted at Egg Mountain, Montana (right), informs visitors that no fossils can be removed from the site.

permission from one of Alberta's two provincial museums, and specimens may not leave Alberta. Quebec museums reserve the right of first refusal on all fossils found in that province or put up for sale. To find out the details, get in touch with the province's department of tourism or with the cultural property officer at a provincial museum.

So much for public land. What about privately owned land? "This one is a no-brainer," says Mark Goodwin, a paleontologist at the University of California Museum in Berkeley. "Ask the landowner."

In practice, it's not always that easy, especially when valuable fossils are involved. The classic how-not-to-do-it story is the saga of the world's most notori-

ous dinosaur, Sue the *Tyrannosaurus rex*. In 1992, friends of commercial collector Pete Larson noticed Sue weathering out of a hillside on the South Dakota ranch of Maurice Williams. Larson paid the rancher $5,000 for the fossil, dug Sue out of the hill, and went to work cleaning the tyrannosaur's bones. The deal went sour when Williams learned that Sue might be worth millions. Years earlier, he announced, he had deeded his land to the government. As a result, Sue was not really his to sell. A paleontological nightmare ensued. The Federal Bureau of Investigation and National Guard raided Larson's business,

The long, curved teeth of *Tyrannosaurus rex.* (above) have been described as "lethal bananas."

Fossilized fish (below) and palm fronds abound in the Green River Formation of Wyoming. The state has relatively liberal fossil-collecting laws.

Larson was tried and sent to prison on unrelated charges, and Sue went on the auction block.

Lessons Learned

Needless to say, the Sue fiasco has given private collectors a lot to think about. Here's what some of them recommend:

● Watch your step. Does the landowner really own the land? A rancher may be leasing the land from the federal government or may have deeded it to the government, as Maurice Williams did. If you have doubts, a visit to the county courthouse can reveal whose permission you really need.

● Be specific. Make sure you

and the landowner understand what you are agreeing to. Are you allowed just to prospect for fossils, or may you collect them as well? If the agreement limits you to prospecting, you will have to strike another deal if anything exciting turns up.

● Write things down. Traditionally, getting permission has been as simple as a beer, a chat, and a hearty handshake. Nowadays, however, more and more fossil collectors are starting to ask for written agreements as a precaution against bait-and-switch tactics or the whims of fickle heirs.

● Deal fairly. After all, the fossils are the landowner's property. "You shouldn't expect to be able to walk away with King Tut's tomb for nothing. Those days are gone," says paleontologist Donald Wolberg, co-author of *Collecting the Natural World*, a legal guide for collectors. "In general, if you treat people well, they'll treat you well."

In short, to stay on the right side of the law, you can't just heave some picks and shovels into your flatbed and head for dino territory. Instead, plan your route in advance. Know where you're going and what laws apply there, and get permission. Once you've dotted your i's and crossed your t's, *then* you can set off for God's country and rattle down that dusty gravel road.

Be a Hero

And if you do stumble across the fossil find of a lifetime – what then?

Essential tools for fossil hunters range from miner's picks (right), for removing rock atop a bone bed, to dental picks, for exposing a bone's edge. A paintbrush (below) helps clear away dirt from a T. rex tooth.

Well, if you play your cards right, you get to be a hero. A tip from hikers led former Utah state paleontologist David Gillette to the burial place of *Seismosaurus*, the longest dinosaur ever found. If you really want to contribute to scientific knowledge, he advises, you should exercise the most difficult virtue of all: forbearance. "Take pictures of it. Don't take anything. Don't disturb it. Don't try to collect it. Then call a responsible paleontologist or a government agency." Finally, before you leave the site, make sure you can find it again. Note the location on a map, and leave a marker (a flag, a stake, a pile of stones) to show where it is.

If all that sounds like common sense, so much the better. "This is not rocket science," says Donald Wolberg. "Don't steal, do it right, and you won't get into trouble. And you may get a *lot* of credit."

Preparing for the Big Dig

If you want to go looking for dinosaur bones, it's best to join an organized expedition. Let experts plan your route, provide food, equipment, and instruction, and arrange for permits and permission. In any case, don't go alone; for safety and company, bring friends. Also bring plenty of water, sun protection, and a topographic map.

Beyond that, these are some tools of the trade for dinosaur fossil hunters:

- Four-wheel-drive vehicle with spare tires

- Notebooks and pens or pencils for making field notes

- Camera and film to document a discovery

- Heavy work gloves and knee pads to spare your skin

- Picks, shovels, and rock hammers for breaking ground

- Chisels, awls, and trowels for excavating

- Whisk brooms, paintbrushes, and dental picks for exposing and cleaning fossils

- Felt markers for numbering fossils

- Old newspapers and tissue paper for wrapping fossils

- Specimen bags (lock-top plastic bags are fine) for sorting fossils

◆

Into the Field

Dinosaur lovers can visit the most significant fossil sites and trackways in North America or join a team of dinosaur diggers under the supervision of leading paleontologists.

Joining a Dinosaur Dig

CHAPTER 9

An orange sun burned in the cloudless turquoise sky, and the rolling landscape unfurled to a boundless horizon. But on that summer day in Montana's badlands, Lou Tremblay, a dinosaur dig volunteer, noticed nothing but the ground two feet in front of him. "I was determined to make a find," he recalls. After all, the first known *Tyrannosaurus rex* was unearthed only about 30 miles away. And just that morning, two fellow volunteers found what looked like the leg of a plant-eating hadrosaur.   ◆   So Tremblay, with head hung low and eyes fixed downward, paced over baked brown clay until finally he stopped, stooped, and scooped up what looked like a bone fragment. "Eureka!" he thought. Where there are shards, there are sometimes skeletons. Sure enough, after a dozen dead ends, he followed a trail of bone bits up the sandy slope to where a smooth, **Amateur fossil hunters** tan patch the size of a baseball pushed up through **can join dinosaur digs** the ground. The bone had been buried **led by some of the world's** at least 65 million years ago – and he was the **top paleontologists.** first person to see this haunting prehistoric relic.   ◆   But that was just the beginning. Using camel-hair paintbrushes, he and fellow volunteer Steve Begin cleared away surface dirt to discover that this knob was only the weathered tip of a long, slender bone. As they had been taught in field school, they snapped some photographs, noted their location in a logbook, and loosened some surrounding soil with a scratch awl. "At this point we knew it was something big," Tremblay says. Their excitement grew as they dug around the bone with garden trowels. Still, they could not have imagined the actual magnitude of their find that day.

Jack Horner looks the part of a paleontologist beside tipis at Camposaur, one of the sites excavated by teams from the Museum of the Rockies.

Preceding pages: Tilted trackway of ankylosaur footprints left 90 million years ago at Grand Cache, Alberta, comes under the scrutiny of paleontologist Phil Currie.

Cretaceous dinosaurs.

"What a thrill," Tremblay says. "I woke up half my family the night I heard the good news." He is not alone. Since the mid-1990s, a slew of museums, research scientists, and institutions have invited the paying public to experience firsthand what was once primarily reserved for professionals. Now many organizations offer everything from half-day dinosaur digs to two-week expeditions in the United States, Canada, and overseas. While some are designed for kids, others are totally authentic field experiences focused around a specific research project. So whether you are the parent of a budding paleontologist, a perpetual student, or an amateur collector, there is a program for you. Here's a sampling:

Short but Sweet

The **Wyoming Dinosaur Center**, in **Thermopolis**, offers day digs at **Warm Springs Ranch** for people short on time, interest, or patience. Warm Springs Ranch sits on the Morrison Formation, deposited during the Jurassic. Most of the more than 1,000 bones already found here come from

Some weeks later Earthwatch project leader Keith Rigby, a paleontologist at the University of Notre Dame, told Tremblay that the rib he found, along with a pelvis, claw, and toe bone found nearby, clearly belonged to a large carnivorous dinosaur. Tremblay's find may even be the largest tyrannosaur specimen ever found. The apparent extent of the corresponding bone bed could make it the world's largest graveyard of late

sauropods, long-necked giants with elephantine bodies, such as *Apatosaurus, Camarasaurus,* and *Diplodocus.*

The Day Digs Program starts at 8 A.M. with a half-hour orientation and van drive to the ranch. Overlooking picturesque red hills at the northern end of the Wind River Canyon, diggers spend the day working alongside scientists in one of several bone beds. There are breaks for a sack lunch and for fossil finders to log their names in the center's bone registry. The field day officially ends at 4:30 P.M. Those who grow weary earlier may return to the world-class museum or visit the preparation lab, where technicians remove bone from rock for display.

The **Old Trail Museum** in **Choteau, Montana**, sponsors a two-day introductory course for groups of no more than eight children and adults. It includes excavation on active sites, preparation, and prospecting for new fossils of hadrosaurs and tyrannosaurs. Instructor Todd Crowell can discuss the egg-laying habits of dinosaurs while juggling rock hammers. Eight-hour days start with a 15-minute lecture, and then participants are off to dig for the morning and prospect after lunch. The museum also offers a five-day introductory family course and an advanced course for alumni of the introductory class.

Dry Mesa Quarry (left) in western Colorado has yielded the bones of gigantic sauropods. A *Supersaurus* shoulder blade found here is the largest single dinosaur bone ever found.

Students (right) explore the site near Buffalo, South Dakota, where Stan, a *T. rex*, was unearthed.

An excavation team (below) sets out with Jack Horner for another day in the trenches at Egg Mountain, a world-famous dinosaur nesting ground.

Family Vacation

The **Dinamation International Society**, in **Fruita, Colorado**, operates a five-day Family Dino Camp at **Mygatt-Moore Quarry** that is fun for both parents and kids. Nearly 150 million years old, the quarry has yielded two kinds of dinosaur eggs and more than eight dinosaur species. They include the chunky *Mymoorapelta*, North America's oldest ankylosaur, and a variety of sauropods.

The Family Dino Camp has a separate-but-equal itinerary that satisfies kids and parents alike. Both age groups dig under shade screens, but while adults excavate real fossils, juniors dig in a neighboring pit for fossil casts to take home. Everyone goes to the lab, but after a brief orientation, kids view a dinosaur film, create dioramas, and sculpt dinosaurs, while parents learn about fossil preparation and other procedures. Paleontologist Jim Kirkland drops by to help parents dig or to lead children on hikes.

Joint activities include picnic lunches and making rubbings of dinosaur tracks and casts of teeth and claws. Field trips go to **Split Rock Dinosaur Area**, **Colorado National Monument**, **Douglas Pass**, and **Fruita's Dinosaur Discovery Museum**.

Sauropod Quarry

The **Dinosaur Valley Museum**, in **Grand Junction, Colorado**, sponsors a six-day expedition-style dig at **Dalton Wells Quarry**, near **Moab, Utah**. This 1,300-foot-long bone bed sits on a 30-foot-wide mesa 200 feet above the valley floor, with dramatic views of the La Sal Mountains and countless sandstone arches and columnlike hoodoos. Situated at the base of the Cedar Mountain Formation, the quarry samples a rare slice of early Cretaceous life, dominated by sauropods. Also excavated here are three kinds of ornithischians, a large fin-backed iguanodontid, a small armadillo-like

Adults Only

The **Royal Tyrrell Museum of Palaeontology** in **Drumheller, Alberta**, offers a thoroughly authentic, adults-only field experience in **Dinosaur Provincial Park**, home to some 200 bone beds containing more than 30 different species and untold thousands of individual bones. About eight large dinosaurs, including duckbilled, horned, and armored species, dominate the collection. The sickle-footed *Troödon* has also been unearthed here, as has one of the world's two complete skeletons of *Parasaurolophus*.

The program, which lasts for a minimum of one week, is fairly rigorous. After a 7 A.M. breakfast, campers leave for the field to prospect, excavate, or study the surrounding fauna and flora until about 4 P.M. Evenings and rainy days are spent working on previously collected specimens in the field station laboratory. At least three professional staff members are on site at all times.

Overseas Adventure

Earthwatch Institute, in **Watertown, Massachusetts**, organizes dinosaur research expeditions to Argentina and other paleontology expeditions to England, Switzerland, Australia, China, and Mexico. Known for its harsh beauty, **Argentina's Ischigualasto Basin**, also called the **Valley of the Moon**, is five miles wide, 40 miles long, and 3,000 feet above sea level. Red cliffs rise from a sandstone and claystone floor that contains a continuous sequence of fossils from the middle through late Triassic. Discoveries include a nearly complete *Herrerasaurus* skeleton, plus the bones of early reptiles such as rhynchosaurs, cynodonts, aetosaurs, protochampids, and dicynodonts which predate the arrival of the first dinosaurs. Data collected here may eventually shed light on a mass extinction of reptiles that occurred in the middle Triassic.

nodosaur, several bipedal theropods, and other specimens yet to be named.

Rod Scheetz, a museum paleontologist, leads this daily expedition. After an 8 A.M. breakfast, teams jump into their Jeeps and spiral up a dirt trail to the mesa. Here they spend the day working in silty mudstone with shovels, dental picks, air-driven chipping hammers, and other tools. They stop only briefly to make their own lunches. The workday ends at 5 P.M., but the long summer days allow for after-dinner activities, such as a scenic drive, rockhounding, or hunting for dinosaur footprints and ancient mollusks known as ammonites. Though children are permitted, this is a no-nonsense adventure.

The trip is led by Oscar Alcober and William Sill of Universidad Nacional de San Juan de Ciencias Naturales. Volunteers prospect for fossils in groups of two to four, mark locations, map localities, gather and wash sediments, excavate, and cover specimens in plaster. Some team members explore new areas by backpack. Evenings are spent chopping firewood, cooking, discussing the day's work, writing in field logs, and classifying and cataloging specimens.

The **Dinamation International Society** in Colorado also specializes in international destinations. Paleontologist Jim Kirkland leads trips to the **Flaming Cliffs** of **Mongolia's Gobi Desert**, where Roy Chapman Andrews discovered dinosaur eggs and nests and where amazing new discoveries await. Participants work with scientists and live in a Mongolian *ger*, a type of tent. They may also take a camel trek through the vast Gobi landscape. Other Dinamation expeditions visit Argentina, Mexico, France, and Canada.

Digging for Credit

The **Museum of the Rockies** in **Bozeman, Montana**, operates a seven-day structured learning program at **Egg Mountain**. Part of the Two Medicine Formation, Egg Mountain is on the eastern slope of the Rocky Mountains. Since 1978, teams led by Jack Horner, the museum's curator of paleontology, have discovered several dinosaur rookeries in the reddish-brown sediment, with six-foot nests containing eggs the size of cantaloupes and even some hatchlings. These fossils provided

the first evidence that dinosaurs nested together. There is also an enormous bone bed of broad-beaked *Maiasaura peeblesorum*.

Like most other field experiences, this program allows participants to prospect for dinosaurs, do small tool and hard rock excavation, and collect geologic data from the arid plains. The week begins and ends at the Museum of the Rockies, where exhibits tell the story of Egg Mountain and *Maiasaura*, the "good mother lizard." There are also lectures, slide shows, discussions, and assorted other programs. Field trips include a visit to **Pine Butte Swamp Preserve**, a habitat for grizzly bears. This program offers academic credit through Antioch College in Washington.

Tail bones of *Diplodocus* (opposite) emerge from Jurassic deposits at Sheep Creek, Wyoming, on a dig led by Bob Bakker.

A lucky digger (above) clasps a horn fragment from a centrosaur, which roamed Alberta in herds. Heavy floods sometimes buried the animals in great numbers.

A crew of volunteers (left) carefully excavates a maiasaur site at Egg Mountain, Montana, where evidence suggests that duckbilled dinosaur parents cared for young.

learn how to prospect, excavate, clean, stabilize, and catalog specimens, and they get hands-on experience in molding and casting fossils. Throughout the course there are lectures and plenty of handouts. The program isn't all work and no play; there are two scheduled social events and a field trip to a site rich in dinosaur footprints.

Career Track

The **Denver Museum of Natural History**'s Certification Program in Paleontology covers everything from collecting and cataloging your own collection to working with museum specimens. Classes take place at the museum, but the program includes field trips to research sites in Utah, Colorado, or Wyoming.

The program's six courses meet four to five times for two to three hours each. Every course combines lectures, lab work, and field trips. Subjects include the rules and regulations of fossil collecting, research methods, report writing, and the history of life as revealed through the fossil record. The program is designed to provide comprehensive knowledge of both paleontological theories and techniques. In addition, two specialized tracks focus on either field work or laboratory methods. The former entails four class sessions, two one-day field trips, and six days on a museum project; the latter requires eight lab sessions.

In New Mexico, paleontologist Adrian Hunt runs a seven-day course accredited by Mesa Technical College. Hunt, curator of the forthcoming **Mesalands Dinosaur Museum**, is a renowned fossil collector and the author of more than 300 scientific articles and several books. In this scenic region, home to one of the world's most complete Mesozoic fossil records, Triassic dinosaurs and their contemporaries are buried in ancient streambeds beneath dramatic red-rock mesas. The program provides an overview of the basic field, laboratory, and museum methods used to study fossils. Students

Courses such as "Paleontology of the Western Interior" and "Curation of Fossils" are also offered. All courses are taught by the museum's curators and staff.

Practical Matters

Denver Museum of Natural History, Adult Programs, 2001 Colorado Boulevard, Denver, CO 80205-5798; tel: 303-370-6303. Each course accepts an average of 25 students. Participants must be at least 17 years old. Prices vary.

Dinamation International Society, 550 Jurassic Court, Fruita, CO 81521; tel: 800-344-3466. Families are lodged at a Grand Junction hotel. The camp, offered twice a summer, is open to 24 people per session. Children must be at least six years old and accompanied by an adult. $875 per adult, $575 per child.

Dinosaur Valley Museum, 4th and Main Streets, Grand Junction, CO 81501; tel: 970-241-9210. Participants sleep in expedition tents and help with meals and camp chores. The dig is offered three times a year for up to 10 people per session. Children under 18 must be accompanied by a paying adult. $699 per person.

Earthwatch Institute, 680 Mt. Auburn Street, P.O. Box 9104, Watertown, MA 02471-9104; tel: 800-776-0188. Participants bring their own tents and sleeping bags. Food is provided, but cooking duties are shared. Expeditions are offered intermittently and are open to 15 people per group. Members must be at least 16 years old, and camping experience is recommended. Prices vary.

Mesalands Dinosaur Museum, 222 East Laughlin, Tucumcari, NM 88401; tel: 505-461-4413. Students are lodged at a motel in Tucumcari. Groups don't exceed 20 people. $400 per person for five-day course, $495 for seven-day course.

Museum of the Rockies, 600 West Kagy Boulevard, Bozeman, MT 59717; tel: 406-994-6618. Participants sleep in genuine Blackfoot tipis; meals are provided. The program, held five times a summer, is open to 25 people per session. With a student-teacher ratio of five to one, there is plenty of supervision. Participants must be at least 12 years old. $1,100 per person.

Old Trail Museum, 823 North Main, Choteau, MT 59422; tel: 406-466-5332. Participants stay at a motel in Choteau. $125 per person for a two-day course, $300 per person for a five-day advanced course.

Royal Tyrrell Museum of Palaeontology, Box 7500, Drumheller, Alberta, T0J 0Y0, Canada; tel: 888-440-424 or 403-823-7707. Participants stay in trailers with semiprivate rooms, men's and women's bathrooms, a laundry room, kitchen, and dining room. Meals are prepared on site. The program is offered throughout the summer, with a maximum of 10 people per session. Participants must be at least 18 years old. $650 per person for the first week, $550 for the second week.

Wyoming Dinosaur Center, Box 868, Thermopolis, WY 82443; tel: 800-455-3466 or 307-864-2997. The student-teacher ratio in the Day Digs does not exceed four to one, and there is no age restriction. Digs are offered daily from late spring to early fall. Cost: $100 per person or $250 for a family of four.

For information on other dinosaur dig programs, see the Resource Directory at the end of this book.

Rock hammer in hand (above), Andrew Veitch inspects the excavation site of Stan the *Tyrannosaurus*, now on display at the Black Hills Institute of Geological Research.

Reference books (right) can help identify puzzling fossils or answer questions that come up in the course of an excavation.

Digging dinosaurs can be a family affair (below), as many programs accommodate adults and children.

Dinosaur Parks and Fossil Sites

CHAPTER **10**

Dinosaurs roamed the entire Earth during their lengthy reign, and North America offered especially rich stomping grounds for the charismatic beasts. Their bones and other traces have been turning up here for well over a century. Although New Jersey lays claim to producing the first fairly complete dinosaur skeleton, a *Hadrosaurus* found in 1858, the badlands of the American West soon lured fossil hunters seeking more and better bones. Pioneering paleontologists rode the railroads west, discovered their mother lodes, and sent hundreds of tons of fossils back to East Coast museums. ◆ From dinosaur nests in Alberta to trackways in Texas, from the sere sagebrush flats of Nevada to eroding bluffs in Nova Scotia, this chapter profiles the most significant places where fossils of dinosaurs, their contemporaries, and some of their successors are found. Some fossil sites lie right off a highway; others require a bit of bushwhacking to reach. Some, like Como Bluff, have been

Exploring bone beds, trackways, and nest sites reveals much about the nature of dinosaurs and the people who study them.

known since the earliest days of dinosaur hunting, while a few are recent discoveries. ◆ These sites span almost the entire age of dinosaurs. To see what some of the earliest species were like, head to Petrified Forest National Park in Arizona. If super-sized Jurassic sauropods suit you better, try Dinosaur National Monument or Dry Mesa Quarry in Colorado. For a glimpse of dinosaur diversity just before the great beasts disappeared, choose Dinosaur Provincial Park in Alberta or Egg Mountain in Montana. Wherever you go, prepare yourself to be transported to a time when dinosaurs ruled the planet.

Camarasaurus leers at a worker exposing fossils in the near-vertical bone bed at Dinosaur National Monument, where 1,600 fossils remain as they were found.

Preceding pages: Dinosaur eggs are sometimes spherical and large; others approach the shape and size of a chicken egg.

Wasson Bluff
Bay of Fundy, Nova Scotia

For information, contact the Fundy Geological
Museum, Two Islands Road, Parrsboro, NS
B0M 1S0 Canada; tel: 902-254-3814.
Tuesday–Saturday, 9 A.M.–5 P.M.,
extended summer hours. $

On a blustery spring day in 1984, amateur
fossil collector Eldon George drove his all-
terrain vehicle along the ocean's edge a few
miles from his home on Nova Scotia's **Bay
of Fundy**. Growing chilled, he ducked into
the lee of a rocky outcropping to get out of
the wind. An unusual rock half buried in
the beach caught his attention. He brushed
some grit off and looked closer. Across this
piece of sandstone were five three-toed footprints, running at odd angles to one another,
as if the creature that made them had per-
formed an elaborate jig. George carefully
extricated the rock and brought it home.

Today the wee tracks are on display at
George's small rock shop in the sleepy village
of **Parrsboro**. What attracts serious fossil
hounds to the shop – and what earned
George's find a footnote in the annals of
paleontology – are the Lilliputian size of
the footprints. Each could be hidden under
a penny. The dinosaur that left these tracks
wasn't much bigger than a sparrow; neither
the species nor age of the gamboling theropod is known, but by all accounts these are
the world's smallest dinosaur footprints.

Boundary in Time

It would be hard to imagine a more efficient
excavating tool than the tides of the Bay of
Fundy. Twice a day, five full stories of ocean
water – the highest tides in the world –
surge in and ebb out, gradually undermining
the 100-foot-high cliffs of sandstone and
basalt that line much of the shore around
the **Minas Basin**. Thus weakened, the cliffs
erode steadily, raining down bits of rock and
the occasional larger slab. Among the detri-
tus are numerous fossils that date from the
dawn of the Jurassic period, one of the most
critical junctures in the evolution of plant
and animal life. Experts estimate that nearly
half of the plant and animal species that
existed in the preceding Triassic period
mysteriously failed to cross over into the
Jurassic, leaving an evolutionary gap that
dinosaurs ultimately filled.

Since George's discovery, paleontologists
have flocked to **Wasson Bluff** to
explore the boundary between the
Triassic and the Jurassic. In 1986,
scientists unearthed more than
100,000 bones and fragments entombed in
the sedimentary rock not far from where
George found the footprints. As recently as
October 1997, another rich cache of prehistoric bones turned up that included early
crocodiles, lizards, sharks, and dinosaurs
both large and small.

When you visit, park atop the forested bluff and wander down the path to the shore. (Plan to arrive near low tide, when the ocean recedes and leaves a wide, safe swath of shore.) Digging isn't allowed on the bluff except by authorized scientists. But anything loose and already on the ground is free for the taking. Head east from Wasson Bluff and you'll wander farther back in time to the Carboniferous period; look for fossils of ferns, calamites (relatives of the modern horsetails), and the stout stems of the lepidodendron.

Fossils on Display

The best place to make sense of the region's rich natural history is the **Fundy Geological Museum** in Parrsboro. This compact but modern museum at the edge of the harbor leads visitors on a brief, intriguing tour, speeding through geological time as if on a freeway. You'll view fossils fresh from the earth (there's a lab where you can observe technicians at work through windows, and ask questions via intercom). Perhaps most intriguing are the dioramas showing the prosauropods – seven-foot-long herbivores that paved the way for Jurassic giants – and other early dinosaurs that ranged across the region some 200 million years ago.

Cliffside walks (below) often turn up new fossils exposed by the bay's tides.

Afterward, you can arrange for guided fossil expeditions with museum staffers or local tour operators. Eldon George himself still leads the occasional tour but has plenty of fossils at his **Parrsboro Rock and Mineral Shop and Museum**. Taste a Colossal Fossil barbecue sandwich at a local restaurant. But above all, wander the eerily remote shores, and have your breath taken away as you seem to peer over the edge of a vast abyss of time.

Sea stacks (opposite) gradually erode with the ebb and flood of the Bay of Fundy, site of the world's biggest tides.

Primitive prosauropods such as *Plateosaurus* (right) grew a fraction of the size of later Jurassic giants. Prosauropod bones have eroded from Wasson Bluff.

Dinosaur State Park
Rocky Hill, Connecticut

Dinosaur State Park, West Street (Exit 23, Interstate 91), Rocky Hill, CT 06067-3506; tel: 860-529-5816.
Tuesday–Sunday, 9 A.M.–4:30 P.M.
Footprint casts can be made May 1–October 31. $

This real-life Jurassic Park makes a perfect paleontological pit stop. Remember those Arthur Murray dance school maps showing where to place your feet? **Dinosaur State Park**

presents the prehistoric version. Nearly 200 million years ago, dinosaurs walked and even swam here, on what was the muddy shore of an ancient lake. Meat eaters and plant eaters, including perhaps the giant and genuine manifestation of Michael Crichton's fantasy "spitter" *Dilophosaurus*, ambled through what is now a convenient highway detour.

Beneath a geodesic dome, talented exhibit designer David Seibert has created a lively, theatrical display around a splendid fossil trackway. A footprint quarry at least three times as large lies unexcavated beneath the lawn. Illuminated by spotlights, hundreds of tracks on a tilted stone slab can be seen from above; a glass-sided walkway passes directly over some of the tracks. All the footprints look fresh, thanks to a thin sheet of mica that covered and preserved the fossil-bearing sediments. Several curious prints show that large meat eaters pushed off the ancient bank to swim in the shallow water. Even in mid-summer, crowds disperse inside the spacious dome, so take time to admire the handsome exhibits, from murals depicting Triassic and Jurassic environments to a full-sized sculpture of *Dilophosaurus*.

Official State Dinosaur

Whether this was the animal that frequented the footprint-rich **Connecticut River Valley** way back when remains uncertain, but its bones have been found from Arizona to China (at that time the world had only a single, giant landmass). Dinosaurs cannot be easily identified from footprints alone, so those without any associated bones receive an "ichnogenus," a name based solely on the prints. In the case of these 20-foot-long carnivores, the ichnogenus is *Eubrontes*. And though enigmatic, in a state full of footprints but lacking major bone beds, *Eubrontes* is the official state fossil.

Tracks from two other dinosaurs are displayed here, too, one a small *Coelophysis*-like carnivore, the other a prosauropod-like plant eater, about 15 feet long. A few intriguing bone bits on display include a cast of the first dinosaur fossil found in North America, a fragment collected in 1818.

You can watch a video of the trackway excavation, which followed the accidental discovery of the site in 1966 by a building crew. A simulated road cut lines one wall, showing how the rocks in the region formed. Pull open drawers in the rock wall to reveal hands-on samples that, along with punchy and informative text panels, make understanding the geology of the Connecticut Valley a cinch.

Don't miss the outdoor exhibits: a clever "walk"

Theropod tracks (opposite) preserved along an ancient muddy shore lie beneath a geodesic dome at Dinosaur State Park.

Dinosaur footprints discovered in Massachusetts in the early 19th century were regarded as a curiosity by local residents.

through Earth's history and a peaceful path through a streamside forest planted with descendants of Mesozoic trees, including ginkgoes, ferns, and evergreens. Best of all is a do-it-yourself footprint casting factory. Bring a container of vegetable oil and a large bag of plaster, and the park will supply rags and rings to make a dinner-plate-sized cast of a three-toed dinosaur track – yours to keep. Just what made these footprints we'll never know, but the animal that slogged through this Mann's Chinese Theater of the Mesozoic certainly deserves to be a celebrity.

Noah's Raven

Dinosaur lovers walk on hallowed ground in western Massachusetts. In 1802, in the town of **Hadley**, 20-year-old farmer Pliny Moody made an astounding discovery: a dinosaur footprint. As the very idea of extinct animals sparked controversy, and the world would not even hear the word *dinosaur* for another four decades, Moody's find was called "Noah's raven," the tracks of a giant, biblical bird.

Three decades later, more ancient footprints turned up in the Connecticut River Valley. The tracks caught the attention of Reverend Edward Hitchcock, an Amherst College professor who devoted his career to diligently assembling and studying the world's largest collection of fossil trackways. Hitchcock's collection, expanded over the years by his successors, now occupies the **Pratt Museum of Natural History**, a dowdy, white-columned brick building at **Amherst College**.

Here as elsewhere, however, dinosaur footprints seem more mysterious when seen *au naturel*, and the **Dinosaur Footprints Reservation**, near **Mount Tom** in Holyoke, offers a scenic spot to do so. Riverside tracks have been attributed to the theropods *Grallator* and *Eubrontes*, though it may take some sleuthing to find them. Just remember the words of Sherlock Holmes: "There is no branch of detective science ... so much neglected as the art of tracing footsteps." Or ask for assistance beforehand at the Pratt Museum (tel: 413-542-2165).

Dinosaur Alley
Maryland

For tour information, contact the Dinosaur Fund, 645 G Street SE, Washington, DC 20003; tel: 202-547-3326. $–$$

"You'll never find anything if you dig!" barks out the bushy-bearded man in a dusty pith helmet. "You have to get down on your hands and knees and scour the surface." The fossil hounds clustered around him listen intently to their guide. After all, Peter Kranz knows more than anyone about uncovering the dinosaurs of eastern Maryland.

Kranz traipses up and down **Dinosaur Alley**, a 10-mile-wide swath of early Cretaceous terrain stretching from Washington, D.C., to Baltimore. Paralleling Interstate 95, it contains the only record east of the Mississippi River of dinosaurs living between 95 and 130 million years ago.

Before the region burgeoned into one of the United States' busiest commuter corridors, giant sauropods lumbered through tropical forests, munching on conifers and fending off feisty cousins of *Tyrannosaurus rex*.

Paleontologist Peter Kranz (right), outfitted in pith helmet and boots, established the Dinosaur Fund to promote Maryland's prehistoric legacy.

Abundant tracks of *Atreipus* (opposite), a late Triassic ornithischian, occur from Nova Scotia to Virginia, but very few of its bones have been found.

These beasts, along with a tenontosaur and the ankylosaur *Priconodon crassus*, left their traces sandwiched between sandy gravel and brightly colored mud in pockets of gray Arundel clay. Floods probably washed this fine clay, along with trees and dead animals, into river meanders cut off from the waters flowing sluggishly toward the Atlantic Ocean.

Millions of years later, in 1858, the tooth of one unlucky creature worked its way to the surface of an iron mine at **Muirkirk**, Maryland. The famous paleontologist Joseph Leidy named the tooth *Astrodon johnstoni* – the first sauropod described from North America and one of few survivors of the older Jurassic group of brachiosaurid sauropods. Local iron mines coughed up more bones in the late 1800s, but most pits were abandoned and flooded by the 1920s.

The All-Important Toe

The treasures of Dinosaur Alley sat virtually undisturbed for decades – until Kranz stormed the scene. In the spring of 1989, he stumbled upon his first dinosaur bone – a theropod toe – at a brick-clay quarry near Muirkirk. Keeping dinosaurs in the news has since become Kranz's self-appointed duty. Late in 1998, his aggressive lobbying paid off when the Maryland legislature declared *Astrodon johnstoni* the state dinosaur. Many bits of *Astrodon* are on display at the **Maryland Science Center** in **Baltimore**, including the largest dinosaur bone ever found on the East Coast, a four-foot-long piece of thighbone.

Kranz had led his group to **Bladensburg**, Maryland. His followers wonder where they will find any fossils as they fight their way through thorny brush along a high chain-link fence. Then, between two cluttered construction lots, a pile of gray dirt rose out of a 50-foot-wide strip of bare soil – the Arundel.

Perched atop the bone-friendly clay in aqua high-tops, khaki shorts, and a gray T-shirt featuring a motherly *Astrodon*, Kranz explains why digging is bad. Dry bone on

the surface stands out as pale blue; covered with dirt, it looks like any other pebble. Finding it difficult to discourage children wielding garden forks and trowels, however, he lets them dig for lignite, jet-black chunks of fossilized wood which, along with the ironstones mined long ago, are signatures of the Arundel. "The last thing that saw that tree before you dug it up was a dinosaur, so in a way, you found a dinosaur fossil," he tells them encouragingly.

Kranz has enlisted the group to help search this forgotten pile before it disappears. That's the problem in eastern Maryland: "Land is invariably owned or covered with buildings or asphalt or vegetation," he laments. "We move from one location to another as they become available." He always keeps an eye out for new housing developments, drainage ditches, or any activity that might reveal another pocket of Arundel, reminding you that "any place you see gray dirt, ironstone, and lignite is a place you want to look."

Kranz dreams of a day when dinosaur buffs can gather at a single site time and again. A Dinosaur Park combining an educational center with an open dig is planned for several wooded acres near the fruitful Muirkirk quarry, but meanwhile Kranz leads fossil tours through his Washington-based, nonprofit organization, the Dinosaur Fund. If hiking doesn't suit you, Dinosaur Fund volunteers will bring the fossils to you in a truckload of Arundel clay. In time, Peter Kranz vows to "make all of the citizens of Maryland into paleontologists."

Dinosaur Valley State Park
Glen Rose, Texas

Dinosaur Valley State Park, Box 396, Glen Rose, TX 76043; tel: 254-897-4588.
The park is always open. The visitor center is open daily 8 A.M.–5 P.M. From Glen Rose on Highway 67, take FM205/Park Road 59 four miles to the state park. $

It was a dance of giants, a slow dance, and most likely one of death. It took place 110 million years ago, along the edges of a shallow sea near what is today central Texas. The unwilling partner was a lumbering *Pleurocoelus* dinosaur, its four thick legs frantically sucking out of the mud. By its side waltzed a hungry *Acrocanthosaurus*, its sharp teeth reaching out toward its prey.

The footprints are still visible today, frozen into the limestone bed of the **Paluxy River** in **Dinosaur Valley State Park** near **Glen Rose, Texas**. Visitors come for many reasons, including the scenic countryside and the clear Paluxy water. But nowhere else in the state is the dinosaur past so tangible: Inner-tubers can stick their hands into the water and touch the huge imprint of a dinosaur foot as they drift above it.

The best time to visit Dinosaur Valley State Park is in the late summer, when the river is low and more of the dinosaur tracks are exposed. Five sites within the park show off the array of trackways – the long trails made by a single dinosaur – found along the Paluxy. Within the state park, and in the

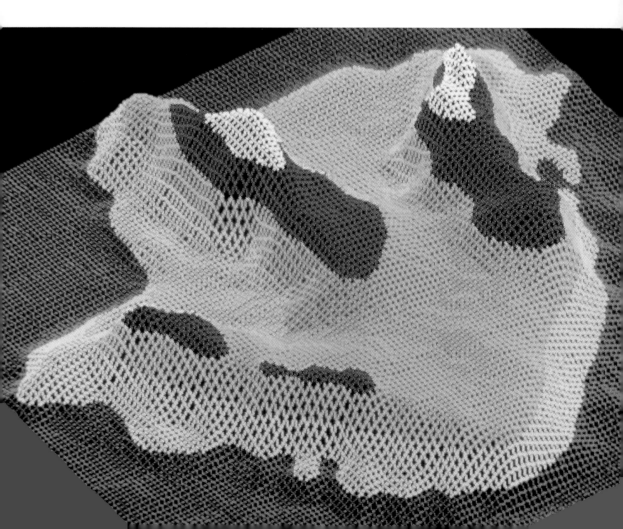

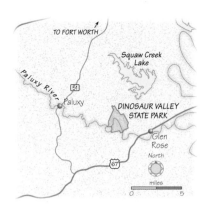

surrounding private land, at least three different species of dinosaur left behind their marks.

Tracks in a Tidal Flat

The most famous are the tracks left by *Pleurocoelus*, a 20-ton example of the long-necked vegetarian dinosaurs known as sauropods. Its footprints, round and blobby, are as big as washtubs. The most common tracks are the pointy, three-toed type left behind by a two-legged carnivore, or theropod. These were most likely made by *Acrocanthosaurus*, an early and smaller relative of *Tyrannosaurus rex* that still measured an impressive 30 feet long. The most curious tracks at Glen Rose are wider and more rounded versions of a three-toed print. They may have been left behind by *Iguanodon*, a two-legged plant eater whose bones were discovered in Texas in 1985.

Around 110 million years ago, the Glen Rose area was a muddy tidal flat, at the edge of a shallow sea that spread and then shrank across central North America for millions of years. The wide flats, framed by bushes and trees, would have made a perfect place for sauropods to browse while theropods stalked.

Local fishermen and moonshiners were the first to

know of the mighty tracks left behind by these creatures. In fact, one of the theropod footprints was built into the bandstand at the Somervell County courthouse in Glen Rose. Paleontologists didn't learn about the tracks until the early part of this century, when geologists discovered the three-toed theropod prints. Building on the area's reputation, locals began carving fake prints into other chunks of rock and selling them during the Great Depression. Although they were never intended to deceive scientists, the Glen Rose carvings nevertheless initiated decades of misinterpretation of the Paluxy River trackways.

Interpreting the Evidence

One of the fakes, however, did put Glen Rose on the map for paleontologists. In 1938, fossil-hunter Roland T. Bird was shown one of the carvings in New Mexico while looking for treasures to bring back to his bosses at the American Museum of Natural History in New York. He knew the carving was fake but immediately set out for Glen Rose, where

Computer image (left) of a theropod track, which was probably left by *Acrocanthosaurus* near Glen Rose, Texas.

Five sites along the Paluxy River (right) in Dinosaur Valley State Park showcase footprint trails made by at least three kinds of dinosaurs.

Only front feet (left) appear in the Mayan Ranch Trackway, once thought to have been formed by a swimming sauropod. Erosion may best explain the absence of rear tracks.

A hiker's foot (right) could fill one of the three toes of this theropod track, whose meat-eating maker probably grew to 30 feet long.

A signpost (below) alerts visitors to the washtub-sized tracks of *Pleurocoelus*, a 20-ton vegetarian that roamed the area around Glen Rose 110 million years ago.

Fearsome carnivore *Acrocanthosaurus* (opposite, bottom) may have stalked sauropods meandering through what is now Dinosaur Valley State Park.

York to be reassembled. Today the footprints can be seen at the American Museum of Natural History, while other chunks are at other museums, including the Texas Memorial Museum at the University of Texas in Austin.

the rock came from, to check out tales of other dinosaur trackways.

Once at the Paluxy, Bird found the real theropod tracks. And then came the big discovery – tracks of at least a dozen sauropods in the riverbed. He contracted for a crew from the Works Progress Administration, diverted the river, chipped out huge sections of trackway, and shipped them back to New

Footprints from around Glen Rose triggered Bird to formulate some of the first theories regarding dinosaur behavior. For example, a trackway from nearby **Davenport Ranch** inspired Bird's theory of dinosaur herding. Rocks at the ranch record at least 23 sauropods moving in the same direction across the area. According to Bird, these lumbering giants must have been moving in a herd – a social behavior that scientists hadn't previously suspected of dinosaurs.

Similarly, at the **Mayan Ranch** trackway closer to **San Antonio**, Bird found footprints

of just the front feet of a large sauropod. Bird interpreted this as evidence that the sauropod could move its massive body only when floating in water. According to this theory, the dinosaur would use its front feet to push itself along in an underwater ballet, its rear feet and tail floating behind. Today, paleontologists think that sauropods had legs strong enough to support their massive bodies on dry land. New examinations of this trackway suggest that Bird may have missed part of the story. There is, in fact, at least one slight imprint of a hind foot along the trackway, and the missing rest may just be due to poor preservation.

The Hunter and the Hunted

At the Paluxy trackway itself, paleontologists still don't agree on Bird's suggestion that the intermingled tracks of sauropods and theropods represent a deadly hunt. At first glance, the evidence seems good. A herd of a dozen sauropods left tracks, followed roughly parallel by the prints of four theropods. One of the theropod's tracks seems to curve into the trail of a sauropod. Indeed, the theropod track has one step missing, as if the carnivore lunged at the other dinosaur's neck, grabbed on with its teeth, and was carried along for one step in a deadly embrace. But recently, some paleontologists have questioned this dramatic scenario, saying there's little evidence the animals changed speed or direction as they would during a pursuit. Many also point out that there's no way of knowing if the theropod tracks were made at the same time as the sauropods', or hours or even days later.

The pursuit legend, however, lives on. Near the entrance to the park stand more reminders: life-size fiberglass models of the sauropod *Apatosaurus* and a *Tyrannosaurus rex*, cast for the 1964 World's Fair in New York and meant to represent the participants in the deadly battle. It was an odd trade for the valuable trackways that had been

sent to New York: *Apatosaurus* and *T. rex* actually lived millions of years after the *Pleurocoelus* and *Acrocanthosaurus* of Glen Rose.

The Paluxy tracks have inspired even more controversy than this. Creationists have long suggested that human footprints exist alongside or even within the dinosaur tracks of Glen Rose. But paleontologists have confirmed that any mysterious tracks at Glen Rose were all made by dinosaurs. The "man-tracks" on a ledge above the main trackway site within the park, for instance, were made by dinosaurs walking oddly, placing a part of their foot down that they wouldn't usually. Scientists view this as a challenge not to the reality of the Glen Rose dinosaur tracks but to themselves to learn why dinosaurs left behind the marks they did.

Clayton Lake State Park
Clayton, New Mexico

Clayton Lake State Park, Rural Route Box 20, Seneca, NM 88437; tel: 505-374-8808.
Always open. $

The landscape around **Clayton, New Mexico**, has long offered respite for travelers. Early settlers stopped at watering holes here as they journeyed along a cutoff of the Santa Fe Trail. And the same was true millions of years ago, when dinosaurs rumbled by. They left their marks within what is now **Clayton Lake State Park**, where visitors can see one of the most significant dinosaur trackways in the country.

It's not surprising that the place is so packed with fossil history. The Clayton Lake area contains Dakota Sandstone, a rock formation that harbors many traces of dinosaurs. Around 100 million years ago, Dakota Sandstone was laid down along the western edge of the shallow sea that covered central North America. The muddy shoreline was the ideal place for many kinds of dinosaurs. Dinosaur footprints in Dakota Sandstone stretch from northern New Mexico to Colorado. Dinosaur Ridge west of Denver, for example, showcases prints in the Dakota similar to those seen here.

Unlike Dinosaur Valley State Park in Texas, the tracks at Clayton Lake are always exposed. Rather than rooting around in a river for footprints, visitors take a wooden walkway right up to more than 500 separate dinosaur tracks. In the morning or early evening, the low-angle sunlight strikes the tracks and brings out their details. Some of the tracks are in danger of disappearing as the sandstone flakes away in wind and rain. Others come into higher definition as the surface slowly erodes.

What the Tracks Say

Still making discoveries at Clayton Lake, paleontologists examine the tracks to learn more about how dinosaurs lived. So far, scientists have catalogued tracks from at least four different kinds of dinosaurs. Most of the prints were left by large, two-legged plant eaters, perhaps hadrosaurs or iguanodonts. Others may have been made by the ornithopod *Tenontosaurus*, whose fossils have been found in Texas, Montana, and Utah. The largest of these tracks would fill a small kitchen sink. Adults and juveniles alike left prints, suggesting that entire dinosaur families milled across this area. About a quarter of the prints, with pointed heels and clawed toes, were made by carnivorous theropods.

The tracks that have gotten the most attention recently lie off the public walkway.

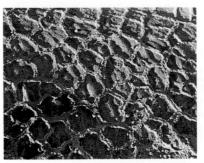

Plant-eating iguanodonts (above) produced many of the 500 dinosaur tracks visible at Clayton Lake State Park.

Mud cracks (left) have petrified in the shale of the Dakota Formation, which preserves dinosaur footprints from Colorado to New Mexico.

These are six small prints accompanied by several shallow, linear depressions. Scientists once interpreted these as the prints of a pterosaur, or flying reptile, in the process of taking off. But new studies suggest that the tracks actually were left behind by a crocodile-like creature, perhaps as it touched the shallow bottom. The size, shape, and spacing of the prints support this theory, which explains the linear depressions as marks of a crocodilian tail dragging across the mud.

By exploring Clayton Lake, paleontologists have deepened their understanding of where and when different kinds of dinosaurs lived. For example, scientists have found that rocks just a bit older than the 100-million-year-old ones here are dominated by the tracks of sauropods, the giant plant-eating dinosaurs. Sauropods make up most of the trackways of that age in Texas, Oklahoma, and Arkansas. But at Clayton Lake and other slightly younger sites, there are no sauropod tracks, only those of other plant-eating dinosaurs. This observation suggests that sauropods temporarily went extinct in North America – only to return around 30 million years later, perhaps by migrating from South America.

A convenient board-walk (below) lets visitors to Clayton Lake State Park get close to dinosaur tracks without damaging them.

Sunlight striking sandstone (right) in the morning or evening brings out details in the dinosaur tracks.

Petrified Forest National Park
Winslow, Arizona

Petrified Forest National Park, Box 2217, Petrified Forest, AZ 86028; tel: 520-524-6228. Open year-round, 7:30 A.M.–5 P.M., extended summer hours. $

Navajos call them "male rains," the brief but violent downpours that pelt the bruise-colored hills of the **Painted Desert** in northeastern Arizona, sending torrents into easily

eroded arroyos and washes. The sand, clay, and volcanic ash that form these colorful badlands were laid down more than 220 million years ago, and their erosion reveals one of the world's greatest treasure troves of fossils from the late Triassic period, when dinosaurs and early mammals were just beginning to roam the planet.

Most famously, the region contains one of the largest concentrations of petrified wood anywhere. Along several short trails in **Petrified Forest National Park**, visitors can amble among stone

logs that record the forms of trees that once grew here. At the south end of the park, the **Giant Logs Trail** behind the **Rainbow Forest Museum**, and **Long Logs Trail** about half a mile north, both allow a close-up look at petrified logs. Along the Giant Logs Trail, some multicolored trunks are as thick as a person is tall, while a few of the trees seen from the Long Logs Trail are more than 150 feet tall. Stripped of bark and branches by an ancient flood, they were quickly buried and resisted decay. Silicon seeping in from the ash slowly and precisely replaced their woody tissues; trace quantities of iron, manganese, and other minerals lent them brilliant shades of red, yellow, and purple.

Tropical Conifers and Triassic Herbivores

Though scientists have figured out what the now-petrified trees looked like, there's been considerable dispute over how they grew: in extensive forests or isolated stands, on dry uplands or wet bottomlands. The ideal place to view the current best guesses about the park's past is the Rainbow Forest Museum, which features murals and reconstructed skeletons and replicas of the creatures that lived among the trees. Even here, visualizing Triassic life is an exercise in the imagination, since the landscape was so different then. What is now an arid grassland, home to prairie dogs, rattlesnakes, and pronghorns, was once a lush forest with wide, braided river channels. Continental drift hadn't yet moved Arizona to its current position; instead it lay closer to the equator, at a low elevation. The climate was tropical, and the place may have looked something like the contemporary Amazon basin. The trees were different: giant conifers and thick-trunked, 30-foot-high horsetails flanked by cycads and tree ferns. It was a world of multihued greenery.

The animals, too, were unlike any found today. The museum displays the skeleton of an aetosaur, a long-bodied, short-legged herbivore with heavy armor plates and formidable shoulder spikes that made it look like it stemmed from the mind of a comic-book artist. Nearby is *Placerias gigas*, a heavy, sharp-beaked plant eater that in both size and stature resembled a rhinoceros. Perhaps most impressive, though, are two predators represented only by skulls. *Metoposaurus* was a huge amphibian – imagine a broad-bodied salamander 10 feet long, armed with razorlike teeth in a two-foot-long jaw. Next to it sits the skull of a phytosaur, a long, lean, large-toothed marine reptile that resembled, but is not closely related to, a crocodile. Phytosaurs grew up to 30 feet long and were the dominant predators in the ancient

Paleontologist Sid Ash (opposite, top), who specializes in fossil leaves and pollen, investigates Triassic shale at Petrified Forest National Park.

Multicolored trunks of petrified trees (opposite, bottom) can best be seen along the park's Giant Logs and Long Logs trails.

Painted Desert rocks (below) of the Chinle Formation yielded remains of the nimble carnivore *Chindesaurus*, among the earliest North American dinosaurs.

sloughs and swamps – lying in mud and water, only eyes and nostrils exposed, waiting to lunge at passing prey.

Formidable as phytosaurs were, they were on the way out. Within a short span of time they were superseded by animals represented here by a single partial skeleton and a reconstruction. The latter depicts *Coelophysis*, a

nimble, carnivorous dinosaur whose bones have been found in the Painted Desert and elsewhere on the **Colorado Plateau**. The skeleton belongs to a small dinosaur named *Chindesaurus*. When it was excavated in the park in 1984, the specimen was dubbed "Gertie," and with an estimated age of 220 million years, it was one of the world's earliest dinosaur fossils. Though older dinosaurs have since been found, paleontologists agree that Gertie is part of the oldest known dinosaur family, the Herrerasauridae. The fast-moving, bipedal predator presaged the giant carnivores who would come to dominate the dinosaur world and captivate the human imagination.

It's not any single fossil animal, though, that makes Petrified Forest a site of global paleontological significance. Rather, it's the whole assemblage present here. Researchers have identified about 200 different ancient plant species, most of them from leaf imprints preserved in mudstone or from fossil pollen. They have found fossil fungus that was responsible for killing some of the trees. They have found fossilized sharks and lungfish, clams, snails, and even insects. They have found coprolites, or fossilized feces, of a number of animals, the examination of which can reveal what foods they ate.

Ancient Bees and Termites

Some recent finds are causing scientists to question long-held assumptions about evolu-

Blue Mesa (opposite) looks bone-dry today, but petrified logs of giant conifers attest to its tropical lushness in the late Triassic.

Sprinting dinosaurs left these traces (right) on Arizona's Navajo Reservation near Tuba City. The three-toed tracks (right, middle) were made by two-legged meat eaters such as *Dilophosaurus*.

Ancient Arizona archosaurs *Desmatosuchus* and *Postosuchus* (below) flank a Park Service paleontologist.

Tuba City Trackway

East of the **Grand Canyon**, on the vast tablelands of the **Navajo Reservation**, ancient sandstone and limestone lie exposed and barren in large horizontal plates covered with a sparse growth of desert shrubs and wildflowers. During the early Jurassic period, over 150 million years ago, these flats may have been ephemeral lakes or riverbeds surrounded by sand dunes. Perhaps wetlands here attracted foraging animals, or the flats were good travel corridors.

What's certain is that dinosaurs roamed the area and left their footprints. Animals that walked upright on their hind legs, probably dilophosaurs, left the three-toed imprints, some over a foot long. One dilophosaur left its fossilized remains nearby, and a skeleton of the 10-foot-tall carnivore can be seen at the Museum of Northern Arizona. But seeing the bona fide footprints is really more humbling. It leaves you wondering which is more impressive: the heft of the animals that left such conspicuous signs of their passing, or the geological good fortune that enables us to view them so many millions of years later.

The site is about five miles west of **Tuba City**, north of Highway 160. A Navajo or Hopi guide can usually be found in town and will show you to the tracks for a small fee.

tion. Paleontologists believed that social insects such as bees and termites developed in close association with flowering plants, which are thought to have evolved some 120 million years ago. The oldest evidence of bees and wasps goes back 100 to 110 million years. Flowers grew large and showy to attract pollinators like bees, which adopted an elaborate social structure to take advantage of numerous sources of pollen.

Over the past few years, however, researchers Tim Demko and Stephen Hasiotis have found ancient bee burrows in some of the Petrified Forest's fossil trees and soils. These burrows closely resemble those made by today's sweat bees, but they are 210 million years old. Termite burrows, too, have been found here. How could social insects evolve so early, with no flowers around? Did they rely on pollen, spores, sap, and rotting wood from the abundant ferns, cycads, and conifers?

Like the summer rains, dramatic but unpredictable, fossil discoveries help clarify the process of evolution, whether of plants, insects, or dinosaurs. The only certainty is that Petrified Forest will continue to provide a window into the distant past for as long as humans are interested in peering through it.

Purgatoire River Trackway
Colorado

Comanche National Grassland, 1420 East 3rd Street, La Junta, CO 81050; tel: 719-384-2181. Office hours Monday–Friday, 8 A.M.–4 P.M.; guided tours Saturday, 8 A.M., May–June and September–October. $$

Sandy Messick, a tour guide for the U.S. Forest Service, is bouncing down a severely rutted dirt road in a four-wheel-drive truck, descending into the **Picket Wire Canyonlands**. "My father built this road back in 1957, for the ranch that used to operate down here," she says. A bounce or two later, she adds with a smile, "It probably hasn't had much maintenance since."

It doesn't seem to have had *any* maintenance. Slipping down a steep canyon wall and running over jumbles of ruts and holes, the road makes for a bone-jarring ride. If it rains, the truck could easily bog down in mud. The payoff, however, is well worth an hour or two of jostling. At the bottom of this canyon in southern Colorado, where the **Purgatoire River** cuts through shale and limestone deposits that were laid down some 150 million years ago, visitors can see one of the most remarkable dinosaur sites in the world. With more than 1,300 footprints embedded in the ground, representing the travels of more than 100 animals, the Purgatoire site is the largest mapped dinosaur footprint area in North America.

Dinosaur Lake

Although local residents knew of the trackway since at least the 1920s – some called it "Elephant Crossing" – not until 1935 was the site brought to the attention of scientists. A schoolgirl named Betty Jo Riddenoure told her science teacher about the tracks, and this prompted the first scientific expedition to the site. In 1938, paleontologists decreed that the tracks had been made by brontosaurs, making them the first such tracks ever reported. But perhaps because of their remoteness, the Purgatoire tracks were largely forgotten for nearly half a century, until researchers at the University of Colorado studied and mapped them in the early 1980s.

Most of the tracks now skirt the edge of the Purgatoire River. But the presence of fossilized plants, mollusks, fish, and crustaceans suggests that in the Jurassic, the area was a lake basin perhaps six miles wide. Dinosaur Lake, as paleontologists call it, sported a semiarid climate similar to the savannas of East Africa today, and, judging by the alternating deposits of shale and limestone, the lake experienced seasonal or longer-term fluctuations in water level. Scientists say the shale layers were laid down as mud in times of high water, while the limestone layers were deposited as coarser sediments along the lakeshore when water levels were low.

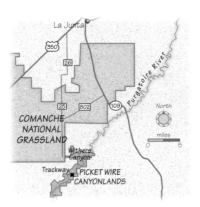

Because their tracks all appear in the limestone, the dinosaurs apparently liked to wander the edge of the lake and perhaps wade in shallow water. Today their tracks appear as clearly defined cavities in four different layers of hard limestone, stretching about a quarter-mile along the river. About 60 percent of the tracks are believed to have been left by *Apatosaurus* visiting the lake. These plant-eating animals stood 14 feet or taller at the shoulder and weighed 33 tons or more. Their roundish footprints, some two to three feet long, look like a series of highway potholes; they undoubtedly gave rise to the "Elephant Crossing" nickname.

The rest of the footprints are smaller and clearly belong to a different animal: Each is an oblong base topped with three rather sinister-looking claw marks. Those tracks, say the scientists, were left by smaller theropods, meat-eating dinosaurs like *Allosaurus*. The size of most two-legged dinosaurs can be readily estimated using such tracks. Hip height is generally about four to five times the track length, so the theropods that roamed about Dinosaur Lake stood from two to eight feet tall at the hip. Those animals, although they weighed much less than the sauropods, were quite fast and ferocious and probably preyed on the huge plant eaters.

Excavation by Flood

When you first wander about the site, it seems that the tracks fall more or less randomly. They can be felt underfoot when crossing the cold waters of Purgatoire and are strewn about the side of the waterway amid sheets of river mud that dry and curl under the baking sun. On closer inspection, though, it becomes clear that at least some of the *Apatosaurus* tracks follow the same path: Five distinct trackways run parallel to one another for some distance. Scientists say it is unlikely that such parallel tracks are a chance occurrence and theorize that the subadult animals must have been moving together along the shoreline. These five trackways have the distinction of being the first published evidence of such gregarious behavior among apatosaurs.

Even after surviving for millions of years, the

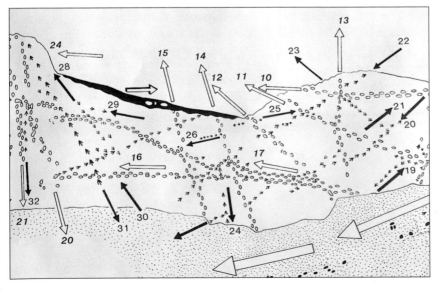

Prehistoric potholes (opposite) were formed by the crushing weight of *Apatosaurus* along the Purgatoire River. Martin Lockley makes a cast of one of more than 1,300 footprints at the site.

Clawed carnivores like *Allosaurus*, perhaps pursuing migrating sauropods, left some of the tracks (above) at the remote Purgatoire River site.

Map detail (left) shows some of the nearly 100 separate trackways preserved at North America's largest mapped dinosaur track site.

Purgatoire site constantly changes. The limestone layers holding the tracks are quite hard, but the soft shale layers between them are easily eroded by the normal flow of the river and by occasional floods. When sections of shale get swept away, the remaining limestone fractures into large blocks; the blocks then break away from the bank and come to rest looking like giant sugar cubes tossed along the river. On the one hand, such changes sometimes reveal cross-sections of footprints and show how underlying layers were compacted by the massive dinosaurs, a process called dinoturbation. They also

may expose entirely new layers of footprints. On the other hand, the erosion is ultimately destroying a world-class paleontological site. The Forest Service, which manages this part of **Comanche National Grassland**, recently took measures to divert the river away from the tracks to prevent further damage.

The Forest Service is also responsible for managing the human impact in Picket Wire Canyonlands (so named, legend has it, because Texas settlers mangled the French pronunciation of Purgatoire). To minimize damage to the canyon's treasures, the agency restricts access – visitors can hike or bike in through Whithers Canyon (more than a 10.6-mile round-trip to the track site), or they can take a daylong Forest Service motor vehicle tour. The tour also visits some traces of more recent history: a rock art site with petroglyphs, the adobe ranch house that the Rourke family occupied for decades, and the crumbling Dolores mission and cemetery, with the century-old headstones of children who died of smallpox. If you opt to go on your own, be sure to get proper directions to the site, take plenty of water, and watch out for cacti and rattlesnakes.

Denver Dinosaur Trackers (above), a group of dinosaur enthusiasts, display a cast of sauropod footprints made from one of the Purgatoire trackways.

Parallel pathways (opposite) indicate that the giant dinosaurs traveled in groups.

Hidden footprints embedded in limestone (right) are unearthed by erosion, but the same process can destroy existing prints.

Dinosaur Ridge
Morrison, Colorado

Friends of Dinosaur Ridge, 16831 West Alameda Parkway, Morrison, CO 80465; tel: 303-697-3466.
Monday–Saturday, 9 A.M.–4 P.M., Sunday, noon–4 P.M.
Morrison Natural History Museum is open Wednesday–Saturday, 1–4 P.M.; call 7 to 10 days ahead for guided tours. $

The grand panorama from atop **Dinosaur Ridge**, at the eastern end of Colorado's **Front Range**, appears to be as far from the influence of the sea as one can get. To the east lie the seemingly endless **High Plains**. To the west, slabs of rust-colored sandstone and conglomerate the size of city blocks thrust from golden prairie, pointing toward the granite massifs of the Rockies.

But as high and dry as this land looks, abundant evidence exists that it once was as low and damp as the Gulf Coast of Louisiana ... and a veritable paradise for dinosaurs.

The evidence for a lower, wetter environment is as subtle as ripple marks in stones, where tides once ruffled the bottom of a lagoon, and as dramatic as a

gigantic, slanted slab of sandstone with dinosaur footprints. The tracks were left by carnivores and herbivores passing along the shore of a vast inland sea that split North America in half 100 million years ago.

Seeing these and other signs of lost worlds does not require an arduous journey to forlorn badlands. It's all conveniently exposed just 15 miles west of **Denver** along the **Alameda Parkway**, a two lane road that angles up and over the ridge near the small town of **Morrison**.

The town gave its name to what may be the most renowned rock formation in the world. The layers of the Jurassic-age Morrison Formation have spilled forth a cornucopia of dinosaur bones throughout the western United States. It all started here at Dinosaur Ridge in 1877 when Arthur Lakes, a school-teacher, made the first major dinosaur bone discoveries in the country. From sandstone that once formed the beds of rivers, Lakes liberated the remains of *Stegosaurus*, now Colorado's state fossil, and of brontosaurs such as *Apatosaurus* and *Diplodocus*, the largest dinosaurs then known.

Hiking through Time

The remarkable fossils and environmental traces visible along Alameda Parkway are protected as a national natural landmark. A small, free museum with guidebooks and exhibits on local geology and paleontology sits at the eastern foot of the ridge, near the intersection of the parkway and Colorado Highway 470. You can hike along the road's shoulder to see the fossils at any time (be mindful of the traffic), or you can time a visit to coincide with one of the "Dinosaur Discovery Days" sponsored by Friends of Dinosaur Ridge, when the road is closed to traffic and guides lead tours and answer questions.

Hiking up and over the ridge from west to east – a little over a mile, with a 200-foot change in elevation – is a journey through geologic

history. You start in the Jurassic shale and sandstone of the upper Morrison, deposited about 150 million years ago on a coastal plain. Near the western foot of the ridge is a covered area where the fossilized remains of a brontosaur can be viewed. (These bones were left behind after Lakes shut down excavation in 1879.) Ribs, back, and leg bones, as well as less identifiable bits and pieces, protrude from boulders and a thick sandstone layer that once formed a riverbed where the jumbled bones were deposited and buried. Here, you can touch a piece of the past without fear of being chastised by a museum guide.

As you walk toward the western crest of the ridge, a sign on the left marks the spot where a layer of sandstone has been distorted in several places by depressions. The key to figuring out how they formed is to remember that this rock, once sand lying along a lakeshore, is viewed edge-on today. Something must have compressed the sand when it was soft, and the layer was later buried and preserved in stone. The size of the depressions – up to three feet across – suggests to paleontologist Martin Lockley, of the University of Colorado at Denver, and to other dinosaur track experts, that they were made by giant sauropods. The regular spacing of some of the tracks suggests that they may have been made by a single animal out for an earthshaking stroll.

Fossil discoveries at Dinosaur Ridge (opposite, top) date back to 1877, when schoolteacher Arthur Lakes uncovered massive bones and attracted the attention of leading paleontologists.

Bulges in sandstone (opposite, bottom) are the underside of footprints made by giant sauropods.

Dakota Sandstone (right) rises above Alameda Parkway. The ridge contains traces of the "Dinosaur Freeway," a possible migration route between Colorado and New Mexico.

A little farther on, the purplish siltstone and mudstone of the Morrison give way to the overlying sandstone and shale of the Dakota Group. These rock layers, about 300 feet thick, were deposited starting 135 million years ago, when the shore of a midcontinental ocean called the Western Interior Seaway began advancing west from Kansas across Colorado. Around 100 million years ago, the shallow sea (at times it was no deeper than 10 feet) stretched from the Arctic Ocean to the Gulf of Mexico. Its western edge eventually reached to where Dinosaur Ridge rises from the plains today, and where the undulating shore once harbored sandy beaches fringed by mangrove swamps.

Dinosaurs in Migration

Just after the road crests the ridge, it turns north and descends the eastern flank. To the left, a slab of yellowish sandstone preserves a series of long, parallel ripples that look as if they were formed just yesterday rather than 100 million years ago. Down the road are more clues to the nature of this ancient environment. Stains on the rock's cream-colored surface resemble rust spots the size of quarters. These may show where mangrove roots once anchored a tree in soft sand. Look closely enough at the rock and you may see impressions of sticks and logs from the former dense, dark tangle of vegetation.

Although the environment here changed from the Jurassic to the Cretaceous periods, it remained a prime place for dinosaurs. The most spectacular evidence for this comes about halfway down the eastern side. A rocky snapshot from the distant past, captured in

Cretaceous sandstone, consists of 37 different trackways comprising 335 individual footprints made as dinosaurs, some alone, others in groups, strolled along the shore.

Part of what Lockley calls the "Dinosaur Freeway," a possible migration route stretching several hundred miles from Boulder, Colorado, to New Mexico, the trackways record the passage of carnivorous, ostrich-like dinosaurs, and plant-eating *Iguanodon*-like ones. According to Lockley, six of the trackways were made by the meat-eating ornithomimids with three-toed, nine-inch-long prints. These bipedal dinosaurs apparently traveled alone.

Larger three-toed tracks, between nine and 18 inches long, were left by at least eight iguanodontids, both juveniles and adults from 12 to 20 feet long that walked on all four limbs. In his "Field Guide to Dinosaur Ridge," Lockley estimates that, based on the distance between their prints, the two-ton

herbivores who probably moved "at a slow walk, about two miles per hour."

Although the iguanodontids were moving in several directions, Lockley's analysis suggests that they occupied groups of similar-sized animals – strong evidence of social behavior. For example, among the larger animals he notes that "at least two pairs appear to have traveled absolutely parallel." And three other animals stuck close to the shoreline itself, if not in lockstep then certainly as part of a group.

At Dinosaur Ridge, seven different layers of Dakota sandstone contain dinosaur tracks. Extrapolating from the density found here and at other sites in the corridor between Boulder and New Mexico, Lockley estimates that the 30,000 square miles of territory along the mountain front could contain 240 billion tracks, though most would still be buried. The shore of the Western Interior Seaway may have been the site of epic dinosaur journeys.

Today, you can make your own journey and leave yet more footprints on Dinosaur Ridge. The concentration of dinosaur signs and remains does not equal that of, say, Dinosaur National Monument a few hundred miles to the west. But the charm of Dinosaur Ridge lies in its accessibility, spectacular surroundings, and exquisitely preserved evidence of a bygone time when dinosaurs flourished.

Paleontologist Martin Lockley (opposite) guides visitors to the east side of Dinosaur Ridge, where a group of iguanodonts left these impressive tracks along an ancient shore 100 million years ago.

Tracks can provide clues to social behavior. These footprints (above) show that young and old dinosaurs journeyed together on all fours.

Diplodocus (left), one of the huge sauropods whose remains were unearthed at the site, used its long, flexible tail to protect itself from predators.

Dry Mesa Quarry
Colorado

Dry Mesa Quarry, U.S. Forest Service, 2505 South Townsend, Montrose, CO 81401; tel: 970-240-5400. The quarry is in a remote section of Uncompahgre National Forest and is only uncovered during the summer excavation season. No charge.

Considering the size of the dinosaurs whose bones have been found at **Dry Mesa Quarry** in western Colorado, including the 100-foot-long *Supersaurus* and the 35-foot-tall *Torvosaurus*, the place itself seems rather small at first glance. Rounding the last bend of a quarter-mile hiking trail, one comes upon not an expansive quarry but a bone-white gash cut into a hillside. The diminutive scale of the excavation makes sense, however, when Ken Stadtman, who directs the dig, explains that the dinosaurs may have arrived here in a flood-induced "bonejam."

"Visualize a dying waterhole in a savanna-like environment," says Stadtman, paleontology curator of the Earth Science Museum at Brigham Young University. "There is a drought, and all the water is disappearing. All the animals are going to this waterhole, and many are dying there. Suddenly, the drought breaks and a flash flood … cuts through the waterhole and carries away lots of skeletons."

Downstream, at the site of the current Dry Mesa dig, "a skeleton probably got caught in the braided channels of water, and like a logjam, everything piled up behind it," says Stadtman. Indeed, 150 million years after the flood, researchers pulling apart the bonejam have found remains of more than two dozen species of animals, allowing Dry Mesa to claim the most diverse fauna of any Morrison Formation site in the United States. Mixed with the jumble of dinosaur bones, scientists have found turtles, crocodiles, lungfish, mammals, and a flying reptile. To date, they have recovered more than 4,000 bones but never a complete skeleton, giving credence to the theory that the disarticulated pieces were all washed there by a flood.

Largest Specimen of All?

Vivian and Ed Jones had explored the high desert canyonlands west of **Delta, Colorado**, since the 1950s, looking for bones and arrowheads. As they hiked the hot, dry hills of junipers and pinyon pines one weekend in 1971, Vivian came across a rather large toe bone. She reported the find to Jim Jensen of Brigham Young University and brought him to the site. The following year, Jensen and others, including Stadtman, began excavating Dry Mesa, soon making several exciting discoveries and also generating a fair amount of controversy.

The first big discovery, in 1972, was an almost complete

Summer visitors (left) help unearth the jumbled skeletons of many vertebrates at Dry Mesa Quarry, including bones from some of the world's largest dinosaurs.

An excavator (opposite, top) carefully removes the remains of such massive sauropods as *Supersaurus* and *Brachiosaurus*.

Scenic mesas (right) surround the quarry site, located in the Uncompahgre National Forest.

skeleton of *Torvosaurus*, a two-ton carnivore not previously encountered that may have rivaled *Tyrannosaurus rex* in size. (The toe bone found by Vivian Jones turned out to belong to *Torvosaurus*.) Later that year, Jensen found evidence of an even larger dinosaur, an eight-foot-long shoulder blade that belonged to what he dubbed *Supersaurus*. At the time it was the largest dinosaur known, believed to be more than 80 feet long and 50 feet high.

In 1979, Jensen found bones from what seemed to be an even larger dinosaur, which he named *Ultrasauros*. While *Supersaurus* has been accepted, other scientists disputed Jensen's claim for *Ultrasauros*, calling it simply a very large specimen of *Brachiosaurus*. "The issue still hasn't been decided," Stadtman says diplomatically.

Nearly 10 years of digging later, in 1988, another monstrous bone emerged from the hillside: a 1,500-pound, six-foot-long pelvis that, Stadtman says, is probably the largest bone complex ever found and most likely belonged to *Supersaurus*. Paleontologists continue to debate who has found the largest

dinosaur in North America. Is it one of the Dry Mesa specimens, or are they overshadowed by *Seismosaurus* from New Mexico? "I would argue that the 1988 *Supersaurus* is larger than the *Seismosaurus*," says Stadtman, "but there isn't enough material to prove that either one is larger."

Several tons of Dry Mesa bones are still encased in plaster jackets and stored under the football stadium at Brigham Young University, waiting to be cleaned. No one can say how much bone remains in the ground at Dry Mesa, and whatever is left might be buried deep in the hillside. Uncovering more bone could require expensive and destructive heavy equipment. For the time being, though, the dig continues each summer, and visitors can watch the excavation from the side of the quarry.

Grand Valley
Colorado

For information, contact Museum of Western Colorado, P.O. Box 20000-5020, 233 South 5th Street, Grand Junction, CO 81502-5020; tel: 970-241-9210.

Besides a pair of dinosaur museums, Colorado's **Grand Valley** offers a trio of trails that touch the past and present of paleontology. Just north of I-70, at the Rabbit Valley exit 25 miles west of **Grand Junction**, the **Rabbit Valley Research Natural Area** includes the **Mygatt-Moore Quarry**, which, since its discovery in 1981, has produced about 2,000 bones from eight kinds of dinosaurs, including *Mymoorapelta*, North America's oldest armored ankylosaur.

The active fossil quarry marks the first stop on the shadeless, 1½-mile **Trail through Time**, where you can see a few real dinosaur bones left in place. Bring boots, water, and the informative trail brochure. Head a short distance uphill to the site where a partial *Camarasaurus* skeleton was found lying on its right side. The skull now resides safely in a museum, but eight articulated neck vertebrae are still partially exposed on a sandstone ledge. Look for gray X's marking the midpoint of each vertebra. A humerus juts out from the base of the rock; another rock nearby broke away from this arm bone but still bears an impression in the shape of the fossil.

The trail winds past angular boulders of conglomerate sandstone, colored with sea foam and rust lichen, and other rocks coated in dark desert varnish. Embedded in some of these darker rocks are tan shards of petrified wood, which are especially noticeable just past the sheltered bench at the halfway point.

Jurassic-age Morrison Formation rock layers, visible from the high point of the trail, have a distinct greenish tint. This means

that they formed under standing water with little air reaching the sediment – advantageous conditions for preserving fossils.

Farther along the trail, four arching sauropod tail vertebrae appear on a rock face. The U-shaped concavity at the base of each backbone distinguishes these as coming from *Diplodocus*, an 80-foot-long vegetarian. An adjacent gap in the rock here contained limb bones, until the block was cut out and carted off by vandals shortly before the trail's dedication in 1986. That's the risk of such an outdoor exhibit, but Bureau of Land Management paleontologist Harley Armstrong, the trail's inspiration and official guardian, is determined to educate potential fossil filchers about laws protecting old bones.

Unmarked rocks near the end of the trail contain reddish dinosaur bone fragments, and an *Allosaurus* leg was found clasped in the roots of a nearby juniper. The last marked fossil stop contains bits of neck vertebrae from what may be either *Camptosaurus* or *Iguanodon*. If the latter, it would be much older than any other specimen of this dinosaur.

Discovery Sites

Along the road to **Colorado National Monument** in **Fruita**, 20 miles east of Rabbit Valley, the trail over **Dinosaur Hill** passes the site where, in 1901, Elmer Riggs of the Field Museum of Natural History bagged one of the finest examples of *Apatosaurus excelsus* ever found. Although the head, neck, and shoulders had eroded away, Riggs got the rear two-thirds of the skeleton, and part of the tail may still lie deep in the hill. A recent excavation found a few more fragments, as well as a shovel and broom dating to Riggs' excavation. Now the site is immortalized with a bronze plaque that misspells the six-ton behemoth's name.

At the head of this one-mile loop trail, you can see atop a boulder the imprint from a

Diplodocus femur. Bronze-headed, lime-green collared lizards dart underfoot as you wind up to the summit, where a bench entices you to admire the view of the **Book Cliffs**, **Grand Mesa**, and the monument.

Just outside Grand Junction, surrounded by subdivisions, is **Riggs Hill**, where Riggs and H.W. Menke struck sauropod gold on July 4, 1900, by unearthing the remains of *Brachiosaurus altithorax*, the largest dinosaur ever found up to that time. Cement "vertebrae" and a plaque mark the discovery site.

Fossil hunter Peter Mygatt (opposite), beside an *Allosaurus* rib, co-discovered the Mygatt-Moore Quarry, where bones from eight kinds of dinosaurs have been excavated.

Dinosaur Hill's trail (below) begins near this imprint of a *Diplodocus* femur and climbs to the site of a 1901 *Apatosaurus* discovery.

Dinosaur National Monument
Dinosaur, Colorado

Dinosaur National Monument, Box 210, Dinosaur, CO 81610; tel: 435-789-2115 or 303-374-2216.
Daily, 8 A.M.–4:30 P.M. (summer, 8 A.M.–7 P.M.). $

To get to the dinosaurs at **Dinosaur National Monument**, you first have to pass by the yellow, knuckle-like knolls of an ancient seafloor. After entering the monument's western gate, you'll see dramatically titled red and gray beds beside the road, which means you've gone farther back in time – roughly 145 million years – to the Jurassic. Dinosaurs await just a short drive uphill.

From the initial discovery in 1909 of eight *Apatosaurus* vertebrae, these beds have harbored one of the most diverse dinosaur assortments of any site in the 700,000-square-mile Morrison Formation, a geologic unit that has spawned excavations of more than a hundred dinosaur quarries. Ten kinds of dinosaurs were swept up in floods and deposited deep in a streambed at the site of the monument's **Carnegie Quarry**. About 400 individuals have already been removed, mostly to build the vast

collection of the Carnegie Museum of Natural History in Pittsburgh.

Today, you can still gape at some 1,600 dinosaur bones left exposed in the quarry wall at Dinosaur National Monument. For those used to complete skeletons mounted in museum halls, the scattered and battered bones here, half entombed and half excavated, create a dramatic tableau of death. Lay a hand on a bone from one of the Jurassic giants, gleaming with preservative coating. Feel the concrete-hard sandstone matrix around it. Imagine the work that went into uncovering and removing all those fossils; then imagine doing it by hand, without power tools, hauling 350 tons of plaster-coated bones in mule- and horse-drawn carts, and taking them 50 miles to the nearest eastward-bound railroad.

Wall of Bones

No longer hauled off to museums, these massive bones, frozen in time, have become the museum. They teach a lesson that the raw data of paleontology doesn't come easily. The idea for the world's first *in situ* fossil exhibit was championed by paleontologist Earl Douglass, who discovered the quarry in 1909 and dug here until 1922, when funding dried up following the death of his benefactor, Andrew Carnegie. (Douglass's vision also included a strip of hotels, but those are thankfully 20 miles away in **Vernal, Utah**, along with gas, food, and other services.) The near-vertical tilt to the ancient streambed made a natural wall, 50 feet high and as long as a football field, around which to build a visitor center. President Woodrow Wilson dedicated the monument in 1915, and it was expanded to its present size of 330 square miles in 1938 to encompass the canyons of the **Green** and **Yampa Rivers**.

Until recently, paleontologists in hard hats perched on the wall, exposing more bone bit by bit. But because this quarry has yielded most of its bounty, staff paleontologists have turned their attention elsewhere. A recent field survey of the monument turned up more than 400 fossil sites – not just dinosaurs but some of the oldest and best-preserved frogs,

salamanders, lizards, crocodiles, and mammals. A pretty complete skeleton of a new species of *Allosaurus* was dug up a half-mile from the visitor center, and a separate early Cretaceous quarry now under excavation contained a rare pair of brontosaur skulls.

Except for a cast of the new *Allosaurus*, still curled in its death pose, the compact exhibits at the public fossil quarry do not reflect the latest finds from these or other new fossil sites within the monument. But there's still much to hold your attention should you avert your gaze from the massive bone bas-relief. Scale models of each of the quarry's dinosaurs, with a relatively sized ranger model for comparison, give a quick gauge of these beasts' dimensions. A beautifully complete, real *Allosaurus* skull can be seen, along with a jaw fragment from this top-of-the-food-chain carnivore that reveals an erupting sharp tooth about to replace a worn, chipped one. Casts of the limb bones, pelvis, and ribs from the most complete juvenile *Stegosaurus* ever found, and a few bones from a *Camptosaurus* embryo, make unusual

displays. You can see a growth series of sauropod ankle bones, or compare the thigh bones of *Diplodocus* and *Camarasaurus*. Although *Camarasaurus* had a shorter neck and tail, its denser, bulkier bones made it weigh around 30 tons, more than twice the mass of the larger *Diplodocus*.

On the quarry face, you can spot a pair of *Camarasaurus* skeletons. One has an arc of tail vertebrae curled above bones of the neck and an intact skull. The ribs, some limb bones, the pelvis, and a few foot bones are scattered across the wall. The second specimen has an eerily protruding skull and neck suspended above a fully articulated leg. Including these two, only 14 complete dinosaur skulls have been excavated from the

The visitor center (opposite, top) at Carnegie Quarry contains a bone bed of half-excavated dinosaur fossils that spans the length of a football field.

Street signs (opposite, bottom) in Dinosaur, Colorado, pay homage to former residents.

Ann Elder (right), a Park Service paleontologist, prepares fossils in the visitor center laboratory.

Utah Field House of Natural History

Before or after a trip to Dinosaur National Monument, stop by the **Utah Field House of Natural History** in **Vernal, Utah**, for grounding in the region's rocks, fossils, and artifacts. A complete *Diplodocus* skeleton straddles the main hall, head and neck swooping down by the admissions counter; walk beneath this behemoth's rib cage for a vivid sense of how huge these creatures were.

Children should enjoy the outdoor sculpture garden with its dinosaur models ranging from scrawny *Ornithomimus* to bulky *Tyrannosaurus*. On display inside are three-toed tracks thought to have been made by *Dilophosaurus* at nearby **Red Fleet State Park**, where trackways can be viewed above the reservoir. The fossil gallery contains leg bones from several dinosaurs and more complete mounts of ancient mammals. Hanging throughout are colorful oil paintings by museum founder Ernest Untermann, which bring to life the prehistoric denizens inside the glass cases. An interesting display on the history of paleontology in Utah includes historic photographs of fossil hunters, and some bones of *Dystrophaeus*, Utah's first dinosaur discovery (and only the second in the West), described by Edward Cope in 1877.

The geology displays will prepare you well for a drive in the surrounding **Uinta Basin**, in which 21 of 26 major rock formations contain fossils. Sample a few by heading north from Vernal on Highway 191, the so-called **Drive thru the Ages**, where whimsical signposts clue you in to the colorful geology, such as the Morrison Formation ("Graveyard of the Dinosaurs") and Curtis Formation ("Home of Fossilized Squid"). For more information, call the museum at 435-789-3799.

The bone wall at Carnegie Quarry (right) is a dense graveyard: Ten kinds of dinosaurs were swept up in floods and entombed here.

Ceratosaurus (left) looms large in the prehistoric sculpture garden outside the Field House.

Dinosaur rewards what time you can give it. At least follow the 10-mile, mostly paved road past **Split Mountain** (after obtaining a "Tour of the Tilted Rocks" brochure). Prairie dogs pop up from roadside burrows. Fremont petroglyphs depicting lizards, bighorn sheep, and people in ceremonial dress adorn the rocks. In late afternoon, golden light emanates from the Entrada sandstone cliffs.

quarry, so most of what's left in place are sauropod femurs, other limb bones, ribs, vertebrae, and shoulder blades. Instead of hounding a ranger for a bone-by-bone breakdown, consult the illustrated booklet "What Kind of Bone Is That?" available at the visitor center. (Ironically, the most common fossil found in the excavation is a mollusk – a unionid clam – which, unlike its quarry mates, still exists.)

Discoveries by Trail

Not to diminish the poignant power of so many fossils in one place, but there's more to Dinosaur than dinosaurs. The fossil wall is literally and figuratively just the tip of the monument. Since roads are few and far between, seeing more of the park requires rafting, backpacking, or a lot of driving. But

The four-mile **Jones Creek Trail** offers a respite from recreational vehicles and a break from the monument's heat, as a steady breeze blows through the canyon formed by towering red Cambrian rocks on one side and pale sandstone on the other. For a shorter, spectacular hike, head to the monument's visitor center outside **Dinosaur, Colorado**, and follow the 31-mile paved road to **Harpers Corner**. There, a moderate, mile-long trail offers jaw-dropping vistas of the monument's canyon country, including the serpentine meanders of the Yampa River canyon and monolithic **Steamboat Rock**, where the Yampa and Green Rivers converge. Had a proposed dam for this site not been thwarted in one of the environmental movement's earliest victories, both river canyons would now be inundated.

Mill Canyon Dinosaur Trail
Moab, Utah

For information, contact the BLM Moab Field Office, 82 East Dogwood, Moab, UT 84532; tel: 435-259-6111. Office hours Monday–Friday, 7:45 A.M.–4:30 P.M. The trail is always open. No charge.

The **Mill Canyon Dinosaur Trail** teaches more about paleontologists than about dinosaurs. It offers an opportunity to see fossils in place, embedded in the rock matrix. Although plenty of ancient bones are visible along this quarter-mile trail, spotting them is a subtle art. The visitor soon gets a sense of the sharp-eyed patience a paleontologist has to practice in the field in order to distinguish fossils from their surroundings – and figure out to which species a bone or fragment belongs.

During the late Jurassic, some 150 million years ago, parts of the now arid and rugged canyon country of southeast Utah were low-lying and wet. If discoveries from recent decades are any indication, they were also rich in dinosaurs. Four different species have been identified along this short stretch of **Mill Canyon**, and numerous bone pieces remain to be identified. Many of the bones exposed along the trail belong to *Camarasaurus*, a large sauropod that grew to a length of 60 feet and a weight of 20 tons. Smaller but still hefty herbivores are represented by *Stegosaurus* – as famous for its tiny brain as for the rows of large plates running down its back – and by *Camptosaurus*, fast-moving and some 20 feet long. These plant eaters were probably preyed upon by *Allosaurus*, a powerful carnivore.

Visitors to the trail can see where grayish bone from these dinosaurs slowly erodes out of buff-colored rock; toward the end of the trail, pebbly conglomerate shows that some of the dinosaurs must have been buried among the fast-accumulating sediments of a riverbank or shoreline. Petrified wood is present, too. Neither wood nor fossil bone

is protected by fences here, but resist the temptation to take souvenirs.

Tracks in Sandstone

Numerous fossils of another sort are also present nearby, for the **Moab** area has lately become known as a hotbed of dinosaur tracks. Areas adjacent to **Arches National Park**, in particular, are rich in theropod tracks that may have been made as the sea rose along a flat shoreline, continuously wetting new tracts of sand that were traversed by numerous animals. One dinosaur track expert has estimated that more than a billion tracks may be present here (though only a small fraction are exposed on the surface), all contained in a single sandstone layer over an area of 300 square miles. From the Mill Canyon Trail, you can look eastward to the fiery red sandstone of **Klondike Bluffs**, home to an extensive dinosaur trackway.

Another site just northeast of Mill Canyon is marked and accessible to the public. Road construction here about three decades ago removed soil from a flat, slightly tilted sandstone pane that reveals impressions of a large sauropod and several carnivorous theropods. Deeply embedded in the rock, and with a diameter about that of an oil drum, the sauropod tracks show that their maker swerved sharply to the right – a rarely noted phenomenon. One of the theropod trails is also unusual, because the animal that made it had an irregular stride – there are alternating gaps of four and five feet between track marks. It's possible that the animal was injured and limping. That such individual markings should survive one-and-a-half million centuries is nothing short of astonishing.

The landscape around Moab is rugged, and much of it is quite difficult to reach; undoubtedly more fossil sites have yet to be discovered. For now, area visitors can most comfortably complete their prehistory circuit by visiting the Bureau of Land Management office in town. A large slab of 200-million-year-old sandstone displayed just outside the entrance

is heavily marked with signs of ancient animals. Along with small dinosaur tracks are scorpion traces and the impressions of the wide feet of a mammal-like reptile named *Brasilichnium* – indicators of the diversity of life here in the distant past.

Bones belonging to *Camarasaurus, Camptosaurus,* and other Jurassic dinosaurs have been left in place along the short trail at Mill Canyon (opposite, top).

Sauropod trackway (above) north of Moab, Utah, shows how the massive animal swerved from its course and turned right.

Allosaurs (left) chase a fleeing *Camptosaurus* into a river toward a rearing sauropod, a scene that could have occurred in Mill Canyon.

Cleveland-Lloyd Dinosaur Quarry
Price, Utah

Cleveland-Lloyd Dinosaur Quarry, BLM Price Field Office, Box 7004, Price, UT 84501; tel: 801-636-3600. Friday–Sunday, 9 A.M.–5 P.M., Easter through September; daily, 9 A.M.–5 P.M., Memorial Day to Labor Day. $

A lumbering *Camarasaurus* wades into a shallow pond to slake its thirst. As the massive dinosaur drinks, its stout, elephantine legs sink into the viscous clay. Struggling to extract its limbs only buries them deeper. The beast bellows an alarm call, which lures a trio of hungry allosaurs to the pond. The carnivores rush in to chomp the flanks of their prey, but before they can reach the helpless camarasaur, they notice their pace slowing. Each step mires the predators deeper in mud until only their thrashing heads remain above water.

Whether or not this scene played out some 147 million years ago is a matter of speculation, but a similar scenario likely did. The **Cleveland-Lloyd Dinosaur Quarry** in central Utah constitutes one of the most puzzling and dramatic dinosaur death traps ever excavated. Unlike the floods that formed the mass dinosaur graveyards at sites such as Ghost Ranch or Dinosaur National Monument, the deposits at Cleveland-Lloyd formed in still water. And unlike most dinosaur deathbeds, where herbivores dominate among the deceased, nearly three-quarters of the bones pulled from the Cleveland-Lloyd quarry come from meat-eating dinosaurs.

The bounty of bones numbers more than 12,000 from a dozen kinds of dinosaurs and represents at least 70 individuals, including 44 *Allosaurus fragilis*. The top predator of the middle Jurassic, *Allosaurus* was widespread and abundant. Some paleontologists suggest that the high numbers found at Cleveland-Lloyd might be because they hunted in packs, at least as juveniles. Though smaller than *Tyrannosaurus*, *Allosaurus* had beefier arms and bigger claws (with three on each hand to *T. rex's* two), so just one out stalking would have inspired intense fear. Smaller carnivores, *Ceratosaurus*, *Stokesosaurus*, and *Marshosaurus*, hunted or scavenged here as well.

The dinosaur bones, stained jet black from manganese oxide in ancient groundwater, were scattered but otherwise preserved remarkably intact and unweathered. Excavation started in 1929, and discoveries began soon after William Lee Stokes, a Princeton student from nearby **Cleveland, Utah**, and the future state geologist, arrived at the site in 1939 with some shovels and a poorly paid assistant. Various teams worked off and on until 1990. Fossils removed from Cleveland-Lloyd have stocked museum displays worldwide, and an unknown number of bones are still buried here.

Bone Densities

Two metal sheds cover the quarry site, where visitors can still see original fossils in place and casts of other bones from a metal walkway just above the excavation. The yardwide pelvis of *Camarasaurus* on display has dinosaur tooth marks carved into it.

More bones, and a mounted *Allosaurus* skeleton, can be seen in the small visitor center on site. There's a cast of the probable *Allosaurus* egg found in 1987, next to a CAT scan that appears to show a tadpole-shaped

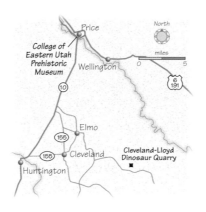

embryo inside; an abnormal shell layer indicates that the egg was retained within the mother as she succumbed in the Cleveland-Lloyd sediments. A site map on the visitor center wall, with thousands of bones outlined, reveals the remarkable density of dinosaur fossils in the surprisingly small site.

Visitors with spare time should enjoy meandering among the red-tinged deposits of the Morrison Formation, the richest repository of dinosaur remains in the United States, on the 1½-mile **Rock Walk Nature Trail**. Or one can take a worthwhile excursion 30 miles north to the **College of Eastern Utah Prehistoric Museum**, in **Price**. There,

four dinosaur skeletons from Cleveland-Lloyd – *Allosaurus, Camarasaurus, Camptosaurus*, and *Stegosaurus* – take center stage, and surrounding cases display deformed toe bones and injured ribs and arm bones from *Allosaurus* (apparently life was tough atop the Jurassic food chain). Upstairs, be sure to see an impressive collection of dinosaur footprints found in the ceiling of coal mines in Carbon County, Utah.

The foot bones of two track makers, *Chasmosaurus* and *Prosaurolophus*, have been mounted above their respective prints, and a nearby footprint cast measures nearly 4½ feet long.

Museums worldwide display the jet-black skeletons characteristic of Cleveland-Lloyd Quarry, a death trap for dinosaurs who sank into thick mud about 147 million years ago. This diorama (left) and a reconstruction of a toothy *Allosaurus* (opposite, top) can be seen at the College of Eastern Utah Prehistoric Museum in Price, Utah.

Quarry map (opposite, bottom) on view at the visitor center reveals the impressive density of dinosaur bones uncovered from the compact excavation.

Berlin-Ichthyosaur State Park
Austin, Nevada

Berlin-Ichthyosaur State Park, HC 61, Box 61200, Austin, NV 89310; tel: 702-964-2440.
Fossil site tours daily, 10 A.M., 2 P.M. and 4 P.M., Memorial Day–Labor Day; weekends, 10 A.M. and 2 P.M. after Labor Day; by reservation in winter. $

Tucked against the western slope of the **Shoshone Range** sits the weathered ghost town of **Berlin, Nevada**. At the turn of the century, gold and silver ore mines supported 250 residents in Berlin and nearby camps. The miners knew about other, stranger stuff here, too, like spool-shaped fossilized bones the size of dinner plates, and, indeed, some reportedly used these bones as dinner plates.

It's hard to imagine today, when one is looking west across a sea of sagebrush to the **Paradise Range**, but in the late Triassic, about 220 million years ago, central Nevada lay beneath an ocean, and in that ocean swam the world's largest ichthyosaurs.

Just as dinosaurs ruled the land and pterosaurs the sky, ichthyosaurs were the masters of Mesozoic seas. Found on all continents except Antarctica, these marine reptiles appeared on Earth around the time of the first dinosaurs and lasted for as long – 160 million years – before succumbing near the close of the Cretaceous. They thrived in a global ocean that encircled the supercontinent called Pangaea. The 57 alleged species that have been found range in size from two to 60 feet long. Built like tunas, with powerful tails and streamlined bodies, ichthyosaurs had eyes up to a foot across, perfect for spotting squid in dark water and snapping them between jaws lined with pointed teeth. Dense ribs girded these reptiles during descents to crushing depths.

A Giant Discovery

The 37 specimens found eroding out of a sandstone hill two miles from Berlin's mine shafts and stagecoach station – fossils of an industrial age – came to scientific attention in 1928. But nearly 30 years passed before Charles Camp and Sam Welles of the University of California Museum of

Paleontology mounted an excavation. Camp described three ichthyosaur species here, the largest being 40-ton *Shonisaurus popul"aris*, up to 50 feet long with six-foot, paddle-like flippers. He developed a scenario in which the creatures were marooned by a receding tide on a bay mudflat, like confused whales that beach themselves. A more recent study concluded that the carcasses simply sank to the bottom of the sea and were buried beneath 600 feet of sediment, although some paleontologists argue that such a gradual burial would be unlikely to produce fossils.

At Camp's urging, an A-frame shelter was built over the fossil site in 1966, leaving in place the remains of either nine or 10 ichthyosaurs – no one can tell for sure. You can peer through windows at either end of the shelter, but it's worth taking a guided tour of the interior. A ranger will point out the various parts of each skeleton, which is helpful since it takes a little imagination to connect the bones and flesh them out into massive marine hunters.

If you've seen pictures of the amazingly intact ichthyosaurs from German shale (where fetuses have been preserved inside the womb or exiting the birth canal), the Berlin specimens are a bit of a letdown. Maybe it's the lack of faces; ichthyosaur skulls contained a lot of cartilage and did not readily preserve as fossils. You'll have to settle for flipper bones, coracoids (which held flippers to the chest), rib cages, and lots of those spool-shaped vertebrae, stacked up like dominoes. In one specimen it's possible to discern the outline of the giant eyeball, larger than that of any vertebrate before or since.

You can't fail to be impressed by the beasts' magnitude. Not only is Nevada's state fossil the world's largest ichthyosaur, some 20 feet longer than the closest contender, but *Shonisaurus* was the largest animal of all in Triassic seas and rivaled in size the world's biggest living fish, the whale shark.

Flipper bones (opposite, top) helped propel huge, streamlined ichthyosaurs through an ocean that once covered central Nevada.

Life-size mural of *Shonisaurus* (left) has some minor anatomical errors but accurately captures the marine reptile's immense size.

Fossil ammonites (above) and other invertebrates have been found at Berlin-Ichthyosaur State Park.

Several skeletons (right) of ichthyosaurs lie beneath a shelter built at the site of the excavation.

Fossil Butte National Monument
Kemmerer, Wyoming

Fossil Butte National Monument, Box 592, Kemmerer, WY 83101; tel: 307-877-4455.
Daily, 8 A.M.–4:30 P.M.; summer, 8 A.M.–7 P.M. No charge.

A ridge at **Fossil Butte National Monument** offers an endless view of high sagebrush desert with little hint of water but for a few aspens lining a shallow draw. Dust that rises with each footprint leaves no doubt that this Wyoming landscape is – what else? – bone dry. Then Vincent Santucci, a paleontologist and chief ranger at the monument, grins and tells you to get ready for a surprise.

A few delicate taps of a hammer against metal wedges between layers of rock pry loose a flat plate of stone that slides back as easily as cutting a deck of cards. Beneath the rocky shroud, exposed for the first time in 50 million years, lies the perfectly preserved skeleton of a fish that swam in the warm, shallow waters of Fossil Lake. Had you been standing here back then, you would have seen a palm-fringed tropical lake teeming with fish, stingrays, alligators, and crocodiles, and strange shorebirds with the body of a flamingo and the head of a duck – descendants of the dinosaurs who last roamed this region 15 million years ago.

Fossil Butte, 10 miles west of Kemmerer on U.S. Highway 30, preserves a slice of that ancient ecosystem in a landscape that now could not be more different.

When the residents of Fossil Lake died, many sank to the bottom. Sediments covered them with a kind of geological security blanket that later hardened into stone and remained buried until the land rose and erosion sliced into southwestern Wyoming to reveal what is left of Fossil Lake. Its remnants lie in what is known as the Green River Formation, a creamy, white layer cake of mudstone, limestone, and volcanic ash that crowns most of the modest buttes and ridges in this fossil-filled landscape.

Re-creating Fossil Lake

Crews building the transcontinental railroad in the late 1860s stumbled into the first major deposits of fossil fish, sparking the interest of scientists and professional collectors who soon came to dig into the past ecosystem of Fossil Lake and two other ancient lakes, Gosiute and Uinta. The monument's 2½-mile **Historic Quarry Trail** leads past a former commercial quarry, quiet now except for the rustling of sagebrush, where you can see the layers of rock hiding ancient treasures. Digging for other than research purposes is now prohibited in the monument but continues at private and state quarries nearby.

FOSSIL BUTTE
NATIONAL
MONUMENT

To see highlights of past excavations, head for the monument's museum-class visitor center. Set into a chalky hillside, the unimposing building is filled with wonders. A fossil alligator, still lying in its bed of stone, reaches practically from floor to ceiling and is accompanied by its ancient relatives, all set off with subtle but graceful lighting. You can almost imagine yourself floating within Fossil Lake back when it swarmed with life. In a glassed-in laboratory, monument staff extract other fossils encased in their rocky tombs.

On summer weekends, the hunt for pieces of the past continues on guided hikes to a research quarry within the monument.

Palms (opposite, top) grew beside tropical lakes in Wyoming 50 million years ago and left their perfectly preserved fronds at Fossil Butte.

The monument's historic quarry (opposite, bottom) is now off-limits to fossil collectors.

Gars (below) swam in the warm, shallow water of Fossil Lake, as did other fish, stingrays, and crocodiles.

There, under the supervision of paleontologists, the tools come out and visitors can try their hand at peeling apart layers of rock like phyllo pastry to see what dwells underneath. Sometimes the amateur diggers may find coprolites (fossilized dung), but frequently they also come upon fish or palm fronds that look as though they had fallen into the sand only yesterday. "Most of the record of the history of life on Earth is still underground," Santucci says. "One of our visitors may make the next important discovery."

Wyoming Dinosaur Center
Thermopolis, Wyoming

Wyoming Dinosaur Center, Box 868, Thermopolis, WY 82443; tel: 307-864-2997.
Daily, 8 A.M.-5 P.M. (extended summer hours). $–$$

A rooster-tail of dust rose from the road as the van sped through chalky gray and red hills. The van snaked its way through a working ranch, then rumbled across cattle guards outside the small town of **Thermopolis, Wyoming**. It clambered up a steep hill on what resembled a worn-out mule trail more than a road.

Across a dry wash, a horizontal strip of the opposite hillside looked like a cake after someone has dragged a finger across the frosting. Then the yellow earth-movers came into view, along with people crouch-ing in the dirt, studying the ground. It was a dinosaur dig. A big one.

In fact, these quarries and others on nearby bluffs had yielded hundreds of dinosaur bones of all kinds since digging began in 1993. More remains rise to the surface almost every day; there are nearly 50 fossil sites on the property that may take more than 150 years to excavate completely.

These dusty boneyards are owned and operated by the Wyoming Dinosaur Center, a cavernous warehouse standing above the **Bighorn River** on the edge of Thermopolis, where visitors gape at towering dinosaur skeletons. Few other places in the world let you watch workers pull bones from the ground, prepare them in a laboratory, and see them on display. It's one-stop shopping for dinosaurphiles.

Mining the Morrison

The Wyoming Dinosaur Center got its start in 1993 when dinosaur enthusiast Dr. Burkhard Pohl and his partners spotted the red layers of the Morrison Formation rising

in the hills outside Thermopolis. They knew the Morrison had yielded many prehistoric remains at famous locales such as Dinosaur National Monument and Como Bluff, so they got permission from the family that owned the land to prospect for fossils.

It wasn't long before dinosaur bones were practically tumbling out of the ground at their feet. They soon bought what they now call the **Warm Springs Ranch** so they could take up digging full-time (as full as Wyoming weather permits) and built the Dinosaur Center to house the steady stream of fossils emerging from the hills.

Painted dinosaur footprints lead down Thermopolis's main street, over the **Bighorn River**, and through a residential neighborhood to the Dinosaur Center. From outside, it looks like a big metal hangar perched on a hilltop. On the inside, it's a whole other world.

Visitors first wind their way past displays tracing the evolution of life leading up to the time of the dinosaurs – a chronology that will be familiar to travelers who have arrived in Thermopolis via the **Wind River Canyon**, which in about 10 miles slices through a timeline of Earth history, including some of the oldest

rocks on the planet. Fossils from around the world preserve primitive plants and simple marine organisms like the ancestors of today's starfish. Huge armored fish the size of small dogs stare at you through exhibit windows. Then you find out about the sharks of the Silurian Period, about 440 million years ago, which were some of the earliest predators on Earth, a hint of the ground-shaking monsters that drew you here in the first place.

The first to come into view are examples of *Coelophysis*, a small forerunner of the better-known tyrannosaurs and one of the first predatory dinosaurs, found in a mass grave in New Mexico. Then there are pterosaurs – flying reptiles, not dinosaurs, but

Triceratops (left), Wyoming's state dinosaur, holds a prominent place at the Wyoming Dinosaur Center's museum.

Agate crystals (above) add color to an old bone, a femur, uncovered at a Wyoming Dinosaur Center excavation.

Prominent paleontologists (right) Barnum Brown, holding pick, and Henry Fairfield Osborn discovered a *Diplodocus* leg at nearby Como Bluff, Wyoming, in 1897.

intimidating nonetheless – gliding above your head in a diorama illustrating the fringes of an ancient sea that during the time of the dinosaurs repeatedly submerged interior North America. Behind you hunches the skeleton of a horn-tailed stegosaur from China, where these armored dinosaurs

with fins riding up their backs may have evolved before venturing out into the rest of the world.

Jumble of Riches

Once you wander into the main hall, however, the specimens do not seem to march in any particular order – one of the museum's strengths and one of its weaknesses. On the one hand, it allows your infatuation to lead you from one Jurassic crocodile to *Hypsilophodon*, a small plant-eating dinosaur that lived in herds like the pronghorn you might see along the highways outside Thermopolis, to the toothy smile of an allosaur. On the other hand, you go back and forth between dinosaurs that did not live at the same times or even sequentially. You wander among them as though they were guests at a cocktail party. At the far end of the hall, a glass-enclosed laboratory is busy preparing other bones for display.

Before or after a museum visit, the Dinosaur Center's van will haul you uphill to the digs and deposit you at their doorstep. During the Jurassic, the region was probably part of a river plain where rafts of dinosaur bones piled up in curves or side channels. They did not all go to

Como Bluff

If you think paleontology is romantic work, consider poor Arthur Lakes, who dug dinosaurs at **Como Bluff** in the late 1800s. He wrote in his journal of huddling "at the bottom of a narrow pit 20 feet deep ... fingers benumbed with cold ... and snow blowing blindingly down and covering up a bone as fast as it is unearthed." Men like Lakes endured such conditions to probe the first great profusion of fossil dinosaurs found in the American West. Como Bluff, Wyoming, supplied many East Coast museums with their first dinosaur skeletons and fueled the intense competition between the two top American paleontologists of the time, Edward Drinker Cope and Othniel Charles Marsh.

Cope and Marsh, each hoping to gain a leg bone up on the other, paid crews to dig up Como Bluff as fast as possible. The diggers pulled out bones of locomotive-sized Jurassic plant eaters and the ferocious *Allosaurus*. Minions for Cope and Marsh spied on each other and even pilfered specimens from the rival camp. (See "Bone Hunters" for more on the Cope-Marsh rivalry.)

It's a testament to the riches of Como Bluff that long after Cope and Marsh found their way into the history books, its dinosaurs have not yet played out. Most of the deposits lie on private land, but crews from museums, including the Tate in Casper, still ferret out new finds, such as the bones of a pterosaur, a flying contemporary of the dinosaurs that resembles a miniature dragon.

Within spitting distance of the historical marker for Como Bluff, about seven miles east of **Medicine Bow** on U.S. 287, is an abandoned cabin built out of around 26,000 dinosaur bones, the so-called oldest house in the world. Fossils are not so plentiful anymore, but at Como Bluff, they're close.

Ichthyosaurus (opposite, top) wasn't a dinosaur but an aquatic reptile with a streamlined body, long snout, and paddlelike limbs. It grew up to 50 feet long.

Fossils emerge from the ground (opposite, bottom) at Warm Springs Ranch, where the dinosaur center runs a dig into Morrison Formation sediments.

Bone Cabin Quarry (left) at Como Bluff got its name from this cabin made of 26,000 dinosaur fossils from the site.

Bob Bakker (below) prospects at Como Bluff for fossils to add to the collection of the Tate Museum in Casper, Wyoming.

waste: Footprints of meat-eating allosaurs and broken allosaur teeth amid chewed-up and trampled bones suggest that one or more allosaurs once made a meal out of a bunch of dead Jurassic vegetarians right where you stand. Another bone bed has produced some of the very few juvenile sauropods known. Yet another site may be an allosaur lair, where juvenile allosaurs waited for parents to return with the disarticulated remains of such prey as *Diplodocus*, *Camarasaurus*, and *Stegosaurus*.

For a fee, visitors can dig alongside experienced researchers. Many visitors have made remarkable finds, and there should be plenty more to come. One of the complications of the Wyoming Dinosaur Center's embarrassment of riches is that whenever crews rev up their earth-movers to clear the ground above known bone deposits, they keep running into new and unexpected heaps of fossils. Then it's time to stop, see what's there, and, as likely as not, get distracted by yet another big discovery.

Red Gulch Dinosaur Tracksite
Shell, Wyoming

For information, contact the BLM Worland Field Office, Box 119, 101 South 23rd Street, Worland, WY; tel: 307-347-5100.
Office hours Monday–Friday, 7:45 A.M.–4:30 P.M. The site is located near Shell, Wyoming, about five miles south of Highway 14 on Red Gulch/Alkali National Backcountry Byway. No charge.

No dinosaurs today, Erik Kvale figured. The geologist from the Indiana Geological Survey, a few of his relatives, and colleague Allen Archer of Kansas State University were exploring dusty badlands in northern Wyoming that Kvale knew as the Sundance Formation – marine sediments deposited by the Sundance Sea, which submerged much of the Interior West during the period known as the middle Jurassic. Fossil shellfish peeked from the ground, but Kvale told the others that dinosaurs living at the time would have stuck to land.

Then something near Kvale's feet caught his eye. It was a footprint: a three-pronged, sharp-clawed footprint the size of a hubcap that screamed meat-eating dinosaur. As he and the others began to look around on that day in 1997, they realized that the sandstone flooring beneath their feet was speckled with dinosaur tracks so well preserved it looked as if the creatures had passed through only a few hours earlier.

They had actually passed through about 165 million years ago, a time when geologists had thought Wyoming was underwater, although the tracks of the landlubbing dinosaurs now prove that at least some of it wasn't. Researchers examining the tracks believe that the dinosaurs left them in the well-sorted sand of a tropical beach, perhaps an island or peninsula in the Sundance Sea. Then the sea level rose, submerging and later

Unknown ceratosaurs akin to *Dilophosaurus* (opposite, bottom) probably made the three-toed tracks (above) at Red Gulch, perhaps while scavenging along a shoreline 165 million years ago.

Scientists (left and opposite, top) will construct computer maps to examine the movement patterns of the various dinosaurs that left parallel and crisscrossing trackways at the site.

burying the tracks beneath layers of sand and mud. Shrimp burrowed down through the mud and into the sand holding the tracks. You can still see their finger-sized burrows around the footprints. Millions of years after the sand and mud had hardened into stone, present-day Wyoming rose in elevation and then erosion went to work, peeling away rocks and sediment until the beachfront of the middle Jurassic came into view once again. A culvert installed by the U.S. Bureau of Land Management, which over-

probably descendants of the first group of meat-eating dinosaurs, called the ceratosaurs, and ancestors of the heavy-weight *Allosaurus* of the late Jurassic and – much later – the blood-chilling *Tyrannosaurus rex*. Of the thousands of footprints, some run in parallel tracks, while others crisscross. Judging from the size range of the prints, some scientists surmise that a family of dinosaurs passed by, perhaps to scavenge shellfish or carcasses along the shoreline.

They left their tracks when Wyoming was a decidedly different place. North America hung at about the same latitude as the Bahamas do today; gentle waves washed the beach. Inland, a scattered subtropical forest of ginkgoes, conifers, and palm-like evergreens called cycads probably lined the horizon.

Kvale, Archer, and others have tried to pry out of the tracks as much detail as they can about the dinosaurs, their behavior, and their environment. They are studying the surrounding geology and using computers to catalog the tracks of each dinosaur and create a detailed map of the site. Check for the latest developments at the small, friendly museum in nearby **Greybull**. Scientists may yet give us a closer look at the dinosaurs that left only their tracks behind. Until then, you can follow in their very formidable footsteps.

sees the site and the surrounding land, washed soil off the dinosaur tracks just in time for Kvale to find them.

Filling in Historical Gaps

The **Red Gulch Dinosaur Tracksite**, as the BLM has named it, opened a window on what had been a blank chapter in the history of dinosaurs in North America. Few known fossils of any kind date to that period, when evolution was turning carnivorous dinosaurs from lightweights into the heavyweight champions that would come to rule the world. The Wyoming beachgoers were

Egg Mountain
Choteau, Montana

For information, contact the Museum of the Rockies Education Department, 600 West Kagy Boulevard, Bozeman, MT 59717; tel: 406-994-6618.
Daily tour at 2 P.M., June 25–August 20. No charge.

The guide shouts over the roar of the hot wind as a dozen visitors peer into a three-foot-deep pit lined with railroad ties. "Does anybody know whose bones these are?" he asks, pointing to blackened leg bones and other fossilized fragments embedded in the gray mud below. A girl of about 10 is quick to answer: "Maiasaurs, duckbills, a whole bunch of them."

Every afternoon from late June to late August, this scene repeats itself in some form here on the wind-scoured badlands 100 miles north of **Helena, Montana**, on the road to Glacier National Park. Dinosaur fans arrive in the small town of **Choteau** (*show*-toe) and detour west 12 miles on a good gravel road to get a glimpse of this site popularly known as **Egg Mountain**. It was here in 1978 that dinosaur hunter John R. "Jack" Horner

and colleagues uncovered the world's first nest of baby dinosaurs and, the next year, the first clutches of dinosaur eggs found in North America. Every year since, Horner's crews have mined a two-by-two-mile square of eroded hills and gullies on an ancient geologic wrinkle known as the Willow Creek Anticline, amassing clues that have revolutionized our view of dinosaur behavior. Each summer, crews from the Museum of the Rockies in Bozeman and The Nature Conservancy, which now owns the site, return to dig, conduct field schools, and lead the daily two-hour public tour.

The first stop is the pit, atop a low ridge overlooking the 20-teepee field camp. Inside lies an exposed section of the densest, most extensive dinosaur graveyard known. Perhaps 30 million fossil fragments from 10,000 animals, all duckbills of a species Horner christened *Maiasaura peeblesorum*, fill a bone bed that's more than a mile long and a quarter mile wide. The site was dubbed "Camposaur" because it was literally discovered in the camp by an

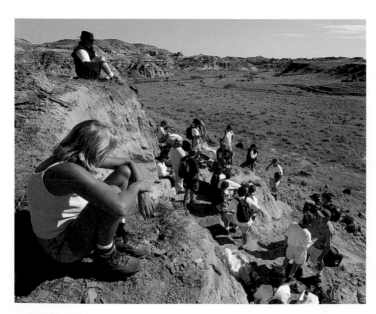

uncomfortable volunteer who couldn't stake his tent or sleep comfortably on the bone-pocked ground. One day 76 million years ago, some catastrophic event – most likely a blast of volcanic gas and ash – overtook the duckbill herd, leaving clear evidence that these ancient grazers lived in social groups just as bison or wildebeests do today.

Seaside Nesting Grounds

The Rocky Mountains, which shimmer blue in the heat haze only 30 miles to the west, were young and dotted with active volcanoes during the Cretaceous. To the east today, the Great Plains stretch for 400 miles. But the Cretaceous continent was split down the middle by an inland sea that lay 200 miles east of this site. These arid plains were shrubby uplands (grasses had not evolved) laced with streams and with shallow alkaline lakes, milky green and devoid of fish.

It was on these uplands that maiasaurs, small but fearsome *Troödons*, and at least one other unidentified dinosaur came to lay their eggs – the first two in colonial nesting grounds.

A few hundred feet from the camp, the guide shows visitors a ravine full of bare mudstone knobs. This was the first of three maiasaur nesting grounds discovered here, from which dozens of eggs, hatchlings, and babies have been removed. These are the finds that led Horner to propose that *Maiasaura* took care of nestbound babies just as modern birds do.

Visitors can also caravan to Egg Mountain, a low hill three-quarters of a mile away where the first intact dinosaur eggs – those of the six-foot meat eater *Troödon formosus* – were found.

The fossil eggs and babies have all been removed to the security of museums. You can see them at the **Museum of the Rockies**, or in a smaller but worthwhile display at the **Old Trail Museum** in Choteau. Only the roped-off rim of a *Troödon*'s mud nest remains, and bits of blackened eggshell that the guide passes around, then carefully retrieves. But from this hill, visitors can usually see crews on hands and knees hoping to uncover some new detail of dinosaur life.

A bounty of duckbilled dinosaur bones (opposite, top) remains to be excavated at Egg Mountain, site of the first dinosaur nests and egg clutches discovered in North America.

Daily summer tours (opposite, bottom) of Egg Mountain visit the spot where the first intact eggs, belonging to *Troödon*, were found.

Tipi camp (right) for field workers lies near the world's densest dinosaur graveyard, with the remains of an estimated 10,000 maiasaurs.

John Day Fossil Beds National Monument
John Day, Oregon

John Day Fossil Beds National Monument, 420 West Main, John Day, OR 97845; tel: 503-987-2333. Daily, 8:30 A.M.–5 P.M. (extended summer hours). No charge.

When dinosaurs roamed North America, much of what is now **John Day Fossil Beds** lay under the ocean. Eventually, the land here began to lift. Massive, mile-thick lava flows blanketed the region. Eruptions of ash and basalt obliterated the seascape but put ground beneath the feet of the dinosaurs' successors: the mammals.

Geologic forces have since lifted and sliced through these rock layers, exposing one of the longest and most complete fossil records of its kind. Dating from 54 million to 6 million years ago, the fossil beds capture the evolution of mammals throughout most of the Tertiary, the geological period between the extinction of the dinosaurs and the Ice Ages.

The oldest layers preserve in great detail the plants and animals that lived in subtropical forests. Strange-looking, rhinoceros-like brontotheres dominated the landscape, along with big predatory *Patriofelis* and the scavenger *Hemipsalodon*. These layers also contain the Clarno Nutbeds, among the finest plant fossils on Earth – seeds and fruit so complete that hundreds of species have been identified. Fossil bananas, palms, and kiwis suggest an ancient climate like Southeast Asia's today.

Younger layers document a slowly drying climate, an increasing variety of habitats, and an explosion of plant and animal types. More than 100 species of mammals have been found in layers dating to the early Miocene, when mammalian diversity peaked in North America. Among the great variety of fossils are saber-toothed cats, "mouse-deer," giant pigs, and distant ancestors of rhinoceroses, camels, and horses. Still younger rocks record open savannas on lush volcanic soils and the invasion of such large Asian mammals as elephants and bear-dogs. Then, toward the end of the Tertiary, familiar herds of grazing mammals replaced the browsers in the cool, dry rain shadow of the young Cascade Mountains.

Touring the John Day Basin

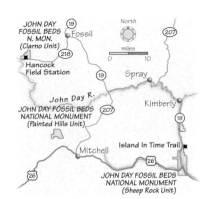

Today, John Day Fossil Beds National Monument is at the scientific heart of this fossil-rich region in eastern Oregon. Paleontologists here actively piece together past ecosystems to learn more about changing climate and how species adapted and evolved. Besides being one of the best fossil-viewing areas in the Northwest, the monument offers a spectacularly rugged landscape of deeply incised canyons just a few hours' drive from **Portland**. Here in the Basin and Range country of central Oregon, the **John Day River** cuts through the Columbia Plateau, creating a beautiful setting for fly-fishing and river rafting.

The past is easy to read in the John Day basin, and the monument has developed several places and activities to enliven the story. The visitor center at **Sheep Rock** displays a variety of mammal and nut fossils plus exhibits about the collectors themselves, from pioneers to contemporary scientists. The showpiece here is a big rhinoceros, *Dicerantherium annectens*. Nearby, the **Island of Time Interpretive Trail** invites visitors to experience the fossil beds firsthand and helps train one's skills as a bone hunter. For those with time to explore the three widely spaced units that comprise the monument, a logbook prepared by the Society of Vertebrate Paleontology makes an excellent driving guide to the deep history embedded in the basin's colorful rock layers.

Volcanic ash (opposite) makes up Sheep Rock Towers, rising above the meandering John Day River.

Eruption and erosion have shaped the landscape (below) in the Painted Hills and the other units of the national monument.

Rustic cabins (bottom) provide classrooms and quarters for weekend courses on the region's natural history.

For families and groups interested in a deeper look, the **Hancock Field Station**, operated in the monument by the Oregon Museum of Science and Industry in Portland, offers weekend programs in paleontology and natural history. Guests stay in rustic cabins and take classes in fossil collecting and stargazing.

Devil's Coulee
Warner, Alberta

Devil's Coulee Dinosaur Heritage Museum, Box 156, Warner, Alberta TOK 2L0, Canada; tel: 403-642-2118. Daily, 9 A.M.–5 P.M., May–September; Monday and Wednesday, 9 A.M.–5 P.M., October–April. Egg site tours daily at 10 A.M. and 2 P.M., July 1–September 30. $ museum, $–$$ egg site tour.

From atop a windswept prairie with a panoramic view of **Devil's Coulee**, an enthusiastic guide beckons visitors for a closer look. Melting glaciers and punishing winds produced this Canadian landscape – a mix of deeply eroded badlands and vegetated coulees topped by prairie, along the flank of **Milk River Ridge** – and in the process partially exposed several dinosaur nesting sites.

About 75 million years ago, this place teemed with duckbilled hadrosaurs, which laid eggs the size of honeydew melons, and smaller egg-laying dinosaurs. Uplands rising from a coastal plain, marked by scattered ponds and shallow rivers, provided nesting habitat for the dinosaurs. Caliche deposits (calcium carbonate) found among the eggshells indicate a semiarid ancient climate. Heavy rains, flooding, or landslides periodically buried and crushed dinosaur

nests, occasionally entombing the embryos. These burials, combined with the buffering effects of abundant clamshells and gastropod shells on the area's slightly acidic water, created optimal conditions for preserving the eggs.

Devil's Coulee is the first dinosaur nesting site discovered in Canada and only the second in the world with fossilized embryos. In 1987, a survey crew headed by Philip Currie, of the Royal Tyrrell Museum of Palaeontology, explored Milk River Ridge and Devil's Coulee. Currie's crew found the first dinosaur egg nest in Alberta along the ridge. Late in the survey, the crew discovered abundant nests, eggshells, and small dinosaur bones in Devil's Coulee, where preparator Kevin Aulenback found part of a dinosaur egg with an embryo's protruding tail. Teams from the Tyrrell have been excavating in the late Cretaceous mudstone, bentonite, and ironstone exposed at Devil's Coulee ever since.

The rugged site has yielded more than 100 eggs, isolated or in clutches, and thousands of eggshell fragments of the hadrosaur *Hypacrosaurus stebingeri*, a few hypsilophodont eggs, eggs of birds and turtles, and fossils of vertebrates, invertebrates, and plants. Fieldwork lately has focused on how nests were built, the number of eggs each held, and how many kinds of dinosaurs nested at the site.

Aulenback prepares dinosaur embryos with dental picks under a microscope. To carefully extract the fragile fossils from the matrix and make casts could take years, but an innovative acid wash that removes

the caliche coating assists the painstaking process.

Get a Close Look

Travelers should visit the small museum in **Warner**, the **Devil's Coulee Dinosaur Heritage Museum**, before joining a tour of the egg site. The museum's displays include full casts of a *Hypacrosaurus* embryo and nest, as well as a brachylophosaur skull, an ankylosaur tail club, dinosaur footprints, and a demonstration table of fossils from Devil's Coulee and the surrounding area. Hands-on educational youth programs provide digs in a simulated bone bed and casting of actual dinosaur footprints. (The Royal Tyrrell Museum in Drumheller also displays nests and eggs from the site.)

Two-hour guided tours leave the museum for Devil's Coulee, where visitors may view the egg sites and a juvenile hadrosaur bone bed, watch technicians at work, or just enjoy the scenery. From atop the coulee, the guide points out major excavation sites

and staked spots where the ground is still littered with dinosaur eggshell fragments and embryo bones. For a good look at these thumbnail-sized fragments, it pays to get down on hands and knees. A trail leads to more egg sites, an excavation of turtle fossils, and to fossilized freshwater gastropods and clamshells.

If time permits, visitors will be led to a hillside quarry filled with young hadrosaurs, where excavation has yielded hundreds of fossils. Paleontologists have hypothesized that the half-grown, 10-foot-long duckbills perished around a shrinking pond during a drought. Among the abundant dinosaur remains are fossils of fish, frogs, salamanders, lizards, and small mammals.

Curled embryo (opposite, top) of duckbilled *Hypacrosaurus* has been reconstructed for display.

Devil's Coulee has yielded more than 100 hadrosaur eggs, including this fragment (opposite, bottom).

The skull of duckbilled *Brachylophosaurus* (above), found in Dinosaur Provincial Park, awaits museum goers in Warner.

T. rex **welcomes** tourists (left) to an information center at nearby Milk River.

Dinosaur Provincial Park
Patricia, Alberta

Dinosaur Provincial Park, P.O. Box 60, Patricia, Alberta TOJ 2K0, Canada; tel: 403-378-4342.
The park is always open; interpretive programs are available Monday–Friday, 8:15 A.M.–4:30 P.M., Saturday–Sunday, 8:15 A.M.–6 P.M., mid-May–mid-October (extended summer hours). $

It took glacial meltwater and rain about 15,000 years to carve out the badlands of southeastern Alberta from the surrounding prairie. It takes a group of visitors about 15 minutes of wandering through dry gullies lined with sandstone and sage to find their first tyrannosaur tooth. The two-inch, triangular tooth is dark brown and shiny, with tiny sawtooth points along the edges. Before it fell from its owner's mouth, it was attached to a hungry dinosaur weighing about seven tons. The excited finders pass it from hand to hand, running their fingertips along the still sharp edges.

Not every fossil comes out of **Dinosaur Provincial Park** this quickly, but this collecting party had several advantages. Led by a paleontologist who had been roaming the area for the last 20 years, they were guided by maps made 50 years ago by scientists who pulled bones from this same hillside. And they were lucky, because a rainstorm the previous week carried away just enough sandstone to expose the tooth while not carrying away the prize itself.

These explorers also had the law on their side. The relatively small park (about 18,000

Glaciers and rain carved the sandstone badlands of Dinosaur Provincial Park (above), one of the world's premier fossil sites.

Paleontologist Phil Currie, at left, leads a dig in the park (right). Thirty dinosaur species thrived here 70 million years ago on a hot, humid coastal plain.

A fossil hunter (opposite) extracts centrosaur bones from a cliff face.

acres) is one of the richest fossil sites in the world. But you can't get into most of it unless you're led by a park interpreter on a scheduled hike or bus tour. And you certainly can't take home a fossil, or even move it, because in Alberta all fossils are protected by law and belong to the province. The tooth discovered that day was marked, photographed, bagged, and sent two hours northwest to the Royal Tyrrell Museum in Drumheller, which keeps tabs on fossil finds in Alberta.

Dinosaurs by the Herd

You can come to the park and have a look, however. As you drive northeast from the town of **Brooks** for about half an hour, you travel over flat prairie and past signs for small farming towns, most of which seem to be named in memory of women, such as Millicent and Patricia. Soon after passing **Patricia**, a sudden dip in the road drives her from your mind as it takes you down through 300 feet of rock and 75 million years of time. Welcome to the park.

It was quite a different place back then, of course. An ancient, inland sea divided North America, and this was a low-lying coastal plain near the shoreline, hot and humid and heavy with vegetation, and laced with branching river channels. "Your first reaction, if we dropped you off in such a place, would be, 'I'm lost in a bayou in Louisiana,'" says Bruce Naylor, director of the Royal Tyrrell, which operates a field station in the park that also serves as a visitor center and exhibit hall for some of the dinosaur fossils. "It wouldn't be until one of those nasties poked his head up that you'd realize you were 70 million years back in time."

This was, in fact, quite a hospitable environment for those "nasties." Tyrannosaurs such as *Albertosaurus* and *Gorgosaurus* roamed the area. Large herds of horned ceratopsians lived and died here, eating the abundant plants and dodging the abundant predators. Hundreds of duckbilled hadrosaurs were around as well. More than 30 dinosaur species have been found within the park.

The park turned out to be just as hospitable for the afterlife of these animals. The Rocky Mountains were rising to the west, and rivers draining from them quickly sealed dead dinosaurs under layer after layer of mud or sand, which hardened into mudstone, sandstone, and ironstone. Millions of years rolled by, and glaciers rolled in. They rolled back, for the last time, about 15,000 years ago as the world entered a warming period. Meltwater from these glaciers formed an enormous lake, dammed by ice. And when the dam broke, floodwaters rushed out, cutting the Red Deer River Valley deep into the sediments.

That exposed the soft mudstone and sandstone in the valley walls to the eroding effects of rain, which carved deep gullies, called coulees. Some of these have side gullies, creating a labyrinthine landscape of striated hills and gulches, some covered with sage and prickly-pear cactus and others bare to the world, their surfaces coated with popcornlike loose rock. As the rain scraped and beat at the rock, carrying away nearly two inches of sediment each year – that's a lot – it unearthed the dinosaur fossils. The process is still going on today.

Dinosaur Graves and Picnic Sites

You can see the results by camping under cottonwood trees on the riverbank, or bunking in Brooks and driving out for the day.

Either way, plan on doing some walking. Wear hiking boots to keep your footing on the slippery sandstone. Bring a hat, sunscreen, insect repellent, and plenty of water – these badlands were not named idly.

Bring along some extra time, too – at least two days for an in-depth visit. The park offers five self-guided trails, which are nice enough. But it's a lot more interesting to go out with a park interpreter, who can get you into areas that are otherwise off-limits and who can also answer questions. Space is limited on these tours, and the park holds half the places for same-day sales, so you'll need to be a little flexible. Reservations can be made by telephone and are strongly recommended.

There are some other advantages to a guided hike. Unless you know why the giant, mushroom-shaped rock formations dotting the park are called "hoodoos," for example, it's good to have someone along who does, someone who can tell you that they form under caps of harder rock like ironstone as water erodes the softer mudstone beneath until the cap balances precariously atop a slender column.

The interpreters offer three different hikes, each about two-and-a-half hours long. For those with sturdy legs, the hike to a *Centrosaurus* bone bed is worth the trip. Centrosaurs were horned dinosaurs, and this site is a mass grave where hundreds of adults, youths, and youngsters perished at once, about 75 million years ago. Their death together indicates that they probably lived together as well, traveling in vast migrating herds like today's wildebeests in Africa. One theory about what killed this group is that the front of the herd halted at a flood-swollen river. The back of the herd, not knowing what was going on, may have surged forward and shoved their traveling companions into the torrent – again, much as wildebeests do today.

After a 20-minute trek up two sandstone ridges – here's where you'll regret wearing

A mudstone formation (opposite, top) is furrowed by erosion at a *Centrosaurus* graveyard, where hundreds of horned dinosaurs died suddenly.

***Tyrannosaurus* balloon** (opposite, bottom) soars above the Red Deer River and the rugged landscape of Dinosaur Provincial Park.

Excavations continue (right) throughout the park, where this hadrosaur skeleton was uncovered. A field station displays some of the fossil finds.

those sneakers – you'll see the remains of an excavation at the site. Part of the hillside is protected by what looks like a large garage door (which, in fact, it is; paleontologists tend to favor low-tech equipment). When the interpreters open it, you can see bits of centrosaur frills, horns, jaws, ribs, and limb bones. They will pass around some fossils for you to examine; look carefully for puncture marks made by the teeth of scavenging tyrannosaurs, who had themselves a picnic at the site. Take a moment to hike up to the **Citadel**, a rock formation overlooking the dig. You'll get a spectacular view of the badlands and get to see more centrosaur bones from this immense bed sticking out from the other side of the hill.

A coulee hike is a little easier, but it focuses more on the current inhabitants of the badlands than it does on the ones who died out 65 million years ago. You'll encounter more of the deceased on what the park glibly calls its **Fossil Safari**, which goes to a dig site in the otherwise inaccessible natural preserve. For the less athletically inclined, the park does have a bus tour, which covers the major features, explains some of the history, and stops at a couple of outdoor displays where you can examine dinosaur skeletons. Each of these gives you a chance to spot a bit of shiny white or brown against a background of muted grays and reds, and feel the thrill of discovering a fossil.

Eastend Fossil Research Station
Eastend, Saskatchewan

Eastend Fossil Research Station, 118 Maple Avenue
South, Eastend, Saskatchewan SON 0T0, Canada;
tel: 306-295-4009.
Daily, 9 A.M.–12 P.M. and 1–5 P.M., September–June;
9 A.M.– 6 P.M., July–August. $–$$

In 1991, on a cattle ranch southeast of **Eastend, Saskatchewan**, paleontologists Tim Tokaryk and John Storer were prospecting for fossils in the coulees of the **Frenchman River Valley**. With them was a local teacher, Robert Gebhardt, who noticed parts of a tooth and tail bone protruding from the hillside. Lo and behold, they were the first pieces from a nearly complete skull and skeleton of a 65-million-year-old *Tyrannosaurus rex*.

Saskatchewan's first *T. rex*, "Scotty" was finally freed during the summers of 1994 and 1995. Eight months of excavation reclaimed the jumble of bones, and four plaster-jacketed blocks, each weighing up to four tons, were carefully transported by a team of Belgian horses and by truck to the **Eastend Fossil Research Station** in October 1995.

Surrounded by rugged prairie, the research station had opened five months earlier in anticipation of Scotty's arrival. After the skeleton was found, paleontologists wanted a convenient facility in which to work on the fossils, and locals lobbied to keep Scotty in the area. The region's wealth of fossils has been known since the 1920s when "Corky" Jones, a local fossil hunter, began making discoveries. Rock deposits in the Frenchman Formation preserve a range of vertebrates from the late Cretaceous – when this area was a subtropical coastal floodplain – that range in size from frogs and salamanders to *Triceratops* and *Edmontosaurus*. In 1995, during a break from the excavation of Scotty, Eastend paleontologists discovered

fossilized feces from a *Tyrannosaurus*. Nearly 18 inches long, the coprolite was chock-full of bone fragments from a juvenile plant-eating dinosaur.

Working on Scotty

Open daily year-round, Eastend Fossil Research Station contains interpretive exhibits, including tyrannosaur teeth and hands-on fossil and geology displays. Visitors can watch preparators in the lab meticulously removing and cleaning Scotty's bones or other fossils. A mural shows all the identified *T. rex* bones to date.

Separating the fossils from surrounding ironstone and mudstone takes years of work. Scotty's skull should be ready for display by 2002, but completing the skeleton will require a decade or so. Then the bones will be cast and mounted in the research station, a satellite facility of the **Royal Saskatchewan Museum** in **Regina**.

In summer, visitors can join a day dig or quarry tour for a firsthand look at field work in a local site known for 35- to 40-million-year-old mammals, including deer, horses, and rhinoceros-like brontotheres. The field station may add tours to dinosaur or other more ancient bone quarries. A few openings are available each year in the volunteer dig program, which requires a

minimum commitment of two weeks.

During July and August, twice-weekly "Fossil Discovery" programs geared for children feature hands-on paleo crafts and activities. Visitors can make casts of dinosaur footprints, open plaster jackets containing miniature dinosaurs, or pick through a sandy matrix to find real fossils. Similar programs are offered twice a month at nearby **Cypress Hills Interprovincial Park**.

Visit the Eastend Museum for a broader sample of local dinosaurs, as well as fossils of marine plants and animals, including many found by "Corky" Jones. A larger museum, scheduled to be built in a year or two, will focus on the science and process of paleontology and archaeology. The museum will feature its own fossil-preparation lab and a spacious gallery where some of the research station's specimens of *Triceratops*, other dinosaurs, and fossil mammals from the Cypress Hills Formation can be shared with visitors.

Day digs (opposite, top) let visitors look for fossils after they tour the research station.

Serrated tooth (above) of Scotty, Saskatchewan's first *T. rex*, is on display at the research station; paleontologists continue the tough task of preparing his remains.

Cretaceous Canada (left) harbored an array of armored, horned, duck-billed, ostrichlike, and meat-eating dinosaurs. *T. rex* was the last of the big carnivores.

◆

Exploring Museums

◆

Museums in the United States and Canada have some of the finest fossil collections in the world. There's no easier way to immerse yourself in dinosaur science than to see the exhibits and take part in interpretive programs.

Museum
Guide

CHAPTER 11

Many paleontologists trace their obsession with extinct life to a formative childhood experience in a museum, when they first encountered the towering skeleton of a dinosaur. *Tyrannosaurus. Allosaurus. Diplodocus.* Any one could do the trick. Maybe tomorrow's top dinosaur paleontologist will choose the calling after being wonderstruck by the rearing mother *Barosaurus* at the American Museum of Natural History in New York, or the sprinting *Giganotosaurus* at the Academy of Natural Sciences in Philadelphia. ◆ Today there are hundreds of dinosaurs to see in museums from coast to coast, ranging from modest, small-town operations to hallowed institutions harboring world-renowned research collections. These fossils have tales to tell, and plenty – the juvenile *Camarasaurus* in Pittsburgh or the *Nanotyrannus* skull in Cleveland, for example – are one-of-a-kind specimens. Some museums focus on fossils from a single site or region; others pursue more catholic interests.

Whether modest, mammoth, or somewhere in the middle, these museums showcase dinosaurs and the science of understanding them.

In addition to bare bones, new displays feature fleshed-out reconstructions of how the animals may have appeared in life. ◆ Museums may put their best bones out on the exhibit floor, or display reproductions instead to save the real skeletons for the experts. But even casts of dinosaur bones can inspire our awe and wonder. Several museums have working preparation labs where visitors can watch as actual dinosaur fossils are painstakingly cleaned. A few even have fossil sites nearby and let you visit or join the dig – another way to inspire a lifelong affection for dinosaurs.

Albertosaurus **model** at Philadelphia's Academy of Natural Sciences morphs from fully fleshed head to skinless torso and bare-boned tail.

Preceding pages: Marine mosasaurs were not dinosaurs but seagoing reptiles related to the largest living lizard, the Komodo dragon.

Peabody Museum of Natural History
New Haven, Connecticut

Peabody Museum of Natural History, 170 Whitney Avenue,
Yale University, New Haven, CT 06511; tel: 203-432-5050.
Monday–Saturday, 10 A.M.–5 P.M.; Sunday, noon–5 P.M. $

Few museums can match the **Peabody**.
Built in 1923, this gothic mini-cathedral to
the history of dinosaur science reflects the
dinosaur-hunting frenzy of Yale University's
most famous fossil expert, Othniel Charles
Marsh. Marsh's wealthy uncle, George
Peabody, financed the museum and facilitated
his nephew's appointment as the country's
first professor of paleontology. It took Marsh

most of his lifetime to acquire one of the
nation's largest collections of dinosaur fossils.

There's much more here than dinosaurs,
of course. You can touch the pineapple-like
bark of a fossil cycad, part of a landmark
collection of seed-bearing plants dominant
through much of the dinosaurs' time on
Earth. You can find skeletal mounts of ancient
mammals and primates, plus exhibits devoted
to Native American cultures beneath the
vaulted ceiling of the first floor. Activities for
kids occupy the second floor in the Discovery
Room, while dioramas of North American
wildlife, a hall devoted to rocks and minerals,
and cultural remains from ancient Egypt fill
the third floor.

The Great Hall of Dinosaurs may seem a
bit fusty, perhaps, but the exhibits are impressive. *Stegosaurus* and *Apatosaurus* skeletons
are especially daunting in the confines of
the hall's central island. Displayed since

Lethal leaper *Deinonychus* (opposite) is shown with its discoverer, John Ostrom, at the Peabody Museum.

Gothic design (right) makes the Peabody seem like a cathedral of American paleontology. Its collection was first assembled under the guidance of Othniel Marsh.

T. rex skull (below right) is displayed in the Great Hall, which features some of the first mounted dinosaurs in North America.

Torosaurus (below) had the largest skull of any land animal; it was named by Marsh in 1891.

1931, the *Apatosaurus* was the first mounted skeleton of the huge dinosaur, known originally as *Brontosaurus*, or "Thunder Lizard." Though scientists have considered the name invalid for decades, it's too well known to ever disappear from the dinosaur lexicon. Originally, this *Apatosaurus* skeleton mistakenly wore the bulkier skull of *Camarasaurus*, but the Peabody has its skulls straight now.

Birth of a New Theory

Apatosaurus has some distinguished dinosaur company here: the sauropod giant *Camarasaurus*, skulls of three ceratopsians or horned dinosaurs, plus skeletons of *Stegosaurus*, *Camptosaurus*, and the sturdy duckbilled *Edmontosaurus* (also one of the earliest skeletons to be mounted in North America). Another notable display features the largest known turtle, *Archelon*, a 12-foot-long contemporary of the duckbills.

The Great Hall also features Yale's great 20th-century contributions to dinosaur science. While exploring the Montana badlands in 1964, Yale paleontologist John Ostrom came across a striking, sickle-shaped toe claw from a dinosaur. From this and other finds, Ostrom named it *Deinonychus*, or "Terrible Claw." The beast provid-

ed evidence that led Ostrom (and his student at the time, Bob Bakker) to launch the modern view of theropod dinosaurs as active, agile, even warm-blooded animals that were ancestors to birds. A man-sized "raptor," or dromaeosaurid, *Deinonychus* appears here dynamically posed as a slashing leaper – the Freddy Krueger of the Cretaceous.

For aficionados of dinosaur art, the Peabody's main attraction isn't a fossil at all but Rudolph Zallinger's 1947 mural, *The Age of Reptiles*. This 110-foot-long panorama won a Pulitzer award and adorned the cover of *Life* and an elaborate spread inside the magazine. Zallinger's masterpiece spans 300 million years of Earth history, including the Age of Dinosaurs. The depictions are somewhat dated, of course, but a recent touch-up has restored the painting to its original vibrancy.

A schedule of changing exhibits highlights new discoveries and research, and an ongoing program of events for families and children offers learning all year long.

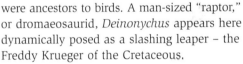

American Museum of Natural History
New York, New York

American Museum of Natural History, Central Park West at 79th Street, New York, NY 10024; tel: 212-769-5000. Monday–Thursday and Sunday, 10 A.M.–5:45 P.M.; Friday–Saturday, 10 A.M.–8:45 P.M. $ (suggested donation)

You want dinosaur fossils? This is the place. The museum spent $48 million redesigning the fossil halls, and while some critics may quibble with some of the changes, one fact is clear: This collection is the most comprehensive, celebrated, and awe-inspiring assemblage of dinosaur fossils in the world. As Cole Porter remarked in a slightly different context, it's the top.

This Victorian pile on Manhattan's Upper West Side, known as the **American Museum of Natural History**, houses the very fossils that inspired Stephen Jay Gould to become a scientist. The dedication of his first book of essays reads, "For my father, who took me to see the *Tyrannosaurus* when I was five." These are the halls whose ambiance that eternal adolescent Holden Caulfield recalls so fondly in *The Catcher in the Rye*. "The best thing in that museum was that everything always stayed right where it was," Holden said. "Nobody'd move .... The only thing that would be different would be you."

For better or worse, Holden's words have a certain irony today. Over the past decade, the whole fourth floor of the museum, home to the matchless collection of fish, reptile, and mammal fossils as well as the dinosaurs, has been refurbished and reorganized. No longer a series of discrete and unconnected specimens – "Greatest Hits of Prehistory," as it were – the floor is now a self-guided tour through vertebrate evolution, a tour meant to teach us that these strange beasts are our own distant cousins, and that extinction is not just a dinosaur thing.

Or so the curators hope. In fact, absorbing those messages may be a stretch for the average visitor, who probably has less than the week it would take to work through, let alone master, these text-heavy exhibits. Fortunately, the fossils themselves, now as ever, stand on their own merits. The two vast dinosaur halls contain 100 or so specimens – no one seems quite sure exactly how many – and an astonishing 85 percent of them are real. (Most museums these days display casts.) The lineup includes not only the iconic skeletons of *Tyrannosaurus rex* and *Apatosaurus* but such treasures as a mummified *Hadrosaurus*, an *Oviraptor* egg with the fetal animal clearly visible, and a *Coelophysis bauri* with the bones of his last meal – another *C. bauri* – still in his stomach.

That's just the beginning. You'll see a growth series of a dozen *Protoceratops* skulls, each so pristine, so perfectly intermediate in size between its immediate casemates, that you suspect someone churns them out to order in the basement. You'll see a 22-foot trackway of dinosaur footprints from 107 million years ago. You'll see one of the museum's first dinosaur acquisitions, a single, mahogany-colored vertebra of *Diplodocus longus*, four feet across. You'll see the world's only intact *Velociraptor* skull. Any of these objects would be the crown jewel of a lesser museum.

Updating the Facts

The aesthetics of the renovation are impeccable. When Holden Caulfield (or his alter ego, author J.D. Salinger) and the five-year-old Stephen Jay Gould roamed these halls, the walls were painted black, and the ceilings were covered with acoustic tiles. "There was essentially no lighting," says paleontologist Lowell Dingus, project manager for

Recent renovation (opposite) of the museum's dinosaur halls brought natural light, anatomically correct mounts, and a new organization based on the shared features of different dinosaur groups.

Barosaurus (left) rears up 50 feet to guard its offspring from an advancing *Allosaurus* in this dramatic diorama.

Early amphibians (below) dominated the land before dinosaurs arose, but many, including this heavy-skulled trematosaur, dwindled just as dinosaurs began to diversify.

the renovation, and so "the dinosaurs looked like creatures from science fiction, not like anything that ever lived." Now the ceilings have been restored to their original heights, 25 feet in some halls. Daylight suffuses the rooms courtesy of new, or newly unblocked, windows. (Some folks complain that the dinosaurs looked bigger and scarier when the walls were black, but you can't please everybody.)

Universal acclaim has greeted the alterations to individual specimens, done to reflect the most current understanding of dinosaur anatomy and behavior. For instance, the beloved *Brontosaurus* finally got a new skull, 20 years after paleontologists demonstrated that it had worn the wrong one since 1905. It also got a new pose; the skeleton that used to look like a big dog ordered sternly off the couch, its tail drooping between its legs, has been remounted with its great tail aloft, since scientists realized that there were no tail marks in sauropod trackways. Makeover

complete, the brontosaur was given its proper name, *Apatosaurus*.

Tyrannosaurus also felt the winds of change. Since his debut in 1915 he had stood upright, like Godzilla, a towering 18 feet. But Godzilla has morphed into a ferocious roadrunner, in acknowledgment of the scientific near-consensus that the modern branch of the *T. rex* lineage survives as birds. He's been mounted in a horizontal, much more birdlike posture, and if the occasional visitor can be heard asking plaintively where the *T. rex* is, only to learn that he's, uh, standing in front of it, well, that's a small price to pay for scientific accuracy.

So, you may ask, "What's not to like?"

In a word, attitude. This seems to be a renovation designed by brilliant scientists for other brilliant scientists, people who in their enthusiasm for their discipline have forgotten how little the rest of us know. Imagine going to a concert expecting to hear "The Three Tenors" and being told that the program had been changed to "An Evening with John Cage," and you'll have a sense of how disoriented a first-time visitor can feel. The displays are educational; they're information-rich; they're exhaustive. But user-friendly they're not. Much of the signage is too technical, and the layout, featuring informational kiosks at evolutionary branching points, is bewildering unless you understand the structure before you start.

***Apatosaurus* vertebra**
(left). The bone's light-weight structure made the sauropod's long, slender neck easier to support.

A New Theory Takes Over

The fossil displays – from armored fishes to dinosaurs to Irish elk – were reorganized in a framework known as "cladistics," a relatively new theoretical approach to evolution that was pioneered in part by American Museum scientists. Cladists, who by now include most vertebrate paleontologists, no longer focus on ancestor/descendant relationships – what gave rise to what – but on groups, or clades, that share particular anatomical characteristics. For instance, the presence of a backbone links humans with dinosaurs as members of the huge vertebrate clade. The dinosaur clade includes two subgroups, courtesy of an anatomical difference in the hipbone.

This is a big switch from the comfortable, chronological narrative that this museum once employed, and that most museums still use. Indeed, the decision to adopt a cladistics was fiercely debated, but in the end, says project manager Dingus, "We decided that people could see the chronological approach lots of places. We wanted to give them something different." The result? Goodbye "Early

Dinosaurs" and "Late Dinosaurs"; hello "Ornithischians" and "Saurischians."

Whether "different" means better for the museum-going, dinosaur-loving public is an open question. Perhaps cladism, like Impressionism, will eventually catch on outside academe; perhaps, like twelve-tone music, it won't. But to get the most out of the exhibits in the interim, try the following: Enter the museum through the relatively dinky 77th Street entrance. The elevator there lets you out at the Orientation Center on the fourth floor, where a video narrated by Meryl Streep explains cladistics, among other things. (You don't even have to listen – and judging from the rows of beautifully designed but empty benches, most people don't – but it helps.) This puts you at the beginning of the evolutionary loop, pointed in the right direction. You'll have to walk through Vertebrate Origins to get to the saurischians, but those early vertebrates are worth seeing, too.

Or you can cut Cladistics 101 and head straight for the dinosaurs. They speak for themselves, which isn't surprising, since some of them have had 100 million years to figure out what to say.

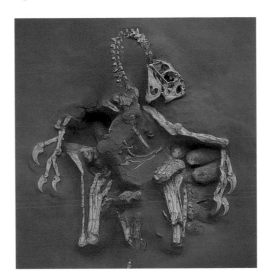

Visitors entering the museum from Central Park West don't have far to wander before encountering dinosaurs like this *Allosaurus* (opposite, top) in the museum rotunda.

Brooding *Oviraptor* (above) died with legs draped around its eggs. This is one of many amazing specimens from the museum's Mongolia expeditions.

Museum technicians (below) spruce up a sauropod skeleton.

New Mounts for Old Bones

The old view of dinosaurs as ponderous, cold-blooded beasts that shuffled through their lives like oversized geriatric elephants was reflected in the way museums mounted their fossil skeletons. Tail-dragging *T. rexes* and plodding sauropods were the norm.

But in the late 1960s, when Bob Bakker popularized the idea of dinosaurs as dynamic, warm-blooded animals, museums started remounting their skeletons in action-packed poses. Previously unwieldy dinosaurs could now leap, lunge, gallop, pounce, and rear up in freeze-frame like the most nimble mammal.

From the appearance of the restored *T. rex* at the Denver Museum of Natural History, it appears that dinosaurs could also kick up their heels and dance like a Radio City Rockette. Another provocative pose is struck by the *Barosaurus* at the American Museum of Natural History in New York, mounted in 1991. A mama is rearing up, her head 50 feet above the ground, to protect her youngster from a snarling *Allosaurus*. Whether the long-necked, 90-foot *Barosaurus* could actually rear up on its hind legs is open to scientific debate, but the scene is a dramatic crowd-pleaser. – *Mary K. Miller*

Academy of Natural Sciences
Philadelphia, Pennsylvania

Academy of Natural Sciences, 1900 Benjamin Franklin Parkway, Philadelphia, PA 19103-1195; tel: 215-299-1000. Monday–Friday, 10 A.M.–4 P.M.; Saturday–Sunday, 10 A.M.–5 P.M. $

The first thing you see when you walk into the **Academy of Natural Sciences** in **Philadelphia** is a 42-foot *Giganotosaurus* leaping over the reception desk as if ready to bound outdoors. It's an impressive mount, the first cast from a fossil skeleton of "the largest carnivore that ever walked the earth," discovered in Argentina in 1995. Take a hard right and you'll be in the museum's Dinosaur Hall, face to face with *Tyrannosaurus rex* (just a smidgen smaller than *Giganotosaurus*).

These two massive predators would have never met in life – they lived about 30 million years apart and on different continents – but here in the City of Brotherly Love, they seem to compete for being the biggest, baddest dinosaur on the block.

With a newly renovated hall, the academy is also competing to reclaim its reputation as a preeminent dinosaur site. It offers just what you'd expect to see in a museum of natural history: murals and text panels and a decent, if not overwhelming, collection of full-size skeletons. Besides the big, bad predators, these include a cast of the horned dinosaur *Chasmosaurus*, the large duckbilled *Corythosaurus*, and the small theropod *Stenonychosaurus* (aka *Troödon*). Also part of the collection is a cast of a rare small-horned dinosaur, *Avaceratops lammersi*, that looks like a baby *Triceratops*. This hog-sized dinosaur, known from a single specimen, is regarded by paleontologist Peter Dodson as a new species rather than a juvenile ceratopsian of a known species.

Aptly named *Giganotosaurus* (opposite), the largest carnivore that ever walked, bounds toward the academy's entrance.

A working lab (right), where staff and volunteers prepare fossils, offers visitors a glimpse of the painstaking labor of paleontology.

Raptors (below) outside the museum's front entrance ready their sickle-shaped claws as they approach unseen prey.

Among the skeletons are life-sized models of dinosaurs caught in active poses. An *Albertosaurus* morphs from bones to muscles to bumpy skin to show how artists and scientists reconstruct what these extinct animals looked like. Just beyond it is a small herd of *Tenontosaurus* protecting the young ones from a vicious-looking *Deinonychus* (the sickle-clawed model for the velociraptor of *Jurassic Park*).

Most of the mounts and models are lighted from below for dramatic effect, but the low lights impede reading the label text, which gives the common and scientific name (with a push-button recording to help with pronunciation), a bit of the animal's natural history, a story about the fossil's discovery, and touchable elements – a tooth, a claw, or other piece of a fossil cast, together with a Braille label and a small raised outline of the skeleton. By comparing the full-sized fossil piece with the skeleton outline, sight-impaired visitors can grasp the scale of each dinosaur.

Museum Firsts

The glitziest exhibit gives a nod to Hollywood's influence on dinosaur popularity.

Inside the Time Machine, a mini-television studio, complete with blue-screen technology, you come face to face (at least on video) with accurate animations of the denizens of *Jurassic Park*. Kids ham it up as they cower from a snarling *Tyrannosaurus*, run from a thundering herd of ceratopsians, or duck as pterosaurs come swooping down. The surprisingly lifelike creatures seem to enter the studio, creating a theatrical performance for parents or others waiting their turn.

If the Time Machine is a bow to the present, tucked into a back corner of the hall is a tribute to the academy's past: the first dinosaur skeleton ever discovered in North America. The 35 bones that make up the reconstruction of *Hadrosaurus foulkii* were dug up in 1858 by academy

Chasmosaurus belli

member William Parker Foulke. A decade later, the academy became the first museum anywhere to display this skeleton and the first to mount a dinosaur in a bipedal position. The *Hadrosaurus* mount resembled an oversized kangaroo, balancing on its tail, but the reassembled cast (the real bones are too delicate to display) has the body balanced over the hips, tail parallel to the ground.

Just beyond the history exhibit is a functioning paleontology lab, where staff and volunteers prepare fossils for research and display. The friendly researchers invite questions and will stroll over with a bone to give visitors a behind-the-scenes peek at their work.

A Mesozoic mural spans 180 million years from the Triassic to the mass extinction of the dinosaurs. As for what killed them off, the museum presents two theories: the quick-and-dirty comet or asteroid impact, and gradually changing environmental conditions. Examine the evidence presented and make up your own mind (although the impact theory seems favored here).

Walking in Dinosaur Steps

While the first floor is somewhat standard fare for museums of natural history, the second floor is something completely different – an interactive mecca of dinosaur exhibits and activities. This section follows a journey through the scientific process of paleontology, from field collection and preparation to debates over how the extinct creatures moved, lived, and reproduced.

The journey starts with the Big Dig, a fossil-filled pit depicting New Mexican badlands. Casts of skeletons lie partially buried under simulated rock (a dense, dust-free mixture of sand, wax, and petroleum jelly) that fossil hunters who are outfitted with goggles, brushes, and chisels work to scrape away. On weekdays (except in summer) the dig may be swarming with goggled students, often so engaged in the process that they have to be dragged away to make room for the next group. During the school year, a part of the dig is usually left open for drop-in visitors.

A section on comparative anatomy shows the similarities and differences between the skeletons of humans, dinosaurs, and other vertebrates. Some touchable dinosaur skulls nearby contain the answers to questions posed about fossil anatomy. Even if you already know the answer, it's still fun to stick your head inside the gaping jaws of a *T. rex* or look through the eye sockets of a *Triceratops*. And it makes a great photo opportunity.

Another fun exhibit invites you to walk like a dinosaur. Step onto a treadmill and start walking (warning: it takes some effort to get it going) and a full-scale mechanical *Dromaeosaurus* made of nuts and bolts walks along with you. The exhibit demonstrates that dinosaur anatomy and locomotion were not so different from our own: Humans and bipedal dinosaurs have joints in the same places, similar muscle groups, and comparable mobility. A set of tracks on the ground nearby lets you compare your gait with that of a dinosaur with erect posture or crawl on all fours with limbs sprawled like a crocodile.

Take a break by sitting inside the mold of a giant sauropod footprint, which offers surprisingly good lumbar support for the weary museum-goer. Then examine clutches of real dinosaur eggs from China, or ponder the current debate about whether dome-headed *Pachycephalosaurus* used its skull as a battering ram or just for sexual decoration. For the aesthetically inclined, another room displays a changing exhibition of original paintings and sketches by world-class dinosaur artists, showing how they flesh out all of those bones.

Elaborate frill (opposite, top) behind the skull distinguishes *Chasmosaurus*.

Tenontosaurus (opposite, bottom) shelters its young from *Deinonychus*, the model for the vicious raptor in *Jurassic Park*.

Examine a *Triceratops* skull (above) or peek into a *Tyrannosaurus* mouth in the museum's upstairs interactive gallery.

Sweet dreams (right) may not be in store for children camped out beneath the menacing *T. rex* during a museum sleepover.

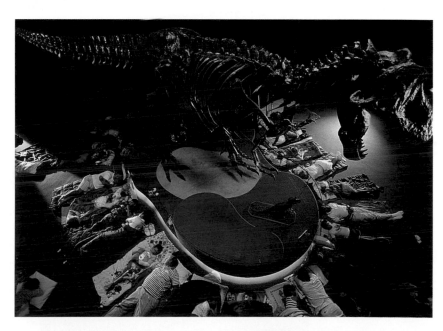

National Museum of Natural History
Washington, D.C.

National Museum of Natural History, Smithsonian Institution, Tenth Street and Constitution Avenue NW, Washington, DC 20560; tel: 202-357-2020.
Daily, 10 A.M.–5:30 P.M., until 6 P.M. in summer. No charge.

To find the most powerful characters in Washington, D.C., head to the White House at 1600 Pennsylvania Avenue – and then keep walking. Continue a few blocks southeast to the large Beaux Arts building with a central dome. There, in the **National Museum of Natural History**, you'll complete your quest in Dinosaur Hall, dedicated to the creatures who ruled the planet for 160 million years during the Mesozoic period. No other incumbent in Washington can match that record.

Dinosaur experts hold the **Smithsonian Institution** in high regard, especially for its late Jurassic species. "It's a very important collection," says Hans-Dieter Sues of the Royal Ontario Museum in Toronto. Sues, who once worked at the Smithsonian, calls the exhibit "one of the top three in the world."

Of the 45 dinosaurs on display, seven have the rare distinction of being "type" specimens, or the original fossils that paleontologists used to name a new species. In fact, the Smithsonian displays a higher percentage of type specimens than any major museum in the world.

Marsh's Trophies

The fossil exhibits trace their ancestry back to 1846, when Congress gave the Smithsonian Institution authority over something called the National Cabinet of Curiosities. The name was a holdover from the days when aristocrats owned elaborate wooden cabinets, in which they stored odd objects ranging from old bones to religious artifacts. The Smithsonian's fossil collection grew dramatically in the early 1900s, when the institution took possession of specimens collected by the famed dinosaur hunter Othniel Charles Marsh, partly as a result of his collecting wars with Edward Drinker Cope (p. 28).

Marsh's legacy still shines in Dinosaur Hall. As visitors work their way toward the back, they happen on one of the prizes collected by Marsh's men in Cañon City, Colorado, in 1883. An ebony-colored, 21-foot-long skeleton of *Allosaurus fragilis* stares down with a wide-open mouthful of daggerlike teeth. Something of a celebrity,

The world's only public display of *Ceratosaurus* (above), a horned carnivore from the late Jurassic, is a crown jewel of Smithsonian fossils.

The unmistakable profile of *Triceratops* (left) can be viewed at the museum's Dinosaur Hall.

Beaux Arts building (opposite, top) on Washington's Mall houses one of the world's top dinosaur collections.

Other reptiles (opposite, bottom) at the museum include the late Cretaceous sea turtle *Protostega*.

this specimen posed for the cover of humorist Gary Larson's *The Prehistory of the Far Side*.

Marsh's *Allosaurus* is considered the most complete currently on display anywhere in the world. More than just a collection of connected bones, the specimen provides powerful insight into the life of this Jurassic predator. Take a close look and compare the two shoulder blades. The left side has an unusual chunk of bone not seen on the right – a sign that the left shoulder broke and healed at some point in the dinosaur's life. The belly ribs were also all broken and healed (although these are not on display). "There are two scenarios we're working with," says Michael Brett-Surman, the Smithsonian's dinosaur specialist. "Either this *Allosaurus* was running and he fell on his left side and broke all his belly ribs and his left shoulder blade, or someone kicked the crap out of him."

Beside the *Allosaurus* is the familiar form of *Stegosaurus*. Made up of bones from 50 different animals, this composite skeleton has a subtle mistake. When the display was mounted early in the 20th century, paleontologists put 19 plates on its back. It was only with the subsequent

discovery of more fossils that they realized *Stegosaurus* had just 17 plates.

A papier-mâché restoration of *Stegosaurus* stands across the aisle from the fossil. A less conspicuous model of a tiny, shrewlike mammal peers out from beneath the car-sized dinosaur, and a glass case to the left displays an assortment of minuscule jawbones from Jurassic mammals, some no bigger than a dime.

Fans of *Stegosaurus* should walk around the center island to view a nearly complete skeleton, positioned on its side as it was found in the field. Brett-Surman calls this

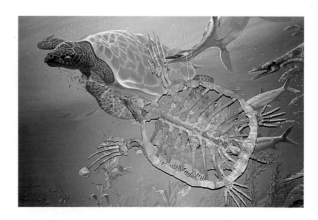

Mosasaurs (left) munched on marine mollusks like nautiloids and ammonites.

A preparator (below) works on *Coelophysis* fossils.

Forty-five dinosaurs (opposite, top) occupy the Smithsonian's gallery, but 87-foot-long *Diplodocus* stands out in the crowd.

Triceratops (opposite, bottom) may have used its horns for defense or in contests between rival males.

one of the crown jewels of the Smithsonian's dinosaur collection. Until recently, it was the most complete *Stegosaurus* known. Shown partly encased in rock, the specimen, nicknamed "the roadkill," gives some idea of how much work it takes to extricate a large dinosaur from the ground.

Next to the roadkill, visitors can spot another example of an ancient injury. The right hipbone of an ornithopod called *Camptosaurus* has a large hole, caused by an injury that never completely healed during the animal's lifetime. Major leg muscles would have originated from the damaged bone, so the injury must have impaired this dinosaur's ability to move.

One of a Kind

The second jewel of the collection lurks on the other side of the aisle from *Camptosaurus*. There, visitors can find a specimen of the late Jurassic species *Ceratosaurus*, a predatory dinosaur displayed nowhere else in the world. A theropod far more primitive than *Allosaurus* and *Tyrannosaurus*, *Ceratosaurus* had an unusual horn on its snout. The

Smithsonian's specimen of this animal has both a skeleton and a skull.

Nearby, another prize hangs against the wall. It's a specimen of *Corythosaurus*, a duckbilled dinosaur with a large bony crest on its head, as though it had been given a haircut in the "mohawk" style. The resemblance may be more than superficial. Experts think *Corythosaurus* and other crested hadrosaurs used their odd-shaped head ornaments to attract attention, particularly from members of the opposite sex. Curators cherish this specimen because impressions of the animal's skin are preserved between some of the tail vertebrae, something rarely seen with dinosaur fossils. Known as "the mummy," this fossil shows that *Corythosaurus* had skin with a scaly, pebbly texture.

The specimen of *Triceratops* next to *Corythosaurus* is a patchwork affair, composed of bones from many individuals. It harbors a secret mistake. When Charles W. Gilmore mounted the skeleton in 1905, he used the hind feet from a hadrosaur – like putting a pig's foot on the skeleton of a bull. Even if it had the right feet, the skeleton would still look a little funny by today's standards. The fossil was mounted at a time when paleontologists thought *Triceratops* had sprawling limbs, like those of a crocodile. Researchers now believe that this dinosaur, as well as most others, stood on erect limbs, rather like an elephant or rhinoceros.

Other outdated ideas show up in the giant *Diplodocus*, an 87-foot-long specimen put on display in 1931. Like most sauropods, *Diplodocus* was built like a suspension bridge, with a long neck and tail extending horizontally from its central trunk and pillar-shaped legs. The Smithsonian version has its tail draped on the ground, but researchers now think that pose is incorrect. "*Diplodocus* wouldn't have dragged its tail," says Brett-Surman. "If you're a dinosaur, especially in a herd, and you drag your tail, you've got a broken tail." In fact, the anatomy of the tail suggests that it went straight back.

Smithsonian curators are currently redesigning some of the mounts. Visitors can sometimes watch as the skeletons are taken apart and reconfigured.

Dinosaur cognoscenti may find some of the exhibit text a bit stale. The Smithsonian last renovated the hall in the early 1980s, and the explanatory panels hail from that era. But the dated descriptions don't subtract too much from the grandeur of these celebrated fossils, residents of an ancient world that transcend all time.

Carnegie Museum of Natural History
Pittsburgh, Pennsylvania

Carnegie Museum of Natural History, 4400 Forbes Avenue, Pittsburgh, PA 15213-4080; tel: 412-622-3131. Tuesday–Saturday, 10 A.M.–5 P.M.; Sunday, 1–5 P.M.; also open Monday in July and August. $

Pittsburgh's hospitals are renowned for organ transplants, but an equally noteworthy head transplant took place down the road in Dinosaur Hall at the **Carnegie Museum of Natural History**. For years after it was dug out of Jurassic rock in Utah in 1909, the most complete skeleton of an *Apatosaurus* ever found was displayed headless at the museum, because a skull found 12 feet from its neck was considered too small and wimpy for such a massive beast. To compound the indignity, it was capped with the wrong head for 40 years while the real head sat forgotten on a basement shelf.

This dinosaur alone is worth a visit to the Carnegie, where a spectacular parade of dinosaurs winds its way through the museum. The procession starts in the lobby with a *Tyrannosaurus rex* mounted in full run to greet visitors, whether busloads of schoolchildren or the Rolling Stones, who stopped in for a private tour when they played Pittsburgh some years ago. With more than 500 specimens from 28 different species, the Carnegie holds one of the largest collections of dinosaur bones in the United States, and the best collection of sauropods – the largest animals known to have walked on Earth.

Bronto Fever

With their long necks and tails, sauropods are familiar to most people. As you enter Dinosaur Hall, stunning sauropods stand single file before you in two columns. The old-fashioned exhibit dates to the end of the 19th century, when industrialist Andrew

Carnegie caught "bronto fever" and was swept up in the race to find the biggest and best dinosaurs for his beloved museum. One Sunday morning in November 1898, Carnegie's eye was caught by a headline in the *New York Journal*: "Most Colossal Animal Ever on Earth Just Found Out West!" The accompanying drawing showed a dinosaur peering into an eleventh-story window of the New York Life Building. Carnegie wanted the behemoth and fired off a note to museum director William J. Holland, instructing him to "Buy this for Pittsburgh." He enclosed a check for $10,000.

Holland immediately set out for Wyoming, where he soon learned that only a single bone of the colossus had been found. But within a year, in excavations in the Morrison Formation of Sheep Creek, Carnegie collectors found another dinosaur that met the philanthropist's standards – a huge *Diplodocus*, which at 84 feet long and 12 tons was one of the longest creatures to ever walk on Earth. Nicknamed "Dippy," it became an instant celebrity. Carnegie built a hall large enough to hold the skeleton and proudly sent casts of it to the British monarch and other European leaders.

Today, you can see the original of *Diplodocus carnegii* – actually a composite of bones from two individuals – in the middle of the left column in Dinosaur Hall. With peglike teeth, it was a plant eater that browsed on low-story vegetation some 120 million years ago.

Until his death in 1919, philanthropist Carnegie funded many dinosaur expeditions. Perhaps the most famous involved the discovery of the richest Jurassic dinosaur quarry, now part of Dinosaur National Monument in Utah, where most of the Carnegie's display skeletons were excavated. The first dinosaur dug out of the quarry was the headless *Apatosaurus*. Named *Apatosaurus louisae* for Carnegie's wife, Louise, it made headlines because at 76½ feet long and 35 tons, it was the longest, most complete specimen of its kind – with or without a head.

Now occupying the middle of the right-hand column, it looks like a buffed-out version of Dippy. Look at its brown, lizard-like head, the wimpy skull discovered near the neck in 1909. When Carnegie director Holland proposed that this small, reptilian skull with fragile, pencil-like teeth belonged on the massive body, other paleontologists scoffed. The prevailing view, put forth by leading dinosaur expert Othniel Charles Marsh and later popularized in movies like *King Kong*, was that brontosaurs like this had huge, boxy heads with large, crushing teeth used in aggressive attacks. Holland lacked the nerve to mount the small skull, so *Apatosaurus* remained sans skull for 17 years. After Holland's death, the skeleton received a cast of a boxy head with power-ful jaws (remarkably similar to that on its distant relative, the splendid *Camarasaurus*).

Forty years later, sauropod expert John McIntosh, of Wesleyan University, visited the Carnegie and reviewed Holland's records of the discovery. He learned of the lizard-like skull and realized that in the ensuing years it had been wrongly attributed to another species. With Carnegie paleontologist David S. Berman, McIntosh retrieved the head, and on October 20, 1979, skull and body were ceremoniously reunited. Similar transplants soon took place on *Apatosaurus* mounts in other museums, a century after Marsh had first placed the wrong head on his prize brontosaur at the Peabody Museum.

Sauropod expert Jack McIntosh admires the back end of the Carnegie's *Apatosaurus louisae*. McIntosh reattached the correct skull to the skeleton 70 years after it was excavated.

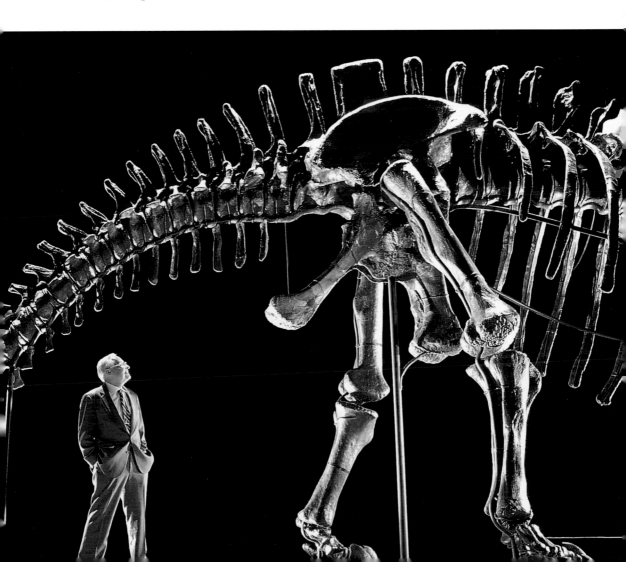

Second Thoughts

Paleontologists have also changed their minds about *Apatosaurus* being a nasty biter. Judging from the weak jaws of it and *Diplodocus*, these two sauropods more likely defended themselves with their power-packed whip tails. But the sturdy jaws of *Camarasaurus* appear much more able to have inflicted a memorable bite. Speaking of *Camarasaurus*, the Carnegie displays a spectacular specimen of it – in fact, the most complete sauropod skeleton ever found – a juvenile mounted on the right-hand wall just as it was found at the Dinosaur National Monument quarry.

As daunting as they are, these vegetarian gargantuas look tame beside the ultimate predator, the *Tyrannosaurus rex* that dominates the far end of the hall. Standing 20 feet tall, this skeleton, found by Barnum Brown in 1902, is the type specimen of the species (used for the initial scientific description of its kind). The story goes that Brown had been inspired to prospect near Hell Creek in eastern Montana by a fossil bone paperweight decorating the desk of New York Zoological Society Director William Hornaday. Apparently, Brown just had a hunch that Hell Creek was the right place to look.

To the right of *T. rex* is *Corythosaurus*, a duckbilled plant eater with tiny teeth. To the left is the skull of *Triceratops*, with its familiar bony frill and horns. *Protoceratops*, a smaller, Asian ancestor of *Triceratops*, rounds out the display.

While most of these specimens date to early Carnegie expeditions, curators continue to prepare fossils from more recent digs and sometimes do it on public view in a corner lab. The primitive dinosaur *Coelophysis*, for example, will soon join the display. An innovative addition is the first truly independent robot docent in any museum, a collaboration with robotics experts from Carnegie Mellon University. During a recent visit, a mob of four-year-olds surrounded the robot, but its video spiel about the life and death of dinosaurs also appeals to adults.

Allosaurus (left) was the top predator in Utah during the Jurassic. Many of the Carnegie's best specimens came from Utah's Dinosaur National Monument early in the 20th century.

A young visitor inspects a *Stegosaurus* (right). The museum's collection of more than 500 dinosaur specimens stems from the foresight and funding of patron Andrew Carnegie.

Cleveland Museum of Natural History
Cleveland, Ohio

Cleveland Museum of Natural History, 1 Wade Oval Drive, University Circle, Cleveland, OH 44106-1767; tel: 216-231-4600. Monday–Saturday, 10 A.M.–5 P.M.; Sunday 1–5:30 P.M. (open until 10 P.M. Wednesday, September–May). $

In 1954, the **Cleveland Museum of Natural History** was gearing up to move from a donated mansion to a new building near the city's cultural hub at University Circle. To capture visitors' imaginations in the hall devoted to past life, the museum's then director envisioned a dramatic display – a giant dinosaur.

So a field party was dispatched westward in search of dinosaur skeletons. Half of the team headed to Colorado, where they learned that a University of Louisiana crew had recently found a dinosaur fossil fragment. The university team generously gave the Cleveland group a map of their site near Cañon City, as well as the bone itself, which turned out to be part of the fourth cervical vertebra of a 70-foot-long *Haplocanthosaurus*.

Three more seasons of digging, mainly by a Yale undergraduate and his team of high school and college students, unearthed the enormous, 200-million-year-old sauropod. After being restored and mounted – minus the head, all but the first four vertebrae, and part of the tail – at the American Museum of Natural History, the 40-percent-complete specimen arrived in Cleveland to great fanfare in 1961. The museum had its showpiece, and "Happy" remains the primary example of its species in the world.

Discovering the Pygmy Tyrant

The other scientifically important specimen in the modest dinosaur displays of the Kirland Hall of Past Life is the world's only known fossil of *Nanotyrannus*. Found in Montana by a museum curator in 1942, the skull was first described as a new species of *Gorgosaurus* and later reclassified as an *Albertosaurus lancensis*. Some scientists even suggested that the small skull came from a juvenile *Tyrannosaurus rex*.

But in the late 1980s, yet another re-evaluation led paleontologists Robert Bakker, Mike Williams, and Phil Currie to conclude that the skull did indeed belong to a primitive tyrannosaurid, but from a new and separate genus. Among the skull's odd features are its wedge shape, narrow beak, and huge crest on top. They named it *Nanotyrannus*, or "pygmy tyrant," a sort of downsized *T. rex*, about the size of a polar bear. A recent CAT scan, which revealed an unusual feature of one skull bone not seen in other tyrannosaurs, bolstered the claim that this specimen was something different.

Also on display is a 20-foot-long *Anatosaurus*, a duckbilled dinosaur from the late Cretaceous Hell Creek Formation in eastern Montana, and a five-foot-long *Triceratops* skull from the same place and slice of time. Along with *Nanotyrannus*, both of these specimens were found during the 1942 field season. A composite *Allosaurus* from the Jurassic of Utah looms 20 feet high.

Behind the scenes, museum staff and volunteers are preparing for a display of a four-by-four-foot block full of *Coelophysis*. The rock contains at least a dozen articulated skeletons of the small primitive predator

that roamed the region of Ghost Ranch, New Mexico, about 225 million years ago.

Besides dinosaurs, the hall features skeletons of saber-toothed cats, a mammoth, and a mastodon. The museum also houses a major collection of fossil fish skeletons, particularly sharks and giant armor-headed fish from the Devonian Period (408 to 360 million years ago). Many of the bones came from the local Cleveland Shale, a rock formation that preserves an ancient shallow sea.

Bony plates (left) on the back of *Stegosaurus*, seen outside the Cleveland Museum, may have helped regulate body temperature by soaking up and radiating heat.

Unlike *T. rex*, *Allosaurus* (above) had powerful arms and three clawed fingers instead of two.

Prize specimen of Cleveland's collection, the world's only *Nanotyrannus* (right) resembles a scaled-down *T. rex*.

Field Museum of Natural History
Chicago, Illinois

Field Museum of Natural History, Lake Shore Drive at Roosevelt Road, Chicago, IL 60605; tel: 312-922-9410.
Daily, 9 A.M.–5 P.M. $

The Louvre has the Mona Lisa, the Smithsonian Institution has the Hope Diamond, and the **Field Museum**, as every fossil aficionado ought to know, has the most famous dinosaur in the world. When Sue the *Tyrannosaurus rex* went on the auction block at Sotheby's in New York in October 1997, the museum teamed up with McDonald's and Walt Disney World Resorts to place a winning bid of $8.4 million, thus scoring what they hope will be the fossil coup of the century.

At present, Sue is a dinosaur in the rough, still being readied for her (or maybe his: scientists aren't sure yet) debut in a new exhibition hall planned for the summer of 2000. Until then, visitors to the Field will be able to glimpse only bits and pieces of the First Fossil, but they can still enjoy all the museum's other dinosauriana, an up-to-date but not-too-glitzy display that gives a big-picture view of the Age of Dinosaurs.

The exhibit starts near the entrance in the cavernous Stanley Field Hall, where you can stroll between the femurs of a 40-foot-tall *Brachiosaurus*. The skeleton, actually a plastic-and-fiberglass model, is based in part on a specimen that the Field Museum's first paleontologist, Elmer Riggs, discovered in Colorado in the summer of 1900. The young, fossil-hungry museum had sent Riggs west to find the remains of a *Brontosaurus*, the largest dinosaur then known. Instead he brought back some-

thing even bigger. A true supergiant, *Brachiosaurus* remained the most massive land animal ever discovered until the 1970s, when it was edged out by more formidable beasts. Unfortunately, Riggs's skeleton was only 20 percent complete, too fragmentary to be put on display. So Riggs went west again, and within a year had unearthed the promised *Brontosaurus* (since renamed *Apatosaurus*). The *Brachiosaurus* model was unveiled at the Field's centennial celebration in 1993.

The next stop for a dino-tour is the museum's upper level. There, in the glass-walled McDonald's Preparation Laboratory, you can watch technicians painstakingly chipping fossils from the rocks with dental picks, air-powered engraving tools, and dabs of polyvinyl acetate, a bone-hardening acrylic. It's a paleontological *Truman Show* with every move visible. Preparators are working on chunks from the front half of Sue (the legs and tail are being prepared at a similar lab at Disney's Animal Kingdom in Orlando, Florida). Then they'll shift to other fossils from the Field's vast holdings.

A few steps away you enter the corridor leading to the main dinosaur display. To get there, though, you'll have to walk through another exhibit, one spanning more than three-and-a-half million millennia. *Life Over Time* gives a refresher course in the history of early life on Earth, starting with a reminder of the sheer vastness of prehistoric time (while a recorded chorus intones the names of the geologic eras) and continuing with the saga of the planet's changing life-forms, landforms, and climate. Even if you don't need to be reminded why DNA is important or precisely when plants colonized terra firma, it's worth pausing to drink in the shadowy serenity of a 300-million-year-old club-moss forest, or to watch one of the video screens that flickers to life as you pass. On the "LOT News," television newscasters, obviously relishing a chance for

Eraptor skull (opposite) is prepared for display; this early dinosaur, a carnivore, walked on two feet and was about the size of a large dog.

Albertosaurus (right) stands over a duckbilled *Lambeosaurus*, whose skeleton was found as intact as it appears in the exhibit.

self-parody, read evolutionary bulletins (including a heart-rending obituary for the trilobites) before signing off with a peppy, "Thanks for watching, and have a nice era." It's great fun and a good orientation to what follows.

Footsteps of the Giant Ones

What follows, of course, are the dinosaurs. You hear them before you see them: a pile-driver-like *Boom Boom Boom* of immense footsteps echoing throughout the 9,000 square feet of the Elizabeth Morse Genius Dinosaur Hall. The displays begin at the beginning, with one of the earliest known dinosaurs, *Herrerasaurus*, a 10-foot-long, 220-pound predator that topped the South American food chain 225 million years ago. The skeleton (another plastic replica; the real bones are in Argentina) and two life-like models at the Field Museum are the only mounted displays in the world.

Next, a ramped walkway takes you halfway round the room and down onto the main floor of the hall. On the left, a bank of small, colorful dioramas illustrate the perils of Mesozoic life. On the right loom the skeletons, real ones this time: a 72-foot-long *Apatosaurus* (the one Elmer Riggs dug up in 1901); a fearsome *Albertosaurus*, smaller cousin of *Tyrannosaurus*, hovering menacingly over a duckbilled

Lambeosaurus; a spiky-headed *Triceratops* (also found by Riggs) near its smaller ancestor *Protoceratops*; and another duckbilled herbivore, the crested *Parasaurolophus*. Behind them, on the far wall, hang two classic paintings by the famed dinosaur artist Charles Knight. In one, apatosaurs wallow in a Jurassic swamp; in the other, a *Triceratops* faces down a *Tyrannosaurus*.

If that sounds retro, never fear. A closer look shows that the hall is thoroughly modern – or even postmodern. For starters, it's hands-on. Press a button on the sign that names any dinosaur, and a child's voice pronounces the name for you, both genus and species. That's a godsend for parents faced with having to bluff their way through jawbreakers like *Herrerasaurus ishigualastensis* and *Parasaurolophus cyrtocristatus*. Speaking of *Parasaurolophus*, a bellows-operated device near its skeleton lets you blow horn solos, just as the animal itself may have done through the hollow bony crest on its head.

Sue's Saga

From Dakota badlands to downtown Chicago, the *Tyrannosaurus rex* named Sue has journeyed perhaps farther in the scientific and legal worlds than any other fossil. Sixty-five million years after the dinosaur died, she became the focus of a saga unprecedented in the world of natural history.

Sue's modern story began in August 1990, when an amateur paleontologist spotted her bones protruding from a hillside near Faith, South Dakota. Susan Hendrickson was prospecting for dinosaur fossils with her boyfriend, Peter Larson, who ran a local fossil-selling company. In the hillside she found him the present of a lifetime – two fragments of vertebrae that led to the most complete *T. rex* ever found.

Hendrickson and Larson soon broke up, but Sue – named for her discoverer – remained. Larson's Black Hills Institute of Geological Research in nearby Hill City picked the dinosaur out of the bluff. Larson gave Maurice Williams, the Sioux rancher who owned the land, a check for $5,000. The check's memo line read: "For theropod skeleton Sue."

But soon everybody knew that the dinosaur was worth a lot more. Two months after the discovery, the Cheyenne River Sioux tribe – to which Williams belonged – laid claim to the fossil. Eventually, enough people became agitated that the government got involved. In 1992, agents of the Federal Bureau of Investigation raided the Black Hills Institute and confiscated Sue. For the next five years, Sue's skeleton languished in custody while the courts decided her fate.

After much suing and countersuing, a U.S. district court ruled that the skeleton belonged to the government, which had held Williams's reservation land in trust. The $5,000 check was no longer valid, and Sue became the rancher's problem. He decided to sell her to the highest bidder.

Sue was auctioned at Sotheby's in New York in October 1997. The Field Museum of Chicago, with help from McDonald's and Disney corporations, bought her for more than $8 million, the highest price ever paid for a fossil. After a contest to rename the dinosaur, the museum stuck with "Sue." Scientists are cleaning and studying her skeleton and plan to display Sue soon. Her bones will finally rest in peace. – *Alexandra Witze*

Children protest (above) the government's seizure of Sue outside the Black Hills Institute in South Dakota.

Graceful curve of a sauropod's neck (right) parallels an archway in the Field's Elizabeth Morse Genius Dinosaur Hall.

model of a *Maiasaura* nest – an irresistible photo opportunity.

Just the Facts, Please

The captions are short but to the point. "What is a dinosaur?" one asks. The dead giveaways have to do with ankles and hip sockets. Prosaic details, yes, but once you learn them, you will look at dinosaur skeletons from a fresh perspective.

Some of the signs make sure you *don't* believe your eyes. "What is wrong with this picture?" inquires a caption to one of the Charles Knight paintings. What's wrong, it turns out, is evidence that *Apatosaurus* lived on dry land, not in swamps, and that *Triceratops* saved its fighting spirit for duels with other *Triceratops*. Alas, Knight's re-creations, so brilliant and stirring just a generation ago, are now fossils themselves, growing dustier by the day.

That kind of tell-all honesty can make it easy to miss just how impressive the exhibits really are. For example, a sign near

Other gadgets are pure kid stuff. "Sniff here for a whiff of *Albertosaurus* breath," invites a sign beside a small vent, adding that "permanent bad breath came from tiny fibers of rotting flesh clinging to its saw-edged teeth." (For all the hype, it's not as bad as a clogged drain.) Down on the main floor, children can touch fossilized dinosaur skin, straddle a five-foot-long *Argyrosaurus* thigh-bone, piece together a felt-board dino-puzzle, or crouch amid the eggs in a fiberglass

Parasaurolophus notes that the skeleton is incomplete because "we haven't filled in any missing pieces." It doesn't mention why. In fact, the skeleton is the official reference or type specimen for the species, its mounting specially designed so that workers could avoid drilling holes in the bones and scientists could remove them one by one for study. Similarly, the sign for the tableau of the hapless *Lambeosaurus* and hungry *Albertosaurus* takes pains to point out that the scene is staged: Though it could have happened as shown, this particular *Albertosaurus* did not, in fact, kill and eat this particular *Lambeosaurus* (whose skull, the sign adds, actually came from another *Lambeosaurus* specimen). What the sign leaves out is that the *Lambeosaurus* is a remarkable fossil. When it was discovered, the bones emerged from the rocks intact, connected, and almost complete – "a dinosaur on the half shell," in the words of the museum's chief dinosaur preparator, William Simpson, and a paleontologist's dream even without its head.

The hall also contains some non-dinosaur fossils, which get short shrift. *Pteranodon* skeletons dangle overhead, frozen in mid-flight – and all but frozen *out* of the captions. Beautifully prepared fossils of Mesozoic fish and marine reptiles, including a 10-foot-long mosasaur, haunt the sidelines in old-fashioned display cases, minimally labeled. Obviously the Field Museum knows who its stars are and is saving the limelight for surefire crowd-pleasers.

After the dinosaurs, a second *Life Over Time* corridor traces the rise of mammals up to the present day. The highlight is another child magnet, a mammoth-bone hut from a 15,000-year-old Ukrainian village. Finally, an exit takes you through a Dinostore stocked with the usual saurian tchotchkes, but

you'll find higher-end stuff in the museum store downstairs.

In sum, the Field Museum's dinosaur displays are fun, fresh, and child-friendly. You can easily see everything in one leisurely visit without suffering the "zone out" you'd get from a bigger, more detailed exhibition. On the downside, once you see it, you've seen it all. Until Sue opens, at any rate, one visit should be enough for adults, unless those adults have children eager for another game of hide-and-seek inside the mammoth-bone hut.

One tip: Go in the morning, especially in summer. The Field Museum shares a parking lot with several other nearby attractions, and spaces near the entrance disappear quickly. Latecomers may face a long, hot walk.

Fort Worth Museum of Science and History
Fort Worth, Texas

Fort Worth Museum of Science and History, 1501 Montgomery Street, Fort Worth, TX 76107; tel: 817-732-1631. Monday, 9 A.M.–5 P.M.; Tuesday–Thursday, 9 A.M.–8 P.M.; Friday–Saturday, 9 A.M.–9 P.M.; Sunday, noon–9 P.M. $ See Resource Directory for listings of other Texas museums.

Of the hundreds of thousands of passengers who fly through the Dallas/Fort Worth International Airport every year, few recognize that the flat, mostly featureless landscape of central Texas is actually a rich repository of dinosaur bones. Probably no one knows it

as well as Louis Jacobs, a paleontologist at Southern Methodist University in Dallas and author of two books about dinosaurs in the Lone Star State.

You don't have to be a professional paleontologist to appreciate Texas dinosaurs. Instead, just visit a few museums in north Texas, where many of the state's dinosaurs come from.

At the **Fort Worth Museum of Science and History**, you can wander through the *Lone Star Dinosaurs* exhibit to learn about the area's rich dinosaurian past. Here, for example, are fossil bones of *Pleurocoelus* and *Acrocanthosaurus*, the two giants whose footprints are preserved in the famous trackways at **Dinosaur Valley State Park** near **Glen Rose**. Be sure to look for the *Pleurocoelus'* three-foot-long humerus, or upper arm bone, to understand how big this creature really was. The *Acrocanthosaurus* bones, including a femur and tail vertebra, come from a skeleton recently found near Fort Worth.

The exhibit also features a skeleton of *Tenontosaurus dossi*, a previously unknown dinosaur species found west of Fort Worth by seven-year-old Thad Williams. This herbivore browsed on four legs but could probably run on its hind legs when pursued. Its hornlike beak allowed it to crop the ferns, cycads, and pine relatives that covered north Texas about 113 million years ago.

Other notable finds in the exhibit are the bones of a baby

Abundant herbivore *Tenontosaurus* (opposite, top) watches some of its distant cousins, the hypsilophodonts, gambol past in Karen Carr's painting from the Fort Worth Museum.

Seventy-foot *Diplodocus* (left), along with a duckbill and other dinosaurs, fills the main hall of the Houston Museum of Natural Science.

Horned dinosaurs (opposite, bottom) were among the last to appear before the K-T extinction.

nodosaur, discovered locally by 12-year-old Johnny Maurice, and a cast of a hadrosaur skull, also found nearby, which may be the oldest known in North America. You'll also see partial skeletons of tiny, plant-eating hypsilophodonts; descriptions of the youngest Texas dinosaurs, those in **Big Bend National Park**; and a dramatic attack scene between an *Allosaurus* and a *Camptosaurus* from Utah.

The exhibit features kid-friendly activities, too, such as the "color-a-dinosaur" on a video touchscreen, an interactive dinosaur quiz, and an "Ask Dr. Jacobs" section. There are dinosaur bones to touch and footprints to sit in. Outside the museum, a DinoDig lets children search for fossils and bones buried in sand. Adults can appreciate the 10 original paintings by artist Karen Carr, from baby nodosaurs being swept away in a flood to the dramatic confrontation at Glen Rose. All exhibit text is in Spanish, too.

Texas Dinosaur Circuit

The **Dallas Museum of Natural History** displays additional Texas fossils. Major skeletal casts include another *Tenontosaurus*, a 32-foot-long mosasaur, or marine reptile, and a *Protostega*, the second-largest sea turtle fossil in the world. There are also a number of fossil fish, among them a large and fierce-looking *Pachyrhizodus*, found in the Dallas area, and a big collection of ammonites. The sauropod *Alamosaurus* from the Big Bend region of West Texas and another skeleton of a hypsilophodont are new discoveries that will be displayed soon.

Other good fossil exhibits can be found at the **Texas Memorial Museum** in **Austin** and the **Shuler Museum of Paleontology** on the campus of Southern Methodist University in **Dallas**, repository of one of the world's top collections of Lower Cretaceous vertebrates. The **Houston Museum of Natural Science** houses a cast of *T. rex* dramatically attacking a duck-billed *Edmontosaurus*, and **Texas Tech University** in **Lubbock** displays the oldest dinosaurs in Texas, from the Panhandle region.

New Mexico Museum of Natural History
Albuquerque, New Mexico

New Mexico Museum of Natural History,
1801 Mountain Road NW, Albuquerque,
NM 87104; tel: 505-841-2800.
Daily, 9 A.M.–5 P.M. $

New Mexico's picturesque mountains conceal a great treasure: the rich variety of dinosaurs buried in their rocks. For the best overview of the state's paleontological history, visit the **New Mexico Museum of Natural History** in **Albuquerque**.

Even before you enter the building, you can tell that New Mexicans take pride in their land's ancient past. Outside stand two life-sized bronze sculptures, one of *Pentaceratops* – a horned dinosaur nicknamed "Spike," whose remains have been found only in

New Mexico – and another depicting *Albertosaurus*, whose isolated teeth and bones have also been found in the state. Once inside the museum's lobby, you are confronted by a life-sized sculpture of the state's official fossil, the small, carnivorous *Coelophysis*.

The museum is laid out as a "walk through time" progressing from the formation of the solar system to the last Ice Age. You start your journey on the second floor in the Origins section, which describes how the solar system and Earth were formed. There, you also learn about New Mexico's oldest rocks, dating back 1.8 billion years, and the earliest trilobite fossils in the state.

Dinosaurs take over when the exhibit reaches the *Age of Giants*. The exhibit features three major skeletal casts: the stout sauropod *Camarasaurus*, the two-legged meat eater *Allosaurus*, and the spiny *Stegosaurus*. Also here are some vertebrae and a partial femur from *Seismosaurus*, perhaps the longest dinosaur ever discovered; it was found near San Ysidro, New Mexico, in 1979. A team led by the museum dug up

NEW MEXICO MUSEUM OF NATURAL HISTORY

Bronze *Albertosaurus* (opposite) looms just outside the museum entrance. Better known from Canada, this carnivore's bones have also been found in New Mexico.

The *Age of Dinosaurs* exhibit (left) includes skeleton casts of *Stegosaurus, Allosaurus,* and *Camarasaurus.*

***Seismosaurus* bones** are encased in stone (below); it may take up to 10 years to prepare them for study and

a partial skeleton of *Seismosaurus* that measured nearly 100 feet long.

From Coast to Volcanoes

Next you step into New Mexico's Seacoast, a hall showcasing some of the marine and shoreline life from the Cretaceous as well as the period's dinosaurs. There's a life-sized model of a mosasaur, a reptile that swam the seas 75 million years ago, and replicas of plants that lived at the time. Other exhibits display fragments of dinosaur eggs, including the oldest known egg of a meat-eating dinosaur, found near Albuquerque by three-year-old David Shiffler. You also see fossilized impressions of dinosaur skin; the only jaw of a *Tyrannosaurus rex* found in the state; a cast of the *T. rex* skull from the American Museum of Natural History in New York; and the skull of a duckbilled dinosaur that may bear marks of an attack by an *Albertosaurus.*

From the seacoast hall, take the Evolator, which simulates an elevator ride through 38 million years of geological history in just six minutes. Downstairs, the final dinosaur exhibit is a fossil preparation lab, where you can watch volunteers chip more bones of *Seismosaurus* out of blocks of stone. Eventually, these bones will be assembled

into a new permanent exhibit of this one-of-a-kind dinosaur. The preparators sometimes come out from behind the huge windows to answer questions. An interactive exhibit near the fossil lab replicates the booming sound that *Parasaurolophus* dinosaurs may have made with the resonating crests on their heads.

The rest of the journey through time takes you through the *Age of Volcanoes*, the Tertiary Period, when great eruptions covered much of the New Mexican landscape after the dinosaurs had disappeared. *Evolving Grasslands* describes how different plants began to spread across the landscape during the same period. Finally, you travel through a Pleistocene cave and enter the last Ice Age, inhabited by a 10,000-year-old mammoth from Tucumcari and the camel-like *Camelops*, a 40,000-year-old creature found in a sand and gravel mine within Albuquerque's city limits.

Ruth Hall Museum of Paleontology

Abiquiu, New Mexico

Ruth Hall Museum of Paleontology, Ghost Ranch Conference Center, HC 77 Box 11, Abiquiu, NM 87510-9601; tel: 505-685-4333. Tuesday–Saturday, 9 A.M.–5 P.M.; Sunday, 10 A.M.–5 P.M. $ (suggested donation)

Sometimes a museum has a star exhibit, but rarely is the exhibit so big that the museum must be built around it. Such is the case with the **Ruth Hall Museum of Paleontology** at **Ghost Ranch, New Mexico**. It showcases an eight-ton block of *Coelophysis* fossils frozen in rock. To paleontologists, Ghost Ranch is a Mesozoic mother lode. More than a thousand individuals of the small, meat-eating *Coelophysis* pepper the rock here, near **Abiquiu**, about 65 miles northwest of Santa Fe.

The rugged, multicolored hills around Ghost Ranch inspired artist Georgia O'Keeffe, who lived nearby, to paint some of her best work. The same hills inspire paleontologists as they uncover one of the oldest and richest concentrations of dinosaur fossils in the world.

Ghost Ranch rocks contain bones from more than a thousand small *Coelophysis* dinosaurs. This skull (above) is the smallest found so far.

Fossil foot and leg surround several *Coelophysis* neck bones (right). Young and old individuals perished together in large numbers.

The story began in 1881. Daniel Baldwin, a collector, found a few fragmentary bones from the Ghost Ranch area and sent them to his boss, Edward Drinker Cope, of the Academy of Natural Sciences in Philadelphia. (Baldwin once worked for Cope's archrival, O. C. Marsh, but quit when Marsh didn't pay him.) Cope studied the hollow leg bones and designated them a new species, *Coelophysis bauri*, after another of Marsh's assistants, George Baur – perhaps because he thought his rival should give more credit to his overworked assistants.

Seventy years later, those reports caught the eye of Edwin Colbert, curator at the American Museum of Natural History in New York. On a trip to prospect fossils farther west, his team stopped in Ghost Ranch in 1947, planning to stay a few days. Impressed by the bounty of bones, they stayed for two summers, chiseling out blocks of rocks filled with *Coelophysis* and shipping them to New York. In the 1980s, paleontologists went back into the quarry and carved out more blocks, including the one that became the museum's centerpiece. Visitors can see the unmarked quarry on the **Kitchen Mesa Trail** that leads into the hills behind the ranch.

Inside a Ghost Ranch Block

The Ruth Hall Museum, named after a local advocate for fossil preservation, occupies just one room next to a small anthropology museum. Visitors can watch fossil preparators chip away at the giant block, which fills the middle of the room. Surrounding it are exhibits describing the geology of the Chinle Formation and the Ghost Ranch discovery. There are casts of an articulated *Coelophysis* skeleton and several skulls, plus a life-sized, 10-foot-long model of what the creature looked like. One exhibit compares a chevron bone from the tail of *Coelophysis* with the same bone in the 100-foot-long *Seismosaurus*.

Other local fossils on display include a cast skeleton of a phytosaur, a long crocodile-looking creature; a microsaur skull only the size of a thumb, and bones from the small crocodilian *Hesperosuchus*. Paleontologists are digging out remains of a new crocodile-like species – a four-foot-long beast protected by more than 500 armored plates – from the giant block of bones.

The Ghost Ranch *Coelophysis* have raised new questions about dinosaur behavior. Why

Red beds (above) of the Triassic Chinle Formation contain *Coelophysis* fossils. Younger Jurassic and Cretaceous sediments also occur at Ghost Ranch.

Paleontologist Lynett Gillette (left) works on the eight-ton block of stone and fossils that forms the museum's central display.

were so many of these creatures in the same place? Carnivores like *Coelophysis* don't usually flock together because of the difficulties of finding enough prey. Colbert and others have suggested that they gathered for a fish-feeding frenzy and that a flash flood swept them away and covered their bodies in silt.

Ghost Ranch also reveals a grimmer side of *Coelophysis* – that it may have been a cannibal. Two of the creatures, now in the American Museum of Natural History, were found with the remnants of baby *Coelophysis* in their stomachs.

Museum of Northern Arizona
Flagstaff, Arizona

Museum of Northern Arizona, 3001 North Fort Valley Road, Flagstaff, AZ 86001; tel: 520-774-5211.
Daily, 9 A.M.–5 P.M. $

The **Colorado Plateau** rises like a great block of stone in the Four Corners region of the Southwest. The plateau is composed of sedimentary layers deposited and compressed into solid rock over hundreds of millions of years and then heaved straight up by the collision of continental plates. Water and wind have sculpted the rock into a dreamscape of canyons, mesas, spires, and arches, and exposed the plateau's geologic history. Within 75 miles of Flagstaff, Arizona, visible rocks date from a thousand to 1.7 billion years old; no place on Earth presents a more accessible and vast span of geologic time.

This arid land, where vegetation scarcely obscures the cliffs and flats, also bares its bones. Fossils found in the plateau's sedimentary storehouse have given paleontologists an excellent idea of what grew, swam, and walked here. And important portions of that record are preserved and displayed at the **Museum of Northern Arizona**, whose researchers have played a primary role in illuminating the region's ancient past.

Grand Canyon Tour

A tour of the museum's geology gallery begins, figuratively speaking, before creatures walked on land. In the depths of the Grand Canyon, rocks 1.2 billion years old bear impressions of stromatolites, microbial communities that to this day form moundlike structures in warm, saline waters. In the past, they lived in shallow marine environments, giving off oxygen that helped create the modern atmosphere before other life-forms evolved.

The exhibits then follow the march of evolution through the rock strata of the Grand Canyon, starting with trilobites and brachiopods, club mosses and conifers,

Pentaceratops is represented at the museum by this lower jaw (above). It is known only from New Mexico's San Juan Basin.

Three *Coelophysis* (left) forage on the Colorado Plateau in the early Triassic.

Coelophysis cast (opposite, top) strikes the classic dinosaur death posture that occurs when neck ligaments tighten.

Five-foot femur (opposite, bottom) of a hadrosaur comes from the New Mexican portion of the Colorado Plateau.

scorpion and reptile tracks, and finally a large shark tooth from the white Kaibab limestone at the rim of the canyon.

You'll find a fair collection of dinosaur fossils, too. A few are regional specialties, such as a mounted reconstruction of a *Dilophosaurus* skeleton 10 feet high and 12 feet long. Found only in northern Arizona, this imposing, early Jurassic predator sports two long bony crests atop its skull. Another local is *Scuttelosaurus*, a small herbivore whose skeleton was found in the Painted Desert northeast of Flagstaff. Heavily armored with bony scales, it could run on two legs but probably preferred to walk on four. Two skulls depict the early dinosaur *Coelophysis*, which has been found at several sites in the region.

More recent dinosaur fossils come from other parts of the Colorado Plateau, most notably upper Cretaceous deposits in the San Juan Basin of northwest New Mexico. The most striking is the five-foot-long femur of a duckbilled dinosaur, a huge herbivore that probably used its wide-flanged lower jaw to strain vegetation from ponds and streams as dabbling ducks do today. Beside it are relics of other giants: the two-foot-long jaw of a ceratopsian and the three-inch-long, serrated tooth of a tyrannosaur.

The age of large beasts did not end with dinosaurs. Fossil bones and teeth of Pleistocene ground sloths, mammoths, and mastodons reveal that animals far larger than today's lived here even after humans arrived. Nearby, the museum's other galleries show how people both ancient and modern have reacted to the stark and scenic landscapes of the Colorado Plateau.

Denver Museum of Natural History
Denver, Colorado

Denver Museum of Natural History, 2001 Colorado Boulevard, Denver, CO 80205-5798; tel: 303-322-7009. Daily, 10 A.M.–5 P.M. (9 A.M.–7 P.M. in summer). $

A large foot poised above your head, about to stomp you flat, is the first thing you see when you enter the **Denver Museum of Natural History**. Your eye naturally follows the foot up to a bony leg, a boatlike ribcage, and then a gaping cavern rimmed with stiletto-like teeth. You are gazing into the gullet of a towering *Tyrannosaurus rex*.

At first glance, he seems frozen at the moment of attack. Then it becomes clear that this is really a theatrical moment. Standing on one leg almost on tiptoes, this 40-foot-long beast is nothing less than a *T. rex* Rockette caught in a chorus-line kick.

Dancing *T. rex* notwithstanding, no dinotainment complex awaits in the exhibits upstairs. You'll find no herky-jerky animatronic dinosaurs in the Denver Museum of

Natural History's *Prehistoric Journey*. Neither will you find the all-bones-all-the-time approach of New York's American Museum of Natural History. *Prehistoric Journey* strikes a happy medium between these extremes.

For sure, there is a diorama with dueling, bear-sized *Stygimoloch* dinosaurs in all their simulated, fleshy glory. There are also plenty of authentic fossil dinosaur bones, including magnificent adult and juvenile *Stegosaurus* skeletons being attacked by an *Allosaurus*, and a *Diplodocus*, whose 50-foot whip tail – more than half the animal's length – curves around much of the gallery space.

Welcome Realism

The defining characteristic of *Prehistoric Journey*, however, is the compelling re-creation of ancient environments. Each one depicts a real place, reconstructed by museum curators from geological and paleontological evidence. A case beside each diorama contains a photograph of the site as it looks today with captions pointing out the relevant geology, as well as fossils from the site (or a similar one) that guided curators in picking the vegetation and animals for the diorama.

The first walk-through diorama deposits visitors in a late Cretaceous forest complete with a real babbling brook. Two bony-headed *Stygimoloch* males, their heads bristling with spiky horns, battle each other for the attention of a female that can be seen deep in the forest. Just as impressive as the dinosaurs is the forest itself, reproduced with breathtaking realism and scientific accuracy. Seven models of broadleaf trees form the canopy. A wrap-around mural and the sounds of buzzing insects and grunting animals complete the illusion. Linger long enough and you'll hear a loud crack-ing and crunching to the right. Look in that direction and you'll meet the orange-eyed gaze of a well-camouflaged *T. rex*. At the diorama's exit is a

case displaying a fossil log from the Cretaceous, its grain so well preserved that it looks as if you could cut this six-foot log into sections and throw it into the fireplace.

The exhibit hall then opens up into a large space housing a host of complete skeletons, many consisting largely of real fossil bone. Among the most impressive are five dog-sized juvenile *Othnielia* dinosaurs running in a pack, all abreast. One looks back over its right shoulder at *Allosaurus*.

At the end of the dinosaur exhibit is another of the subtle but compelling artifacts that make a visit to the museum particularly rewarding. It doesn't look like much, but this four-inch-long piece of layered rock records evidence of a momentous event: the mass extinction 65 million years ago in which the dinosaurs perished. An actual segment of the famous Cretaceous–Tertiary, or K–T, boundary, the rock contains iridium and bits of shocked quartz from the impact of the massive asteroid or comet now strongly implicated in the dinosaurs' deaths.

A final diorama displays a lemurlike primate with a baby clinging to her back in the jungle canopy of Eocene Wyoming. If the tyrannosaur at the museum's entrance is caught in a dance of death, this primate of 50 million years ago is frozen in a symbolic leap from a tree limb into the future. Millions of years later, her descendants will evolve the ability (and sense of irony) to dig up a *T. rex* skeleton, cast it in high-tech materials, and pose it like a member of the Rockettes.

Allosaurus lunges at *Stegosaurus* (opposite, top) as the relatively small herbivore, *Othnielia*, looks on. All three creatures lived in western North America during the late Jurassic.

Fossil evidence suggests that duckbilled dinosaurs (opposite, bottom) walked on four legs with their rigid tails outstretched.

A T. Rex in an active pose (right) greets visitors entering the Denver Museum of Natural History.

Fossils in the rough are cleaned and displayed in the preparation laboratory (above).

Dinosaur Valley Museum
Grand Junction, Colorado

Dinosaur Valley Museum, 4th and Main Streets, Grand Junction, CO 81501; tel: 970-241-9210.
Monday–Saturday, 9 A.M.–5 P.M., and Sunday, 9 A.M.–4 P.M., April 1–September 30; Tuesday–Sunday, 10 A.M.–4 P.M., October 1–March 31. $

Grand Junction, Colorado, may be the only place where a sidewalk stroll includes a peek at people exposing dinosaur bones in a store-front window. The sight will likely stop you in your tracks, if you haven't already spotted the rusted metal *Dimetrodon* sculpture out front or the turquoise head and torso of *Allosaurus* bursting through a plaster wall.

One of three branches of the Museum of Western Colorado, **Dinosaur Valley Museum** opened in 1985 in a vacant department store.

Beyond its otherwise unassuming entrance, this museum packs plenty of informative and innovative displays into a compact space. Exhibits here run the gamut from bare bones to rumbling robot dinosaurs in the flesh – something for every taste and age group.

Youngsters should head straight to the popular Kids' Quarry. Instead of unconvincing plaster copies, junior paleontologists get to play with real bones – big ones. The 10-foot-wide pit contains crushed walnut shells that can be brushed away with whisk brooms to uncover any of a dozen sauropod fossils. Children can match each bone with its numbered outline on a map to the site, then find the corresponding number on a chart of a sauropod skeleton.

The museum's curator of paleontology, Rod Scheetz, believes that visitors should be able to see and touch actual fossils. Hands-on bones include a hadrosaur femur and the humerus from an adult *Camarasaurus* and juvenile *Apatosaurus*. Other bone displays have points to make about size and growth. A series of thighbones from seven different

dinosaurs spans the range from a three-inch-long *Dryosaurus* bone to the five-foot *Apatosaurus* version. Casts of thighbones and unguals, or claws, of *Allosaurus* from Utah's Cleveland-Lloyd Dinosaur Quarry vividly show some of the dozens of allosaurs entombed at this unique site.

Local Discoveries

Colorado's state fossil, *Stegosaurus*, shows up as a complete mounted skeleton; its body armor, a pointed dorsal plate and tail spikes, are still framed by the plaster field jackets. A young hadrosaur is another local find. The beast's humerus, tibia, braincase, vertebra, and skull fragments were uncovered in the **Book Cliffs**, which form a scenic backdrop to Grand Junction. The cliffs are composed of Mancos Formation shale, remnants of a Cretaceous ocean. Researchers speculate that the dinosaur carcass was swept out to sea and promptly buried.

Other specimens, including the Kids' Quarry bones and an *Apatosaurus* pubis and tailbone bearing deep gashes from the teeth of an *Allosaurus*, come from the **Mygatt-Moore Quarry** west of town, where the museum sponsors day digs for anyone who wants to try dinosaur hunting. Trained volunteers also staff the fossil preparation lab, but anyone can try out an air-powered chisel in an adjacent case and grind away on a block of rock.

A new exhibit features discoveries made during ongoing excavation at the **Dalton Wells Quarry** near **Moab**, Utah. Abundant bones from eight kinds of early Cretaceous dinosaurs, including a pair of previously unknown sauropods and the formidable carnivore *Utahraptor*, have already been found there.

A complete skeleton of a recently discovered kind of armored ankylosaur, *Gastonia burgei*, sporting spikes and scutes, is a highlight of this display.

A few moving, rubber robot dinosaurs can be found here. Made by Dinamation, which runs its own **Dinosaur Discovery Museum** in nearby **Fruita**, they include the usual suspects: *Tyrannosaurus*, *Triceratops*, *Apatosaurus*, and *Stegosaurus*, plus a *Pachycephalosaurus* stripped to its steel skeleton except for head, hands, and feet.

The museum's innovative approach keeps you wondering what lies around the next bend. It's a bit like prospecting for fossils. You're never quite sure what you'll find next.

A combination of traditional mounted skeletons (left) and kid-friendly exhibits appeals to the young and the old alike.

Fleshed-out reconstructions (above) and rumbling robot dinosaurs add color and movement to the displays of bare bones.

Green River Formation fossils include an exquisitely preserved turtle (right), fish, alligator, crayfish, and crickets. One rock slab contains hundreds of herring.

The Dinosaur Museum
Blanding, Utah

The Dinosaur Museum, 754 South 200 West, Blanding, UT 84511; tel: 435-678-3454.
Monday–Saturday, 9 A.M.–5 P.M., April 15–October 15 (until 9 P.M. in summer, closed in winter). $

Sculpting extinct animals is both an art and a science. Though a fine artist's talent and sense of style are required to create compelling work, the sculptor must also adhere to strict rules of anatomy. When the sculpture is destined for a museum of natural history, there's scant room for guesswork. Since no live models are available, dinosaur sculptors look to the nuances of bone structure for clues about body proportion and posture.

Stephen and Sylvia Czerkas are regarded as two of the foremost dinosaur artists in the business today. Their life-size and lifelike creations grace the halls of fine institutions across the country, including the Natural History Museum of Los Angeles County, California Academy of Sciences, and Philadelphia's Academy of Natural Sciences, to name just a few. In 1995, the couple founded a small but excellent **Dinosaur Museum** in their adopted hometown of **Blanding, Utah**. It was a particularly fortuitous choice of location: As it happens, an important Permian fossil site is located nearby, and its rare (and huge) petrified logs, 275 million years old, form an integral part of the museum's collection.

Re-creation through Time

The museum's three major galleries (a fourth is in the works) trace the evolution of dinosaurs. The collection ranges from the skeleton of an Argentine *Herrerasaurus*, which, at 225 million years old, is among the earliest dinosaurs, to that of a large Mongolian tyrannosaur, *Tarbosaurus*, which lived during the late Cretaceous not long before the dinosaurs died out. The *Tarbosaurus* is shown fleeing the deadly grasp of a fearsome *Deinocheirus*, whose clawed, eight-foot arms and shoulder blades are suspended in midair. The museum also does a good job of showing how our understanding of dinosaurs has changed over time. A series of antique etchings, models, and books contrasts outmoded ideas of dinosaurs as sluggish, plodding reptiles with a modern view of them as dynamic, fast-moving creatures that cared for their young.

This contemporary perspective comes across clearly in the Czerkas's own sculptures. A huge *Allosaurus* in the main gallery, painted in woodland camouflage colors, seems ready to lunge off its platform; maiasaur nestlings evoke an image of maternal care. In a back gallery, the skull of an *Albertosaurus*, a large North American carnivore, is bare bone on one side; the other side was sculpted by Stephen Czerkas to show muscle and skin. Accompanied by photographs that illustrate the sculpting process, this is a graphic demonstration of how artists and paleontologists manage to put flesh on often fragmentary fossils.

Other exhibits emphasize how the current understanding of dinosaurs has arisen out of recent discoveries. Rare fossilized impressions of dinosaur skin, on display in one case, enable sculptors to clad their creations accurately. A display of fossil eggs from Montana and Mongolia illustrates how scientists have come to reinterpret dinosaur reproduction and child rearing. One entire room is devoted to the topic of fossil tracks, a fascinating branch of paleontology that has revolutionized our knowledge of dinosaur behavior.

The Czerkases have also delved into popular culture. A long hallway that bisects the museum is lined with posters from every imaginable dinosaur movie, from *The Lost World* to *Jurassic Park*. The posters serve as a reminder that dinosaurs are not only extinct animals from the dim recesses of time. They're part of the human psyche as well.

Dinosaur artists Sylvia and Stephen Czerkas, with their depiction of *Carnotaurus*.

Earth Science Museum
Provo, Utah

Brigham Young University, Earth Science Museum, 1683 North Canyon Road, Provo, UT 84602; tel: 435-378-3680. Monday, 9 A.M.–9 P.M.; Tuesday–Friday, 9 A.M.–5 P.M.; Saturday, noon–4 P.M. $

At first glance, the single, L-shaped room housing the public exhibits in Brigham Young University's **Earth Science Museum** might not promise to hold one's attention for long, but a closer look reveals some pretty special specimens. Your gaze will surely be drawn to that seemingly ubiquitous Utahan dinosaur diorama: the conflict between *Allosaurus* and *Camptosaurus*. Here the tableau has been handled with artful athleticism. The *Allosaurus* skeleton, spanning the length of a teardrop-shaped pedestal, turns sharply to the left in pursuit of the prey, poised as if ready to leap off the diorama.

This dynamic display was designed by

"Dinosaur Jim" Jensen, a legendary bone hunter rarely photographed without his pith helmet. Jensen's career contributed greatly to the museum's collections, and much of an estimated 130 tons of jacketed dinosaur bones he and colleagues dug up still resides beneath the nearby football stadium. His greatest fame, perhaps, came with the discovery of two gargantuan dinosaurs at **Dry Mesa Quarry** in Colorado: *Supersaurus* and *Ultrasauros*. Though paleontologists now tend to regard the latter as an especially large specimen of the sauropod *Brachiosaurus*, you can still gawk at the cast of the nine-foot-long scapula-coracoid bone that led Jensen to name the new genus in 1979. Then turn around and compare this immense bone with the shoulder blade on *Allosaurus*.

A huge painting nearby depicts a quartet of *Ultrasauros* wading across a shallow swamp. *Supersaurus*, *Apatosaurus*, and smaller sauropods also enter the busy scene, filled with other dinosaurs, reptiles, and mammals in a lush setting of ferns, cycads, and conifers.

Beside the *Ultrasauros* specimen is a massive *Brachiosaurus* arm bone that's also a cast – well, mostly. The actual fossil resides in Washington, D.C., at the Smithsonian Institution, but Jensen and current curator Ken Stadtman returned to where it had been found and located the missing piece, a muscle-anchoring ridge called the deltoid crest. They attached this part to their cast, which is now more complete than the original bone.

Fossil Rareties

An intriguing original fossil is the only known specimen of *Diceratops hatcheri*, a horned dinosaur that lacks the nose horn of its more common cousin, *Triceratops*. The six-foot skull was found in Wyoming in 1891, and since then some have said it's just a weird-looking example of *Triceratops*. Other experts see enough distinctive features, such as the thin-walled braincase, to warrant keeping the singular specimen in its own genus.

Be sure to step into the gift shop, if only to view the case that contains a rare chunk

The nine-foot shoulder blade (opposite) of *Ultrasauros*, perched atop a reconstruction of how the leg might have looked, is one of the museum's most extraordinary specimens.

Tons of dinosaur bones (left) stored beneath the neighboring football stadium are still encased in plaster field jackets.

A *Stegosaurus* skeleton (below) found in 1997 is a virtually complete specimen.

of duckbilled dinosaur skin. Found in eastern Utah, the fossil preserves the pebbly, ridged texture of the skin as well as exposing in cross-section the muscle tendons and tailbones.

The real prize of this museum, though, consists of what most visitors cannot see. Rows of shelves stacked floor to ceiling hold a comprehensive collection of Jurassic dinosaur fossils. Highlights include the massive vertebrae, pelvis, and limb bones of *Supersaurus*, remains of three species of sauropod calves from the **Cactus Park Quarry**, and much of the jet-black *Allosaurus* bones and an aborted allosaur egg from the **Cleveland-Lloyd Quarry**. (A cast of the egg appears in the exhibit hall, alongside examples of normal and diseased allosaur toe, arm, and back bones.)

Another curious carnivore in the collection is *Torvosaurus* from Dry Mesa, which combined the puny forearms of a tyrannosaur with even bulkier upper arms than *Allosaurus*. The museum hopes to mount a skeleton of this imposing beast, which would be the only one in the world.

Utah Museum of Natural History
Salt Lake City, Utah

Utah Museum of Natural History, President's Circle at University Street, University of Utah, Salt Lake City, UT 84112; tel: 801-581-4303.
Monday–Saturday, 9:30 A.M.–5:30 P.M.; Sunday and holidays, noon–5 P.M. $

It's hard to avoid the state fossil, *Allosaurus*, at the **Utah Museum of Natural History**. Behind the ticket counter, a near-life-sized model extends its claws and flashes green eyes. Toss two bits into the gaping jaws and he talks: "My name is Al. What's yours?"

Not too intimidating, perhaps, but upstairs in the Earth Science Hall, a pair of allosaurs torment a poor, plant-eating *Camptosaurus* lured from its nest of eggs and hatchlings. The larger predator cocks its head toward the prey. The smaller allosaur has sunk its teeth into the shoulder of the camptosaur, which recoils with a grimace of pain frozen across its skeletal mouth. Behind them, a *Stegosaurus* brandishes its mace-like spiked tail.

Despite the action and emotion in this display, the antagonists still strike the tail-dragging posture that was in vogue when the mounts were made a quarter-century ago. Instead, so current theory goes, their heads and tails should be balanced over the legs like a seesaw. And the *Stegosaurus* should have a second row of plates running along its back.

Quibbles aside, the skeletons from Utah's famous **Cleveland-Lloyd Quarry** are still impressive. Except for the *Stegosaurus*, entirely a replica, the mounts contain a mix of actual fossils and casts of the real thing. Now the museum prefers not putting actual bones in its dinosaur mounts, reserving the

Featured diorama (left) at the Utah Museum depicts two allosaurs attacking *Camptosaurus* near a *Stegosaurus*. All four skeletons came from Utah's Cleveland-Lloyd Quarry.

Dinosaur footprints (above) made 80 million years ago were discovered in Utah coal mines.

Vibrant dinosaurs (opposite, top) adorn a wall mural painted by Utah schoolchildren.

Smooth stones (opposite, bottom) were found with sauropod bones at the Long Walk Quarry. The stones, or gastroliths, may have been swallowed by the giant beasts to grind up food.

real thing for small satellite cases around the hall. For instance, the original skull from the smaller *Allosaurus* specimen is here, as well as a unique display of an *Allosaurus* brain-case cast removed from one of the Cleveland-Lloyd skulls.

Work in Progress

At the preparation lab on the ground floor, you can sit on a bench shaped like a sauropod humerus and watch the prepara-tors at work, or ask questions through an

intercom. All the bones you'll see there are real, maybe *Allosaurus* fossils tinted red by iron oxide, or some of the bizarre and deli-cate specimens – including sauropods no one seems to recognize – coming out of the museum's **Long Walk Quarry**.

The soft Long Walk bones come welded to a rugged rock matrix, a challenging combi-nation, so expect to find preparators putting in many hours on these specimens. One plaster field jacket on display reveals another curious aspect of the early Cretaceous site, the large number of apparent gastroliths scattered among sauropod remains. Long Walk Quarry may ultimately confirm that such smooth red, gray, and brown stones ground up food in the gizzards of the herbivorous giants.

Back upstairs, a flexible fence among the old-fash-ioned dioramas corrals *Dinosaur Builders,* a "living exhibit" that features a changing array of casts made from dinosaurs found worldwide. You may catch workers assembling all the bits and pieces for a mount of a complete skeleton,

such as *Saurophaganax*, an allosaurid recently discovered in Oklahoma.

Follow the geology displays around to the far corner and see some wonderful original vertebrate fossils from the Green River Formation, including a gar with sparkling scales whose relatives still swim in the Mississippi, and a freshwater stingray found today only in tropical South America. An adjacent case contains exquisite casts of a few of the 600 species preserved at Solnhofen, a limestone quarry near Munich, Germany, best known for preserving all known speci-mens of the ancient bird *Archaeopteryx*. It's displayed here, along with two species of the flying reptiles *Pterodactylus* and *Rhamphorhynchus*, plus the tiny dinosaur *Compsognathus lingipes*.

Take a moment to swing through the Biology Hall and view a five-foot-tall "trunk" of a *Tempskya* tree fern. Herbivorous dinosaurs roaming this part of Utah 130 million years ago, when it was flat swamp-land, probably munched on similar plants.

Black Hills Institute of Geological Research
Hill City, South Dakota

Black Hills Institute of Geological Research, 217 Main Street, Hill City, SD 57745; tel: 605-574-4289. Monday–Friday, 9 A.M.–5 P.M. $

An early inkling of the Black Hills Institute emerges from a grainy photograph of Peter Larson, age eight, and his brother Neal, age five, at their home in rural South Dakota. Next to them is a table-top full of fossils and a post bearing a hand-lettered sign that says "MUSEUM." Peter acquired a passion for fossils at an early age and began picking up scraps of bone and teeth of extinct camel- and rhinoceros-like creatures eroding from South Dakota hillsides. Years later, he and Neal partnered with fellow fossil collector Robert Farrar in a commercial enterprise called the **Black Hills Institute of Geological Research**, based in a former auditorium in Hill City, South Dakota. The institute has gathered an impressive collection of dinosaur fossils that will someday serve as the cornerstone of a full-fledged museum.

Stan Joins the Collection

The trio is well known for excavating Sue, the remarkably complete *Tyrannosaurus rex* discovered in South Dakota in 1990. It was to be the centerpiece of their proposed museum. But the Federal Bureau of Investigation, with help from the National Guard, seized the dinosaur, and after a long court battle, Sue was sold at auction to the Field Museum of Natural History. The disappointed institute founders didn't give up: They have since unearthed another *T. rex*, named Stan, that now stands in the institute's free exhibit hall and will someday preside over the museum.

Indeed, gazing around the current exhibit hall, it's hard to imagine a place with more spectacular dinosaurs in such a small space. Beside Stan is a horned *Triceratops* skull, a *Camarasaurus* skull, a cast skeleton of *Albertosaurus*, dinosaur eggs from China, a replica of a *T. rex* skull from the American Museum of Natural History, and a cast skeleton of a meat-eating dinosaur known as *Acrocanthosaurus*. Posing in a corner is an ostrich-like dinosaur, thought to be a close relative of *T. rex*, which stands nearby.

While dinosaurs certainly catch a visitor's eyes first, they are actually outnumbered by top-notch exhibits lining the walls in a kind of glassed-in menagerie of life on Earth. The cases brim with glittering ammonites, fossilized beds of crinoids that swayed in the current of long-gone seas, and the ancient

Lethal weapons even after 75 million years, some *T. rex* teeth (left) remain sharp enough to slice through flesh.

The Larson siblings (opposite, middle) Peter, Neal, Jill, and Mark had a modest start in the museum business. Now Peter and Neal run the Black Hills Institute.

Peter Larson (opposite, bottom) shows off the skull of Stan, the *Tyrannosaurus* that will preside over the institute's future museum.

Black Hills Institute workers (right) have a reputation for first-rate fossil preparation; major museums have acquired specimens found by institute expeditions.

French dinosaur eggs (bottom, right), shown in comparison with a chicken egg, are among the institute's many changing exhibits.

mammals – some similar to today's rhinos and camels – that roamed the savanna-like landscape of what is now the Midwest some 35 million years ago. Keep in mind that many specimens are for sale, so repeat visitors can expect continually changing exhibits. The unconventional background of the institute's founders has not given short shrift to science: Displays here are as scientifically accurate and up-to-date as those of any modern museum. In fact, major museums through-out the world have acquired specimens and exhibits from the institute.

In the institute's vast treasure chest of a shop, it's easy to get the feeling that you're actually in the private research collection of

a well-endowed museum as you pull open broad wooden drawers full of prehis-toric riches. Ammonites. Trilobites. Dinosaur bones. Primeval shark teeth. Chunks of mammal jaws. Carefully pick them up and cradle them in your hand. Whether or not you decide to take one home (prices begin at a dollar and go way up from there), you have intimate contact with the past that most museums could never offer.

Museum of the Rockies
Bozeman, Montana

Museum of the Rockies, 600 West Kagy Boulevard,
Bozeman, MT 59717; tel: 406-994-2251.
Monday–Saturday, 9 A.M.–5 P.M.; Sunday, 12:30–5 P.M.
(extended summer hours). $

"One place through all time." That's the motto of Montana's **Museum of the Rockies**. But make no mistake about it, the time most dear to its curator of paleontology, famed dinosaur hunter John R. "Jack" Horner, is the Mesozoic Era. Specifically, the late Mesozoic, about 80 million years ago, when you might have seen a 30-foot-long duckbilled dinosaur gathering mouthfuls of berries to take back to its young in a colonial nesting ground, or felt the earth tremble as a herd of 10,000 three-ton duckbills tromped over the savanna.

Across a wide sweep of central and eastern Montana, quirks of geology, wind, and water have exposed Mesozoic sediments chock-full of dinosaur fossils. Since 1978, when Horner and colleagues discovered what had been a nest of baby dinosaurs and then the first clutches of dinosaur eggs ever found in North America, his teams have collected and cataloged more than 25,000 dinosaur specimens, including three *Tyrannosaurus rex* skeletons. This museum, on the Montana State University campus in Bozeman, houses one of the largest dinosaur collections in the country, including six previously undiscovered species.

It's not bones, however, that make the museum's Berger Dinosaur Hall unique. Indeed, you won't notice many bones at first. When Horner and his crews crawl over caliche and mudstone in the blistering heat, they search for ideas, not just skeletal trophies. In Horner's imagination, the Mesozoic remains a vital, vivid era when a remarkably successful lineage of animals

Baby duckbill *Maiasaura* (opposite) emerges from an egg in this detailed reconstruction.

Maiasaura, "good mother lizard" (left), gazes toward Jack Horner, the paleontologist who named her and whose ideas about her maternal instincts are presented in the exhibits.

Triceratops (below) roamed in herds during the late Mesozoic much as bison do today.

was pioneering many of the life strategies still used by vertebrates: living in large social groups, flocking together to nest, and taking care of their babies. From his fossil finds, Horner envisioned dinosaur lives in a way no one had before. And it's this vision that strikes you in the two-story hall.

Looming above you on a raised platform is a life-size, rosy-brown duckbill, her vaguely camel-like face lowered to a nest full of big-eyed babies as she delivers a mouthful of leaves and berries. This is the dinosaur that Horner christened *Maiasaura peeblesorum*, "good mother lizard," after finding at least three colonial nesting grounds. Some of the nests contained unhatched grapefruit-sized eggs, others 14-inch hatchlings, still others three-foot babies. These were fast-growing, nest-bound babies with worn teeth that helped convince Horner that a parent had to be supplying them with solid food.

Mesozoic Marvels

The scene looks deceptively simple, but it took years of collecting, analyzing, and interpreting data to envision it. And that's the process into which Horner hopes to draw you. You're invited to look through a microscope at thin cross sections of bone from baby and adult birds,

crocodiles, and maiasaurs to judge for yourself his evidence that these dinosaurs grew as rapidly as warm-blooded birds. Take a hand lens from the rack and scrutinize bits of plant matter in a chunk of fossilized dino dung. Run your hands over bronze casts of eggs, a baby *Maiasaura* skull, or dinosaur skin imprints left in the mud of a Cretaceous floodplain. On a relief globe of the Mesozoic Earth, trace the Colorado Sea that once pushed inland from the Gulf of Mexico to Canada, confining Montana creatures of that era between a shifting shoreline to the east and the newly emerged Rockies to the west.

In a corner of the hall, a *Quetzalcoatlus*, a flying, birdlike reptile known as a pterosaur, stands 10 feet tall in a coastal forest of palmettos, horsetails, ginkgoes, and cycads near the ancient shoreline. Its

batlike wings are folded at its sides while more of its kind soar overhead, suspended from the ceiling or painted into a mural.

Horner would be the first to tell you that scientific interpretations must be subject to change, and so must museum exhibits that seek to go beyond bones. Look to the right, beyond the *Maiasaura* scene, for instance, and you'll see two slender, six-foot meat eaters known as *Troödon formosus*. One is brooding a nest full of six-inch, potato-shaped eggs; another walks near a nest where eggs are hatching and young *Troödons* are piling out to feed on the carcass of a small plant-eating dinosaur

that Horner named *Orodromeus makelai*.

Until 1998, a fiberglass *Orodromeus* was tending those eggs. That's because within the same patch of badlands that contained the *Maiasaura* nesting grounds, Horner's crews had found two dozen skeletons of young *Orodromeus*, but only a few *Troödon* remains among a dozen clutches of such eggs. Not until 1996, when a preparator chipped away sediment from bone inside an unhatched egg, did Horner confirm that the embryo was actually a *Troödon*.

So what were all the orodromiad skeletons doing there? Did the fierce, pack-hunting *Troödon* bring *Orodromeus* carcasses back for their young to eat? Were they good parents, too? Stay tuned, Horner advises, the story is still unfolding.

New Interpretations

There are bones on display here, too. The only known *Troödon* skeletons are here, including the partial skeleton of a baby, displayed in a wall case along with the partial skeleton of a young *Orodromeus* and casts of *Maiasaura* nestlings. In another wall is an up-ended, six-foot-tall chunk of bone-studded sediment – a tiny portion of

A preparator (left) works on *T. rex* bones.

T. rex skull (opposite, bottom). Studies of the predator's braincase suggest that it had stereoscopic vision and keen senses of smell and hearing.

Robert Bakker (right), curator of Wyoming's Tate Mineralogical Museum, poses with an *Apatosaurus* femur.

Museum with a Mission

For decades, Wyoming has been a net exporter of dinosaur bones, supplying centerpieces for large East Coast museums but keeping few of the best specimens at home. **The Tate Mineralogical Museum** in **Casper, Wyoming**, aims to change that. Its attitude is summed up on a T-shirt with a picture of the state dinosaur, a *Triceratops* known as Lady Stephanie, and the slogan, "Keep 'em in Wyoming."

If you're in the mood for a small collection with a friendly staff rarely too busy to give you a personal tour, then it's worth stopping at this free museum tucked away on the campus of Casper College.

The museum is interactive in the old-fashioned way. Visitors are invited to pick up many fossils and use magnifiers to study them closely. Its preparation laboratory – visible through glass windows – stays busy cleaning up the remains of many Wyoming dinosaurs, including an arthritic allosaur named Rip van Allosaur that probably died of old age.

The imaginative displays and often whimsical text spring from the fertile mind of the Tate's curator, Robert Bakker, a consultant to *Jurassic Park*, author of *The Dinosaur Heresies*, and a crusading proponent of dinosaurs as fast, smart, and caring (at least toward their own family) forerunners of today's birds. *Tyrannosaurus rex* was not a lizard numskull but "a 10,000-pound turkey with a really bad attitude," Bakker says. His sketches of dinosaurs hang on the walls here, and he has arranged most of the museum's dinosaur bones, such as the *T. rex* skull seemingly ready to chomp away at you, in the sort of active poses they would have held in real life. True dinophiles can attend the Tate's yearly conference, usually held in June. The event is open to professionals and amateurs and features lectures, field trips, and fossil hunting. For information, call the Tate at 307-268-2447. – *Michael Milstein*

a two-square-mile bone bed known as "Camposaur" that may have contained the remains of 10,000 maiasaurs overtaken by a blast of volcanic gas and ash one day 75 million years ago. At 30 bones per cubic meter, it's the largest concentration of dinosaur bones known in the world.

A while back, Horner began displaying some of the most unusual trophies from the basement research collections in a "glass menagerie," a 30-foot-long display case on the mezzanine above the dinosaur hall, at the entrance to an interactive playroom for children. There you'll see dinosaur skulls – the bone fragments carefully reassembled onto plaster forms – from Montana plant eaters such as *Einiosaurus procurvicornis* (featured by the U.S. Postal Service on its dinosaur stamp series), *Avaceratops lammersi*, *Tenontosaurus tilletti*, *Hypacrosaurus stebingeri*, and *Brachylophosaurus*. The latter, the best-preserved dinosaur skeleton ever found in Montana, is still under preparation.

Beyond the dinosaur hall, sharing a largely empty space with a life-sized robotic rubber *Triceratops*, is a glass-front "fossil bank" where volunteers are at work cleaning bones and answering questions. Someday *Triceratops* will give way to a new Cenozoic display. (Much of the museum is devoted to the very recent Holocene, a mammalian saga of gold miners, settlers, and Native Americans.) The museum also boasts a lively, interactive Paleozoic section where you can look at "a day 370 million years ago" when tropical seas sloshed across much of the region. But for those who share Horner's passion for dinosaurs, the action here will always be in the Mesozoic.

Royal Tyrrell Museum of Palaeontology
Drumheller, Alberta

Royal Tyrrell Museum of Palaeontology, Box 7500, Drumheller, Alberta T0J 0Y0, Canada; tel: 403-823-7707.
Tuesday–Sunday, 10 A.M.–5 P.M.; closed Monday except holidays; extended summer hours. $

Dinosaurs are all over the town of **Drumheller, Alberta**. The biggest one is a sculpture of a huge, green tyrannosaur near a bridge over the Red Deer River. A gleaming statue of a cowboy riding a bucking *Triceratops* stands in front of the rodeo grounds. And a sign with a toothy Allosaur at the edge of town says, "WELCOME TO DRUMHELLER, HOME OF THE DINOSAUR EMPIRE."

The capital of this empire is the **Royal Tyrrell Museum**, one of the world's largest and most comprehensive fossil collections, set about ten minutes northwest of town on a highway called the **Dinosaur Trail**. Canada's crown jewel of paleontology is housed in a large, modern, glass-and-granite structure surrounded by the eroded sandstone hills that provide it with most of its fossils. Even as the museum was being built in 1984, paleontologists crossing the construction site found the lower jaw of a *Troödon*, the first ever discovered.

The exhibits include more than 30 complete dinosaur skeletons, a great variety of prehistoric mammals, and about 800 other fossils from various periods during the last 3.5 billion years. It is a spectacular, state-of-the-art display, and about as far from a musty natural-history museum as you can imagine.

Attack of the Theropods

Your first dinosaur encounter upon entering the museum and weaving through the throng of children pulling levers and pushing buttons in the hands-on science hall is an exhibit labeled *Extreme Theropods*. It's not just a name to appeal to the skateboard-and-baggy-jeans set. These meat-eating dinosaurs *were* extreme in the size and strength of their jaws and teeth, which gape over your head and cast menacing shadows on the wall, thanks to some clever lighting. It's like walking into a bar and finding it filled with hungry and nasty creatures three times your size. There's a skeleton of a *Sinoraptor* poised to strike with vicious-looking claws; a giant *Daspletosaurus* with nasty bite marks in various stages of healing on its bones; and an *Allosaurus* looming out of the darkness with glinting teeth. And this is only the beginning. You haven't gotten to the main dinosaur gallery yet.

The hollow crest of *Parasaurolophus* (left) may have been used to emit mating calls.

An *Albertosaurus* pursues a terrified *Struthiomimus* on the museum's front plaza (opposite, top).

Dinosaur fever in Drumheller extends to public art, like this cowboy riding a bucking *Triceratops* (opposite, bottom) at the rodeo grounds.

A Varied Menu

First you get to walk through the *Burgess Shale*, an underwater world from over half a billion years ago where tiny animals started to develop teeth, tentacles, hard bodies, and jaws. Re-creations of these creatures are blown up 12 times bigger than life-size and appear to swim beneath your feet as you step across a plate-glass floor, revealing much about the nature of early life.

A multimedia exhibit farther on explores the origins of early reptiles and features a complicated evolutionary tree and a sample of the bones that scientists use to determine which creature sits on which branch. Interpretive text is brief and to the point and aims to give the big picture rather than mire you in murky details. For further elaboration, however, the museum employs strolling performers, one of whom might stop and extol the virtues of a particular lineage. "I got the crocodile blues," sings one woman in wraparound shades and a beret. "All my glory days are through./ Me and the dino boys used to rule the land./ But now they're dead and gone./ And my only rival left is you."

A few steps farther and the main dinosaur hall opens before you like a landscape filled with giant, long-necked sauropods, imposing tyrannosaurs, trucklike *Triceratops*, and their relatives. Some are skeletons; others are full-scale models. You could easily spend hours wandering the gallery, comparing the forms and lifestyles of different beasts, getting up close with no glass museum cases in the way.

But don't focus exclusively on the giants. The museum has a lot of small but

fascinating surprises. Look closely at a pterosaur shinbone, for instance, and you can see a *Velociraptor* tooth embedded in it; the dinosaur was apparently scavenging a few scraps of meat from the pterosaur's carcass. Up on the wall, a slab of rock shows a big fossil fish, *Xiphactinus*, with a smaller fish caught in its gullet, a last meal not fully digested. And if you've ever wondered what the Cretaceous version of gingerroot looked like, you can find it here.

After the dinosaurs, and a short video on what might have happened to them, comes a gallery devoted to prehistoric mammals. According to museum director Bruce Naylor, North America once had a diversity of mammals that "made Africa today look pretty pathetic."

The period following the extinction of dinosaurs was a time of evolutionary experimentation, Naylor explains. "We had the first lions and camels. Primates were here, but they were experimenting at being rodents. Horses got out of the gate really fast, and began trying out larger body sizes. But then someone changed the rules. This used to be a much wetter place, like today's Gulf Coast, with swamps and lakes. Then it became much drier, and turned into the harsh badlands we see now. These animals died out or moved. We missed it by about 10,000 years."

The gallery reflects the great diversity of prehistoric mammals, though some visitors may find it difficult to take their eyes off the giant mastodon skeleton that dominates the hall.

Field Trip

You can also see the people who prepare and study the fossils. A large, aquarium-like window lets you peer at preparators chipping bone out of rock or making casts. And if you're tired of merely looking, you can try your hand at being a paleontologist for a day.

For a reasonable fee, the museum will bus you about 20 minutes away into the badlands, where a team of field workers is excavating a bone bed of horned dinosaurs. Museum paleontologists point out bones eroding out of the earth, hand you a tiny pick and a bucket, and show you how to uncover the specimen about a half-inch at a time. And that's what you'll do for the next six hours. You'll get lunch, water, and a lot of encouragement (and insect bites and a sunburn if you're not careful), and you'll undoubtedly gain a better understanding of what paleontologists actually do. You don't get to keep your finds, however. All fossils belong to the people of Alberta, which means the provincial government, which means the museum.

If you would rather pass on the hands-on experience, you can simply watch others dig. You get to ask questions and tour the excavation site. The digs are open only in summer. Be sure to call ahead; it's an extremely popular program.

Ceratopsians like *Arrhinoceratops* (above) were especially abundant in Alberta during the Cretaceous.

No glass cases (left) come between visitor and dinosaur, making for an intimate museum experience.

Badlands (right), starkly beautiful in the afternoon sun, surround the museum. Forty species of dinosaurs have emerged from Alberta's Dinosaur Park Formation, which formed about 75 million years ago.

California Academy of Sciences
San Francisco, California

**Golden Gate Park, San Francisco, CA 94118;
tel: 415-750-7145.**
Daily, 10 A.M.–5 P.M. (extended summer hours). $

*L*ife Through Time, the evolution exhibit at the **California Academy of Sciences** in **San Francisco**, is short on large, dramatic dinosaur mounts but long on context, with a few surprises: the addition of live animals that have been around since before the dinosaurs. The decade-old exhibit takes a familiar, chronological approach to natural history, with a video introduction to the development of life from single-celled creatures to dinosaurs and beyond.

A bank of computers near the entrance houses *Lifemap*, an interactive program developed at the academy, which follows the evolutionary relationships between groups of plants and animals. It's worth spending some time here to learn which characteristics unite, say, sauropod and theropod dinosaurs.

Life began in the seas, and the next room contains some remnants from that distant past. Tanks with live horseshoe crabs, starfish, lungfish, and a preserved coelacanth show some of the life-forms that have endured for 600 million years.

Kids may want to race through life's transition to land to see the dinosaurs, but they should slow down to see the live Chinese giant salamander and chuckwalla lizard, or watch an animated video about how and why life moved from water to land. Near a diorama of a Carboniferous forest is the first fossil cast, a 10-foot-long synapsid *Dimetrodon*. The label sets the record straight that this sail-finned creature was "definitely not a dinosaur."

Enter the Dinosaurs

Dinosaurs fill the next room. The largest mount shows an *Allosaurus* chasing, and ready to chomp, a *Camptosaurus*. Predator and prey perch at the end of a trackway cast with two sets of fossilized footprints, evidence that helped scientists reconstruct the primal scene. An adjoining room shows what was happening with sea creatures during the age of the dinosaurs. It includes a cast of the largest fish ever found, an ocean diorama containing nautilus and squid models, and a real ammonite fossil of gigantic proportions.

The strangest-looking model hangs overhead in the next hall. It's *Quetzalcoatlus*, a pterosaur with a 45-foot wingspan, resembling an overgrown pelican with fur. Across the room, a display of bulky sauropod legs contains some real fossils that visitors can touch.

The biggest attraction for kids here is the *Terrible Claw* diorama showing a hunting pack of three fleshed-out *Deinonychus*, lunging from a forest with their sicklelike claws poised to slash. It's the best photo-op in the exhibit, where parents coach their kids, "Okay, act scared now," before snapping a picture. Around the back of the diorama, a furtive, shrew-like mammal cowers near the gurgling creek. A submerged crocodile and some insects complete the Cretaceous scene.

Just beyond the diorama is the *Tyrannosaurus rex* corner. Overhead, at its proper height, is a cast of the mighty predator's skull. The impressive view of its teeth and head makes you feel like an hors d'oeuvre. A section of a jaw and a real tooth allow a closer, albeit fragmented view.

A diorama depicting a fossil dig in Montana has a crushed *Triceratops* skull and some other real bone fragments along with the tools of the trade: chisels, brushes, and field notebooks. An entertaining video shows how fossils are found and how much work it takes to bring them back from the field.

That's the "end of the line" for dinosaurs in *Life Through Time*, except, as the text panel reminds you, for the birds. If you can't bear to part with dinosaurs, though, head for the main entrance of the museum, which is dominated by a skeleton cast of *T. rex*.

A fearsome hunter, Deinonychus lunges from a lush forest in the *Life Through Time* exhibit.

Natural History Museum of Los Angeles County
Los Angeles, California

Natural History Museum of Los Angeles County, 900 Exposition Boulevard, Los Angeles, CA 90007; tel: 213-763-3466.
Monday–Friday, 9:30 A.M.–5 P.M.; weekends 10 A.M.–5 P.M. $

Despite being among the largest and oldest museums in the country, the **Natural History Museum of Los Angeles County** got into the dinosaur business relatively late. In the 1960s, museum leaders realized that they were missing the boat on these crowd-attracting magnets and raised money for a series of dinosaur-collecting expeditions to the Hell Creek Formation in Montana. The out-of-state forays netted an impressive array of duckbilled dinosaur skeletons, *Triceratops* skulls, and the skull and foot of a *Tyrannosaurus* (the largest and most complete *T. rex* skull then known).

These fossils, along with others bought or swapped in exchange for pieces from the museum's extensive collection of Ice Age mammals and other vertebrates, form the core of the dinosaur displays.

The biggest attraction is the *Dueling Dinosaurs* mount in the main foyer of the museum's upper level. In a dramatic reconstruction using real and cast bones, a towering, gap-mouthed *Tyrannosaurus* is about to munch a fleeing *Triceratops* (the scene is re-created outside the museum entrance with full-scale bronze statues). Ringing the dinosaur skeletons are text labels and beautiful color illustrations describing the people behind the project, the natural history of the two animals, and other forms of life at the end of the Cretaceous.

From here, enter the Dinosaur Hall just beyond the foyer to see more dinosaurs. You'll first walk through a marine exhibit complete with the sound of surf. A 30-foot plesiosaur (the bright yellow label cautions you that this is "NOT a dinosaur") is mounted here, along with a giant pterosaur (also not

Schoolchildren (above) with prehistoric souvenirs.

Dueling dinosaurs (right) recreate a diorama inside the museum featuring the skeletons of *Tyrannosaurus* and *Triceratops*.

A hatchet-shaped crest caps the head of this lambeosaur (opposite, top), a duckbilled dinosaur found in the Americas, Europe, and Asia.

Carnotaurus (opposite, bottom), discovered in Argentina, had bony horns above its eyes, conical studs along its back and sides, and puny arms.

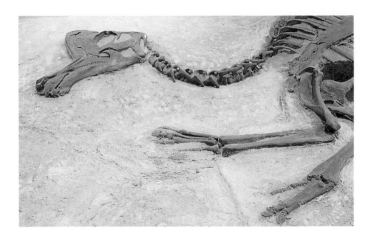

Many of the fossils are mounted as they would have appeared in the field or lab. A rare baby duckbill, *Edmontosaurus*, is partially encased in plaster, its head twisted around in a death pose. Another larger duck-billed dinosaur is displayed with an impression of its horny beak, a feature not usually fossilized. A changing exhibit displays a fossil skeleton in a protective field jacket and shows how fossils are received and prepared in a working paleontology lab.

There are some other inventive mounts here. A cast of *Armargasaurus*, a member of the sauropod group, is laid out on the ground in all its 50-foot glory. Except, as the text label points out, there's something missing. Visitors are left to figure it out for themselves, but it's not hard to guess that the creature is sans skull, a common condition of fossils from this small-headed group.

If you like primal scenes, you can find another pair of fighting fossil skeletons, this time *Allosaurus* and *Camptosaurus* locked in staged battle, with a razor-toothed *Allosaurus* model posed nearby.

a dinosaur), and some really huge clam and oyster fossils. A geological chart orients you in time before entering the next hall, which announces its all-star cast with a red neon sign proclaiming, "Dinosaurs!"

Highlights of the hall include a cast of the complete skeleton of a *Mamenchisaurus* from China, the longest-necked dinosaur ever discovered, some very realistic, life-sized models of *Allosaurus* and *Carnotaurus*, and real fossil skulls of *Triceratops* and *Tyrannosaurus*. Big purple labels, looking a bit dated, give brief descriptions of each fossil animal and how it was collected. You might consider bringing an eight-year-old along to help with pronunciation, however, because the labels don't provide guidance with tongue-twisting scientific names.

Rare Duckbill and Headless Sauropod

The *Carnotaurus* model deserves special mention. Created by paleontology artist Stephen Czerkas, this full-scale model took seven years to make and was the first sculpture created of this recently discovered dinosaur. It was an especially curious-looking creature, with ornamental studs on its skin and bull-like horns atop its head. A cast skeleton behind the sculpture, together with some model plants, complete the scene.

George C. Page Museum of La Brea Discoveries
Los Angeles, California

George C. Page Museum of La Brea Discoveries,
5801 Wilshire Boulevard, Los Angeles, CA 90036;
tel: 323-857-6311.
Monday–Friday, 9:30 A.M.–5 P.M.; weekends, 10 A.M.–5 P.M. $

The Los Angeles County Museum is the place to see dinosaurs in Southern California, but if you want to get blown away by fossils, drive across town to the **Page Museum** and the **La Brea Tar Pits**. The Page Museum, opened in 1977, seems a bit defensive about the lack of dinosaurs here (a fact that's pointed out in two videos), but it does house the world's largest collection of Ice Age mammals and birds – more than 30 skeletons total. There's a ground sloth the size of a bear, a trio of saber-toothed cat skeletons (*Smilodon*, the official state fossil of California), and a wall display with over 400 dire-wolf skulls.

All these fossils, plus millions more in the museum's collection, were excavated from the nearby tar pits. The deposits, actually asphalt and not tar, seep up from an underground petroleum reservoir. Between 40,000 and 10,000 years ago, these pools of sticky asphalt ensnared all manner of creatures, from snails to *Smilodons*. The grazing animals, including camels, giant sloths, and mastodons, stuck to the pits like flies to flypaper. Anticipating an easy meal, predators and scavengers descended upon the trapped herbivores and got stuck, too. In all, 650 animal species and nearly four million individual fossils have been recovered from the tar pits over the last 100 years, an embarrassment of riches beyond the imagination of most paleontologists.

The Page Museum reflects the diversity of animal life in the Los Angeles Basin during the Pleistocene Epoch. In addition to skeletons of sloths, wolves, and saber-toothed cats, you'll see mastodons (for the kids, there's also a cheesy animatronic version of a woolly mammoth, complete with fake fur), western camel, bison, lions, short-faced bears, and hundreds of birds. There's even the skeleton of a woman who died or was deliberately buried in a pit over 9,000 years ago. All the skeletons on display are real, but most specimens have been assembled

Dire-wolf skulls (left) reclaimed from the La Brea Tar Pits fill an exhibit case at the Page Museum.

Saber-toothed tigers (opposite, top) spar outside the Page Museum. Inside are three skeletons of the ferocious feline.

A *Mastodon* (opposite, bottom) was the largest of more than 600 kinds of animals captured in sticky pools of asphalt.

GEORGE C. PAGE MUSEUM
LA BREA DISCOVERIES

from the bones of many individuals.

In addition to fossils, an interactive exhibit shows how difficult it is to free metal "limbs" (representing animal legs) from sticky asphalt. You can also see researchers and volunteers clean and sort bones inside a glass-walled prep lab.

The Page Museum, on "Museum Row" in **Hancock Park**, is a short stroll from the only working fossil dig within a major city, **Pit 91** (there are more than 100 pit excavations in the area). In the summer, when the pit is softened by the California sun, researchers and volunteers pick through the fragrant, gooey asphalt, extracting blackened bones, fossil fragments, and plant material. An observation deck above the 15-foot-deep dig gives you a bird's-eye view of the messy, painstaking work. The ongoing research at Pit 91 will examine every fossil fragment from the tiniest seedpod to the largest mastodon skull, in order to complete a

picture of life during the last Ice Age. The evidence so far indicates that Los Angeles was cooler and more humid during the Pleistocene, resembling San Francisco's present climate. Present-day Angelenos have something to be thankful for.

FURTHER READING

History of Paleontology

American Dinosaur Hunters, Nathan Aaseng (Enslow Publishers, Inc., 1996).

Archetypes and Ancestors: Paleontology in Victorian London, 1850-1875, Adrian Desmond (University of Chicago Press, 1982).

The Bone Hunters, Url Lanham (Columbia University Press, 1973).

The Bonehunters' Revenge: Dinosaurs, Greed, and the Greatest Scientific Feud of the Gilded Age, David Rains Wallace (Houghton Mifflin, 1999).

Bones for Barnum Brown: Adventures of a Dinosaur Hunter, Roland T. Bird (Texas Christian University Press, 1985).

The Dawnseekers: The First History of American Paleontology, Robert West Howard (Harcourt Brace Jovanovich, 1975).

Discovering Dinosaurs in the Old West: The Field Journals of Arthur Lakes, Michael F. Kohl and John S. McIntosh, eds. (Smithsonian Institution Press, 1997).

O. C. Marsh: Pioneer in Paleontology, Charles Schuchert and Clara Mae Levine (Yale University Press, 1940).

Richard Owen: Victorian Naturalist, Nicolaas Rupke (Yale University Press, 1994).

Natural History

A Cold Look at the Warm-Blooded Dinosaurs, R. D. K. Thomas and E. C. Olson, eds. (Westview Press, 1980).

The Complete Dinosaur, James O. Farlow and M. K. Brett-Surman, eds. (Indiana University Press, 1997).

The Complete Idiot's Guide to Dinosaurs, Jay Stevenson and George R. McGhee (Alpha Books, 1998).

Digging Dinosaurs: The Search That Unraveled the Mystery of Baby Dinosaurs, James Gorman and John R. Horner (HarperPerennial, 1996).

Dinosaur! The Definitive Account of the "Terrible Lizards" from Their First Days on Earth to Their Disappearance 65 Million Years Ago, David Norman (Macmillan General Reference, 1995).

The Dinosaur Heresies: New Theories Unlocking the Mystery of the Dinosaurs and Their Extinction, Robert T. Bakker (Kensington Publishing Corp., 1996).

The Dinosauria, David B. Weishampel, Peter Dodson, and Halszka Osmolska, eds. (University of California Press, 1990).

Dinosaur Lives: Unearthing an Evolutionary Saga, John R. Horner and Edwin Dobb (HarperCollins, 1997).

The Dinosaur Society's Dinosaur Encyclopedia, Don Lessem and Donald Glut (Random House, 1993).

The Dinosaurs of North America, Dale Russell (University of Toronto Press, 1989).

Dinosaur Tracks, Anthony Thulborn (Chapman and Hall, 1990).

Dinosaur Tracks and Other Fossil Footprints of the Western United States, Martin Lockley and Adrian P. Hunt (Columbia University Press, 1995).

Dinosaur Tracks and Traces, David G. Gillette and Martin G. Lockley (Cambridge University Press, 1989).

Discovering Dinosaurs in the American Museum of Natural History, Mark A. Norell, Eugene S. Gaffney, and Lowell Dingus (Alfred A. Knopf/Nevraumont Publishing, 1995).

Encyclopedia of Dinosaurs, Philip J. Currie and Kevin Padian, eds. (Academia Press, 1997).

The Evolution and Extinction of the Dinosaurs, David E. Fastovsky and David B. Weishampel (Cambridge University Press, 1996).

The Great Dying: Cosmic Catastrophe, Dinosaurs, and the Theory of Evolution, Kenneth J. Hsu (Harcourt Brace Jovanovich, 1986).

Hunting Dinosaurs, Louie Psihoyos with John Knoebber (Random House, 1994).

The Illustrated Encyclopedia of Dinosaurs, David Norman (Crescent Books, 1985).

Kings of Creation: How a New Breed of Scientists Is Revolutionizing Our Understanding of Dinosaurs, Don Lessem (Simon & Schuster, 1992).

The Mistaken Extinction: Dinosaur Evolution and the Origin of Birds, Lowell Dingus and Timothy Rowe (W. H. Freeman, 1998).

An Odyssey in Time: The Dinosaurs of North America, D. A. Russell (University of Toronto Press, 1989).

Palaeontology: An Introduction, E. W. Nield and V. T. Tucker (Pergamon, 1985).

Predatory Dinosaurs of the World, Gregory Paul (Simon & Schuster, 1988).

Tracking Dinosaurs: A New Look at an Ancient World, Martin Lockley (Cambridge University Press, 1991).

The Ultimate Dinosaur Book, David Lambert (DK Publishing, 1993).

Regional Titles

California Jurassic Park! Dinosaurs and Other Prehistoric Creatures That Once Roamed Our State, Carole Marsh (California Books, 1999).

Colorado's Dinosaurs, John T. and Janice L. Jenkins (Colorado Geological Society, 1993).

Dinosaur Lake: The Story of the Purgatoire Valley Tracksite, Martin G. Lockley, Marquardt Lori, and Barbara J. Fillmore (Colorado Geological Society, 1997).

Dinosaurs in Maryland, Peter Kranz (Maryland Geological Society, 1989).

Dinosaurs of New Mexico, Spencer G. Lucas (New Mexico Academy of Science, 1993).

Dinosaurs of the East Coast, David Weishampel and Luther Young (The Johns Hopkins University Press, 1996).

Dinosaurs of Utah, Frank De Courten (University of Utah Press, 1998).

Dinosaur Stalkers: Tracking Dinosaur Discoveries of Western Colorado and Eastern Utah, Bob Silbernagel (Dinamation International Society, 1996).

A Guide to Lower Cretaceous Dinosaur Footprints and Tracksites of Paluxy River Valley, James O. Farlow (Baylor University, 1987).

The Little Dinosaurs of Ghost Ranch, Edwin H. Colbert (Columbia University Press, 1995).

Lone Star Dinosaurs, Louis Jacobs (Texas A & M University Press, 1995).

Tyrrell Museum of Palaeontology and the Drumheller Valley, Tyrrell Museum (Wildland Publishing, 1987).

A Vanished World: The Dinosaurs of Western Canada, Dale A. Russell (National Museum of Canada, 1977).

The Dinosaurs of Wyoming, Gerald E. Nelson, ed. (Wyoming Geological Association, 1994).

Guidebooks

A Cambridge Field Guide to Prehistoric Life, D. Lambert (Cambridge University Press, 1985).

Dinosaur Safari Guide, Vincenzo Costa (Voyageur Press, 1994).

Dinosaurs (Audubon Society Pocket Guides), Joseph Wallace (Knopf, 1993).

Dinosaurs, Eugene S. Gaffney (Golden Books Publishing Company, 1990).

Dino-Trekking: The Ultimate Dinosaur Lover's Travel Guide, Kelly Milner Halls (John Wiley & Sons, 1996).

Magazines & Journals

Dinosaur Report
The Dinosaur Society, 200 Carleton Avenue, East Islip, NY 11730; tel: 800-346-6366.

Dinosaur Discoveries
Tiger Publications, P.O. Box 8759, Amarillo, TX 79114; tel: 806-655-2009.

Dinosaur World
1208 Nashua Lane, Bartlette, IL 60103; tel: 630-289-7018.

Fossil News: Journal of Amateur Paleontology
1185 Claremont Drive; Boulder, CO 80303.

Journal of Paleontology
Paleontological Society, Box 1897, Lawrence, KS 66044; tel: 913-843-1221.

Prehistoric Times
145 Bayline Circle, Folsom, CA 95630-8077; tel: 916-985-7986.

DINOSAUR MUSEUMS

Academy of Natural Sciences
1900 Ben Franklin Parkway, Philadelphia, PA 19103; tel: 215-299-1000.

American Museum of Natural History
Central Park West at 79th Street, New York, NY 10024; tel: 212-769-5000.

Black Hills Institute of Geological Research
217 Main Street, Hill City, SD 57745; tel: 605-574-4289.

California Academy of Sciences
Golden Gate Park, San Francisco, CA 94118; tel: 415-750-7145.

Canadian Museum of Nature
P.O. Box 3443, Station D, Ottowa, ON KIP 6P4, Canada; tel: 613-990-2200.

Carnegie Museum of Natural History
4400 Forbes Avenue, Pittsburgh, PA 15213; tel: 412-622-3283.

Cleveland Museum of Natural History
1 Wade Oval Drive, University Circle, Cleveland, OH 44106-1767; tel: 216-231-4600.

College of Eastern Utah Prehistoric Museum
155 East Main Street, Price, Utah 84501; tel: 801-627-5060.

Dakota Dinosaur Museum
1226 Simms, Dickinson, ND 58601; tel: 701-227-0431.

Dallas Museum of Natural History
3535 Grand Avenue, Dallas, TX 75226; tel: 214-670-8457.

Denver Museum of Natural History
2001 Colorado Boulevard, Denver, CO 80205; tel: 303-370-6357.

Dinosaur Depot
330 Royal Gorge Boulevard, Cañon City, CO 81212; tel: 719-269 7150.

Dinosaur Discovery Museum
550 Jurassic Court, Fruita, CO 81521; tel: 970-858-7282.

Dinosaur Footprints Reservation
c/o The Trustees of Reservations, P.O. Box 792, Stockbridge, MA 01261; tel: 413-298-3239.

The Dinosaur Museum
754 South 200 West, Blanding, UT 84511; tel: 435-678-3454.

Dinosaur Valley Museum
4th and Main Streets, Grand Junction, CO 81501; tel: 970-241-9210.

Drumheller Dinosaur and Fossil Museum
335 1st Street East, Drumheller, AB T0J 0Y0, Canada; tel: 403-823-2593.

Earth Science Museum
Brigham Young University, 1683 North Canyon Road, Provo, UT 84602; tel: 801-378-3680.

Field Museum of Natural History
Lake Shore Drive at Roosevelt Road, Chicago, IL 60605; tel: 312-922-9410.

Fort Worth Museum of Science and History
1501 Montgomery Street, Fort Worth, TX 76107; tel: 817-732-1631.

Fundy Geological Museum
Two Islands Road, Parrsboro, NS B0M 1S0, Canada; tel: 902-254-3814.

George C. Page Museum of La Brea Discoveries
5801 Wilshire Boulevard, Los Angeles, CA 90036; tel: 323-857-6311.

George S. Eccles Dinosaur Park
1544 East Park Boulevard, Ogden, UT 84401; tel: 801-393-3466.

Houston Museum of Natural Science
1 Hermann Circle Drive, Houston, TX 77030; tel: 713-639-4600.

Las Vegas Natural History Museum
900 Las Vegas Boulevard North, Las Vegas, NV 89101; tel: 702-384-3466.

Milwaukee Public Museum
800 West Wells Street, Milwaukee, WI 53233; tel: 414-278-2702.

Morden and District Museum
P.O. Box 728, 111B Gilmore Street, Morden, MB R6M 1N9, Canada; tel: 204-822-3406.

Museum of Geology
South Dakota School of Mines, 500 East Joseph Street; Rapid City, SD 57701; tel: 605-394-2467.

Museum of Northern Arizona
3001 North Fort Valley Road, Flagstaff, AZ 86001; tel: 520-774-5211.

Museum of Texas Tech University
4th Street and Indiana Avenue, Lubbock, TX 79409; tel: 806-742-2442.

Museum of the Rockies
Montana State University, 600 West Kagy Boulevard, Bozeman, MT 59717-0272; tel: 406-994-3466.

Museum of Western Colorado
P.O. Box 20000-5020, 233 South 5th Street, Grand Junction, CO 81502-5020; tel: 970-241-9210.

National Museum of Natural History
10th Street and Constitution Avenue NW, Washington, DC 20560; tel: 202-357-2020.

Natural History Museum of Los Angeles County
900 Exposition Boulevard, Los Angeles, CA 90007; tel: 213-763-3466.

New Mexico Museum of Natural History
1801 Mountain Road NW, Albuquerque, NM 87104; tel: 505-841-8837.

Nova Scotia Museum
1747 Summer Street; Halifax, NS B3H 3A6, Canada; tel: 800-341-6096.

Peabody Museum of Natural History
Yale University, P.O. Box 6666, 170 Whitney Avenue, New Haven, CT 06511; tel: 203-432-5050.

Pratt Museum of Natural History
Amherst College; Amherst MA 01103; tel: 413-542-2165.

Raymond M. Alf Museum
The Webb School, 1175 West Baseline Road, Claremont, CA 91711; tel: 909-624-2798.

Royal Ontario Museum
100 Queen's Park, Toronto, ON M5S 2C6, Canada; tel: 416-586-5551.

Royal Saskatchewan Museum
2445 Albert Street, Regina, SK S4P 3V7, Canada; tel: 306-787-2815.

Royal Tyrrell Museum of Palaeontology
Box 7500, Drumheller, Alberta T0J 0Y0, Canada; tel: 403-823-7707.

Ruth Hall Museum of Paleontology
Ghost Ranch Conference Center, Abiquiu, NM 87501; tel: 505-685-4333.

Saskatchewan Museum of Natural History
College and Albert Streets, Regina, SK S4P 3V7, Canada; tel: 306-787-2815.

Science Museum of Minnesota
30 East 10th Street, St. Paul, MN 55101; tel: 612-221-9488.

Shuler Museum of Paleontology
Southern Methodist University, Dallas, TX 75275-0395; tel: 214-768-2000.

St. Louis Science Center and Dinosaur Park
5050 Oakland Avenue, St. Louis, MO 63110; tel: 314-289-4444.

Tate Mineralogical Museum
Casper College, 125 College Drive, Casper, WY 82601 tel: 307-268-2447.

Texas Memorial Museum
University of Texas, 2400 Trinity Street, Austin, TX 78705; tel: 512-471-1604.

University of California Museum of Paleontology
University of California, Berkeley, CA 94720; tel: 510-642-1821.

Utah Field House of Natural History and Dinosaur Garden
235 East Main Street, Vernal, UT 84078-2605; tel: 435-789-3799.

Utah Museum of Natural History
University of Utah, President's Circle, Salt Lake City, UT 84112; tel: 801-581-4303.

University of Michigan Exhibit Museum
1109 Geddes Avenue, Ann Arbor, MI 48109-1079; tel: 313-764-0478.

University of Wyoming Geological Museum
P.O. Box 3006, Laramie, WY 82071-3006; tel: 307-766-4218.

Virginia Museum of Natural History
1001 Douglas Avenue, Martinville, VA 24122; tel: 703-666-8600.

Wyoming Dinosaur Center
Box 868, Thermopolis, WY 82443; tel: 307-864-2997.

FOSSIL SITES

Berlin-Ichthyosaur State Park
HC 61, Box 61200, Austin, NV 89310; tel: 702-964-2440.

Clayton Lake State Park
Rural Route, Box 20, Seneca, NM 88437; tel: 505-374-8808.

Cleveland-Lloyd Dinosaur Quarry
BLM Price Field Office, Box 7004, Price, UT 84501; tel: 801-636-3600.

Devil's Coulee Dinosaur Heritage Museum
Box 156, Warner, AB TOK 2L0, Canada; tel: 403-642-2118.

Dinosaur National Monument
P.O. Box 210, Dinosaur, CO 81610; tel:
303-370-6387.

Dinosaur Provincial Park
P.O. Box 60, Patricia, AB T0J 2K0,
Canada; tel: 403-378-4342.

Dinosaur Ridge
Friends of Dinosaur Ridge, 16831
West Alameda Parkway, Morrison,
CO 80465; tel: 303-697-3466.

Dinosaur State Park
West Street, Rocky Hill, CT 06067
3506; tel: 860-529-5816.

Dinosaur Valley State Park
Box 396, Glen Rose, TX 76043; tel:
254-897-4588.

Dry Mesa Quarry
U.S. Forest Service, 2505 South
Townsend, Montrose, CO 81401; tel:
970-240-5400.

Eastend Fossil Research Station
118 Maple Avenue South, Eastend, SK
S0N 0T0, Canada; tel: 306-295-4009.

Egg Mountain
Museum of the Rockies Education
Department, 600 West Kagy
Boulevard, Bozeman, MT 59717; tel:
406-994-6618.

Fossil Butte National Monument
Box 592, Kemmerer, WY 83101; tel:
307-877-4455.

**John Day Fossil Beds National
Monument**
420 West Main, John Day, OR 97845;
tel: 503-987-2333.

Mill Canyon Dinosaur Trail
BLM Field Office, 82 East Dogwood,
Moab, UT 84532; tel: 435-259-6111.

Petrified Forest National Park
Box 2217, Petrified Forest, AZ 86028;
tel: 520-524-6228.

Purgatoire River Trackway
Comanche National Grassland, 1420
East 3rd Street, La Junta, CO 81050;
tel: 719-384-2181.

Red Gulch Dinosaur Tracksite
BLM Worland Field Office, Box 119,
101 South 23rd Street, Worland, WY;
tel: 307-347-5100.

**Smoky River Coal Ankylosaur
Tracksite**
c/o Grand Cache Chamber of
Commerce, Grand Cache, AB,
Canada; tel: 780-827-3790.

Warner Valley Tracksite
BLM Dixie Resource Area, 225 North
Bluff Street, St. George, UT 84770; tel:
801-673-4654.

DINOSAUR DIG PROGRAMS

Dinamation International Society
550 Jurassic Court, Fruita, CO 81521;
tel: 800-344-3466.

Dinosaur Research Expeditions
Montana State University, Hagener
Science Center, P.O. 7751, Havre, MT
59501; tel: 800-662-6132 (ext. 3716) or
406-265-3716.

Earthwatch
680 Mt. Auburn Street, P.O. Box 9104,
Watertown, MA 02471-9104; tel: 800-
776-0188.

Exposaur Excursions
P.O. Box 781, Drumheller, AB T0J
0Y0, Canada; tel: 403-823-4973.

Mesalands Dinosaur Museum
222 East Laughlin, Tucumcari, NM
88401; tel: 505-461-4413.

**Old Trail Museum and Paleontology
Field School**
823 North Main, Choteau, MT 59422;
tel: 406-466-5332.

Timescale Adventures
P.O. Box 356, Choteau, MT 59422;
tel: 800-238-6873 or 406-466-5410.

Western Paleo Safaris
P.O. Box 1042, Laramie, WY 82073;
tel: 888-875-2233 (ext. 7737).

Wyoming Dinosaur Center
Box 868, Thermopolis, WY 82443;
tel: 307-864-2997.

ORGANIZATIONS

Dinamation International Society
P.O. Box 307, Fruita, CO 81521; tel:
303-858-7282.

Dinosaur Fund
645 G Street SE, Washington, DC
20003; tel: 202-547-3326.

Dinosaur Nature Association
1291 East Highway 40, Vernal, UT
84078-2830; tel: 800-845-3466.

Dinosaur Society
200 Carleton Avenue, East Islip, NY
11730; tel: 516-277-7855.

Dino-Trekking Club
1042 15th Avenue, Longmont, CO
80501.

Dino University
505 Eighth Avenue, 18th Floor, New
York, NY 10018.

Society of Vertebrate Paleontology
60 Revere Drive, Suite 500, Northbrook,
IL 60062; tel: 847-480-9080.

TOURISM INFORMATION

Arizona Office of Tourism
1100 West Washington Street,
Phoenix, AZ 85007; tel: 800-842-8257
or 602-542-8687.

California State Division of Tourism
801 K Street, Suite 1600, Sacramento,
CA 95814; tel: 800-462-2543 or 916-
322-2881.

Colorado Travel and Tourism
1625 Broadway, Suite 1700, Denver,
CO 80202; tel: 800-265-6723.

Connecticut Office of Tourism
Department of Economic and
Community Development, 505
Hudson Street, Hartford, CT 06106;
tel: 800-282-6863.

Illinois Bureau of Tourism
100 West Randolph Street, Suite 3-
400, Chicago, IL 60602; tel: 800-226-
6632 or 312-814-4732.

Maryland Office of Tourism
217 East Redwood Street, Baltimore,
MD 21202; tel: 800-644-7386.

Nevada Tourism
Capital Complex, Carson City, NV
89710; tel: 800-237-0774.

New Mexico Tourism
Lamy Building, 491 Old Santa Fe
Trail, Santa Fe, NM 87503; tel: 800-
545-2040 or 505-827-7400.

New York State Division of Tourism
P.O. Box 2603, Albany, NY 12220-
0603; tel: 800-225-5697 or 518-474-
0603.

Nova Scotia Department of Tourism
Box 130; Halifax, NS B3J 2M7, Canada;
tel: 800-341-6096 or 902-424-5000.

Pennsylvania Office of Tourism
Room 400, Forum Building,
Harrisburg, PA 17120; tel: 800-847-
4872 or 717-232-8880.

South Dakota Department of Tourism
711 Wells Avenue, Pierre, SD 57501;
tel: 605-773-3301.

Texas Tourism
P.O. Box 12728, Austin, TX 78711; tel:
512-478-0098.

Tourism Saskatchewan
500-1900 Albert Street; Regina, SK
S4P 4L9, Canada; tel: 800-667-7191 or
306-787-2300.

Travel Alberta
P.O. Box 2400, Edmonton, AB T5J
2Z4, Canada; tel: 800-661-8888 or
403-427-4321.

Travel Montana
Deptartment of Commerce, 1424 9th
Avenue, Helena, MT 59620; tel: 800-
541-1447 or 406-444-2654.

Utah Travel Council
Council Hall, Capitol Hill, Salt Lake
City, UT 84114; tel: 800-200-1160 or
801-538-1030.

**Washington, D.C., Convention and
Visitors Bureau**
1212 New York Avenue NW, Suite
600, Washington, DC 20005; tel: 202-
789-7000.

Wyoming Division of Tourism
I-25 at College Drive, Cheyenne, WY
82002; tel: 800-225-5996 or 307-777-
7777.

GOVERNMENT AGENCIES

Bureau of Land Management
U.S. Department of the Interior, 1849
C Street NW, Washington, D.C.
20240; tel: 202-208-5717.

U.S. Fish and Wildlife Service
U.S. Department of the Interior, 1849
C Street NW, Washington, D.C.
20240; tel: 202-208-5717.

U.S. Forest Service
U.S. Department of Agriculture, 14th
and Independence Avenue SW, S
Agriculture Building, Washington,
D.C. 20250; tel: 202-205-8333.

National Park Service
Office of Public Inquiries, P.O. Box
37127, Washington, D.C. 20013; tel:
202-208-4747.

PHOTO AND ILLUSTRATION CREDITS

INDEX

Note: page numbers in italics refer to illustrations